compassionate

therapy

JEFFREY A. KOTTLER

compassionate therapy

working with difficult clients

Jossey-Bass Publishers · San Francisco

For sales outside the United States contact Maxwell Macmillan International Publishing Group, 866 Third Avenue, New York, New York 10022

Printed on acid-free paper and manufactured in the United States of America

 The paper used in this book meets the State of California requirements for recycled paper (50 percent recycled waste, including 10 percent post-consumer waste), which are the strictest guidelines for recycled paper currently in use in the United States.

Library of Congress Cataloging-in-Publication Data

Kottler, Jeffrey A.
    Compassionate therapy : working with difficult clients / Jeffrey A. Kottler.—1st ed.
        p. cm.—(The Jossey-Bass social and behavioral science series)
    Includes bibliographical references and index.
    ISBN 1-55542-422-8
    1. Psychotherapist and patient. 2. Resistance (Psychoanalysis)
3. Countertransference (Psychology) I. Title. II. Series.
RC480.8.K68 1992
616.89'14—dc20   91-30554
                                                          CIP

FIRST EDITION
HB Printing   10 9 8 7 6 5 4 3 2 1   *Code 9226*

THE JOSSEY-BASS

SOCIAL AND BEHAVIORAL SCIENCE SERIES

contents

Part Four: Managing Difficult Cases

preface

This book is about those clients who defy the textbooks. These are the cases that challenge therapists to the limits of their abilities and patience. They are the ones whom I have thought about most and talked about most with colleagues in the hope of finding a breakthrough.

In some cases, these difficult clients drove me to the brink of exasperation; nothing I tried with them seemed to make the slightest difference. And yet from working with them, I learned more about myself and about doing therapy than from any supervisor or instructor I ever had. It is the truly difficult clients who do not obey the rules we think are so important. They force us to be more flexible, creative, and innovative than we ever thought possible. And they require us to look deep inside ourselves to examine every one of our own unresolved issues that get in the way of our being compassionate and effective—both as professionals and as human beings.

Contents of the Book

The primary purpose of this book is to present a thorough grounding in the nature of client resistance, to describe the various models currently in use, and to help readers integrate what is known into a perspective that allows them to see therapeutic conflict as a constructive, albeit challenging, dialogue. The book is intended primarily for experienced clinicians who have logged considerable hours with clients who are sometimes uncooperative. Beginners and laypersons may also find the realistic portrayals helpful in showing that the therapeutic process often takes paths other than those plotted out in the usual textbook blueprints.

Several threads are interwoven throughout the content of this book: a conceptual discussion of the nature of client resistance and why some people present difficulties for a therapist; my personal experiences in the struggle to reach clients who seemed inaccessible; and practical suggestions for dealing with difficult cases. Some of the key questions that will be addressed include the following:

- What makes some people so difficult to work with?
- How is client difficulty different from client resistance?
- How do client expectations and therapist perceptions collide to create therapeutic impasses?
- What are the similarities between ourselves and those clients we struggle with the most?
- Why are conflicts of power at the root of most difficult therapy relationships?
- Why do we take client resistance so personally—as if something were being done to us?
- What guiding principles are most important when working with clients who do not follow the usual rules?

These questions all lead us to consider the situations in which therapists find themselves in trouble.

1. When clients are determined to be uncooperative (active resistance)
2. When clients cannot help but be uncooperative (entrenched patterns of being difficult)
3. When therapists do not know something (missing important information and knowledge)
4. When therapists believe they know something that they really do not (invalid assumptions)
5. When therapists cannot do something very well (poor execution of interventions)

6. When therapists will not do something (lapse of respon-
    sibility)
7. When something in the therapist is getting in the way of
    being helpful (unresolved issues)
8. When therapists have lost their compassion

Each of the four parts of this book is intended to help the
reader follow a systematic process of thinking more constructively, feeling more compassionately, and intervening more effectively with clients who are perceived as uncooperative.

Organization

Working with Difficult Clients is divided into four parts. In Part
One, "What Makes Clients Difficult," four chapters explore the
reasons that dealing with some people in therapy is such a
struggle. Their characteristics, behaviors, resistant strategies,
and manipulative games are described in detail and illustrated
with a number of cases. In addition, the interactive nature of
therapeutic impasses is examined in Chapter Four, which looks
at the circular communication problems created by the unrealistic expectations that therapists and clients have of one
another.

Part Two, "When the Therapist Is Difficult," contains three
chapters in which issues related to countertransference and the
therapist's own unresolved narcissistic needs are explored. Particular attention is given to how certain clients are "taught" to be
difficult by their therapists who are unable or unwilling to be
flexible. Also described are those therapists who are likely to
have more than their fair share of difficult clients because of
certain beliefs they hold and games they play out in their
sessions.

The third section of the book, "Some Very Difficult Clients," deals specifically with the kinds of clients who are most
often experienced as difficult to treat by a wide variety of practitioners. Illustrated liberally with case descriptions, each chapter
describes the behavior, dynamics, and communication patterns
of these clients, including special treatment problems and sug-

gestions for more effective therapeutic outcomes. These cases include clients who are manipulative (Chapter Eight), controlling (Chapter Nine), hostile (Chapter Ten), combative (Chapter Eleven), boring (Chapter Twelve), and passive (Chapter Thirteen).

The last part of the book, "Managing Difficult Cases," is directed solely at presenting those principles, strategies, and interventions that are most helpful to the therapist in working with difficult cases. Chapter Fourteen discusses the ways practitioners can more effectively confront their unresolved transference issues; Chapter Fifteen deals with the therapist's inner world as it relates to feeling more compassionately and thinking more constructively about different cases. Chapter Sixteen focuses on solidifying therapeutic alliances and capitalizing on insight processes, and Chapter Seventeen covers action-oriented strategies that have proved helpful in resolving impasses. The last chapter, Chapter Eighteen, summarizes the principal messages of the book in the form of "Rules of Engagement" for working with difficult clients.

Acknowledgments

I am most indebted to the difficult clients whom I have encountered during the past decade. Through their creativity, persistence, and dedication to finding their own unique path to enlightenment I have been pushed far beyond my own comfortable little world. Like most so-called learning experiences, these journeys with obstructive or rebellious clients were extremely taxing and frustrating. Only after we reached our destinations (or abandoned the search) could I look back with fond memories and say to myself, just like a kid who has crawled off a roller coaster after screaming nonstop in terror, "Gee, that was fun! I can't wait to do that again!"

I am also grateful for the wisdom and advice offered by colleagues who have consulted with me over the years about difficult cases, and to those who reviewed and reacted to this manuscript.

Las Vegas, Nevada   Jeffrey A. Kottler
January 1992

*This book is dedicated to
my father, who taught me about compassion,
and my son, who helped it to grow.*

the author

JEFFREY A. KOTTLER is an associate professor of counseling and educational psychology at the University of Nevada, Las Vegas. He studied at Oakland University, Harvard University, Wayne State University, and the University of Stockholm, and received his Ph.D. degree from the University of Virginia. He has worked as a therapist in a variety of settings including hospitals, mental health centers, schools, clinics, universities, corporations, and private practice.

Kottler is the author or coauthor of *Pragmatic Group Leadership* (1983), *Ethical and Legal Issues in Counseling and Psychotherapy: A Comprehensive Guide* (1985, 2nd ed., with W. H. Van Hoose), *On Being a Therapist* (1986), *The Imperfect Therapist: Learning from Failure in Therapeutic Practice* (1989, with Diane S. Blau), *Private Moments, Secret Selves: Enriching Our Time Alone* (1990), *The Compleat Therapist* (1991), and *Introduction to Therapeutic Counseling* (1992, 2nd ed., with R. W. Brown). He has also completed an audio program with Jossey-Bass: *The Reflective Therapist: Confronting the Personal and Professional Challenges of Helping Others* (1991).

compassionate
therapy

PART ONE

What Makes Clients Difficult

CHAPTER ONE

The Nature of Resistance

I have long been perplexed by the differences between what I was told by supervisors, teachers, and authors about how therapy was supposed to work and how it actually plays out in my office. I feel continually assailed by the claims of numerous workshop presenters and writers who claim they have discovered the latest miracle cure that works with almost everyone. The implication is that if my clients do not improve when I use these methods, it must by *my* fault. So I find myself wondering: am I the only one who still struggles, after all these years, with difficult clients?

In beginning the research on this topic I came across a number of works on dealing with severely disturbed or resistant clients. One edited volume by Giovacchini and Boyer (1982) seemed especially promising—that is, until I read the introduction, "Most clinicians have unreasonable patients sometime during their careers, often when they are still residents or beginning practitioners" (Giovacchini, 1982, p. 19).

Great! So I am supposed to have outgrown this? By now I should not encounter difficult clients anymore? I should be able to circumvent any problem, work around any resistance, neutralize any obstruction that gets in the way of a therapeutic cure?

The author later admitted that he occasionally felt frustrated, angry, out of control, hurt, or misunderstood in response to some of his unreasonable clients. I immediately felt a sense of kinship. As I dug deeper into the volume of scholarly treatises on what to do with regressed, paranoid, or borderline clients,

3

how they would be putty in our hands if we simply followed the analytic prescription for resolving transference neuroses, I discovered a small, comforting essay. In this chapter (Adler, 1982, p. 39), the author acknowledged the helplessness that therapists feel when confronting uncooperative clients: "I finally had to conclude that feelings of helplessness and hopelessness were part of the burden I had to bear as a therapist, and that I was not alone in experiencing them. I also began to see that these feelings tended to come up with greatest intensity with certain kinds of patients. And, in spite of my best intentions, I found myself repeatedly hopeless, helpless, and furious with those patients and fantasizing ways to get back at them or get rid of them."

As embarrassing as such admissions are—that certain clients really get to us in ways that disrupt our lives—I believe this circumstance is more universal than we have been led to believe. Further, by discussing openly those kinds of clients with whom we struggle the most, we put ourselves in a better position to sort out their dysfunctional behavior from our own and to formulate treatment strategies that are more likely to be successful.

Why Some Therapists Have More Difficult Clients Than Other Therapists

The whole subject of difficult clients is a bit awkward to discuss, for if we admit we have such people in our practice, we may be saying as much about ourselves as we are about them. The experts in our field have not made it easy for us to talk about our problem clients; the tendency of these experts is to publicize only those interventions that work, quietly ignoring their efforts that have failed dismally. As a result, some of us feel that we are the only ones who ever encounter difficult and resistant clients.

We often end up blaming ourselves when we cannot get through to a particular client, even though, according to Purcell and Wechsler (1991), it is the unavoidable outcome of some of our own unresolved issues that we can never hope to fully resolve. "Ignoring our personal issues reinforces the myth that as competent therapists we should be able to work effectively with all clients at all times, and under all circumstances" (p. 65).

We are further intimidated by the master therapists we see "live in concert" or on videotape who seem to handle problem clients with great deftness and ease, as if this minor glitch in the program can be easily corrected by waving a magic wand or instituting some ingenious strategy that becomes obvious only *after* they have explained it.

It is not just extraordinary charisma and skill that allow the most prominent practitioners to handle easily any difficult client who comes their way; they also have the luxury of screening prospective clients carefully and selecting only those who are most motivated and best suited to their approach. Masters and Johnson, for example, reported phenomenal success rates for their sex therapy cures in the 1970s, rates that could never be matched by other clinicians. This success is explained, in part, by their elaborate screening procedures that weeded out potentially difficult cases; also, those who were accepted in the program were highly motivated to succeed as they had traveled hundreds of miles and paid thousands of dollars to participate. Most of us do not have an unlimited supply of clients from which we can choose our favorites, all of whom have adequate financial resources and an intense desire to change. We are thus bound to encounter a clientele different from those who journey to Mecca (Anderson and Stewart, 1983a).

The more indigent the population we are working with, the more involuntarily they are forced into treatment, and the less famous we are in clients' eyes, the more often we will encounter clients who are uncooperative. No doubt this resistance can also be a function of the therapist's age, experience level, training, skill, personality, and therapeutic approach. Given all things equal, some practitioners do encounter more clients who are difficult because of the ways the therapists work, because of their lack of flexibility, and especially as a result of how they interpret behavior and define resistance.

Perspectives on Change and Resistance

The subject of difficult clients is treated by almost every existing therapeutic model, beginning with Freud's original conceptions of the client's efforts to repress threatening material unconsciously ([1914] 1957). In addition to this psychodynamic formulation of client reluctance, the phenomenon has also been defined as (1) an unwillingness to disclose (Rogers, 1958), (2) noncompliance with prescribed assignments (Shelton and Levy, 1981), (3) a struggle for interpersonal dominance (Watzlawick, Weakland, and Fisch, 1974), (4) nonacceptance of the therapist's legitimacy as a source of influence (Strong and Matross, 1973), or (5) a specialized form of communication (Erickson, 1964). Most simply, resistance can be defined as whatever the client does, deliberately or unconsciously, to prevent, circumvent, or otherwise block the progress of therapy (Puntil, 1991).

Developing a taxonomic classification of the twenty-two most common forms of client resistance, Otani (1989a) divided them into several basic categories that include withholding communication through silence, restricting meaningful content, engaging in a manipulative style of responding, or violating the basic rules of therapy. These kinds of resistance, with examples of characteristic behavior for each, are shown below:

Withholding Communication

Being silent
Making infrequent responses
Making minimal responses
Engaging in incessant
  rambling

Restricting Content

Making small talk
Intellectualizing
Asking rhetorical questions
Engaging in obsessive
  rambling

Being Manipulative

Discounting
Being seductive
Externalizing
Forgetting

Violating Rules

Missing appointments
Delaying payment
Making improper requests
Displaying inappropriate
  behaviors

The way therapists interpret these various client behaviors depends on their operating theory of how and why people change. Resistance can be viewed as an inevitable and natural component of change or as a signal that therapy is headed in the right direction. The gestalt therapist, for example, defines resistance as the client's avoidance of expressing genuine feelings. The behavior therapist labels clients difficult if they do not follow through with assigned tasks. And the client who follows therapeutic directives, but uses denial or repression to avoid dealing with other issues, will be seen by the psychoanalyst as defensive and resistant (Anderson and Stewart, 1983b).

Some of the more common theoretical views of resistance are also described by Dowd and Seibel (1990). A review of these interpretations of client behavior shows that some practitioners do not equate resistance with being difficult; they see in the client's obstructive actions a potential for progress if used effectively. Other therapeutic approaches view client resistance as an enemy that must be overcome if the client is to make any lasting changes. I have organized these various perspectives on a continuum from viewing resistance as the therapist's enemy to seeing resistance as a friend:

Resistance as Enemy

Problem Solving: Resistance is the enemy and must be overcome

Psychoanalytic: Resistance must be interpreted and counteracted

Behavioral: Resistance is annoying noncompliance with assigned tasks

Social Influence: Resistance is viewed neutrally as a form of communication

Cognitive Behavioral: Resistance is a natural component the change process

Systemic: Resistance is a way to maintain the structural integrity of the family

Existential: Resistance is a means of legitimate self-expression

Strategic: Resistance is embraced and paradoxically prescribed

Resistance as Friend

The continuum, of course, is a simplification of some very complex and varied perspectives. It is not meant to pigeonhole a theoretical orientation into a particular slot; rather it allows practitioners to classify their ideas about client behavior as primarily negative, positive, or neutral. This evaluation will determine, in part, how the therapist interprets and subsequently responds to resistant behavior.

Some Types of Resistance and What They Mean

A therapist's treatment of a difficult client depends not only on his or her general theoretical orientation but also on the particular meaning a certain client behavior has at a given moment in time. Resistance can be a normal and healthy way for clients to stall action until they have had the opportunity to explore thoroughly the consequences of changing. In other cases it can stem from more severe underlying character disorders. It can be used to avoid discomfort; it may arise from the fear of success. Resistance can be motivated by self-punishment or reflect a rebellious disposition. It can even be caused by neurological disease or meddling family members.

In the context of sexual dysfunctions, Munjack and Oziel (1978) classified various types of resistance according to their underlying causes. If we adapt their schema to a more universal client population, we can identify five discrete types of resistance, all motivated by different origins and thereby treated by different methods.

In *Type I* resistance clients simply do not understand what the therapist wants or expects. They may be relatively unsophisticated about how therapy works or may be very concrete thinkers. When requested to explain how he happened to arrive in therapy, one client says that he took the bus. He is not trying to be sarcastic or avoidant; he just does not understand the intent of the question. The source of the client's difficult behavior in Type I resistance can be the client's naivete, the therapist's incomplete communication, or a combination of both factors. Once the source of misunderstanding is identified, the therapist is able to clarify the expectations, roles, and objectives of therapy while concentrating on being very precise in future communications with the client.

In *Type II* resistance the client does not comply with assigned tasks because she lacks the skill or knowledge necessary to do so. The client is not being obstinate; she just cannot do what the therapist is asking. "How are you feeling right now?" the therapist asks a young woman who seems upset. She repeatedly replies, "I don't know," with increasing exasperation because she really does not know; at that moment she cannot put her feelings into words. The solution to this form of client difficulty is also relatively straightforward: ask clients to do only what they are able to do at the time, at least until they are able to develop new options.

Type III resistance involves a lack of motivation; clients show marked apathy and indifference in response to whatever the therapist does. This behavior can be the result of previous failures in therapy or a self-defeating belief system. Ellis (1985) has postulated that most forms of client reluctance result from the client's unrealistic demands that the world be a certain way ("It's not fair that people treat me this way") and self-sabotaging internal statements ("My situation is hopeless and I will never improve"). Some clients are especially difficult, not just because of the presence of these dysfunctional thoughts but because the clients resist any challenge to consider their validity.

Type III resistance also results when the client does not perceive any incentives to cooperate: "Why should I get all worked up over talking with you? Nothing will change anyway. Whether I get my act together or not, my wife is still going to leave me. At least I get time off as long as I stay depressed."

The intervention strategy for this type of resistance also logically flows from its source; the therapist should concentrate on instilling hope and positive expectations in the client as well as identifying possible sources of motivation and reinforcement for him. For this unmotivated man, he was helped to realize that even if he had no urge to improve his mood for himself or to save his marriage, he had to consider the effect of his behavior on his children. It made sense for him to lighten his mood and try to get on with his life for the sake of his children, who were suffering because of his neglect.

Type IV resistance is the "traditional" guilt- or anxiety-induced variety recognized most often by psychoanalysts. Defense mechanisms are no longer working effectively. The client starts to back off as repressed feelings begin to surface. Work can be proceeding smoothly and consistently until a nerve is struck, and then sometimes deliberately, but often unconsciously, the client does everything possible to sabotage further progress. Fear is often the overriding force — fear of embarrassment when revealing personal material to a stranger, fear of the unknown, fears that are triggered by prior experiences with well-meaning helpers, fear of being judged, fear of the anticipated pain that will accompany facing one's problems (Kushner and Sher, 1991). The antidote for these types of resistance is the bread and butter of insight-oriented psychodynamic treatment: offer support, work on trust in the relationship, facilitate greater client self-acceptance, and interpret what is occurring.

Type V resistance results from secondary gains the client receives as a result of his symptoms. In general, most examples of self-defeating behaviors that we see in clients (or ourselves) follow several basic themes (Dyer, 1976; Ford, 1981). Look, for example, at a client with a chronic somatizing disorder that is resistant to any and all interventions. Whether he has a complex factitious disease, a Munchausen syndrome, or a more pedestrian form of hypochondriasis, the client enjoys a number of benefits that make change especially difficult.

Whether we are speaking of symptoms as diverse as guilt, obsessive rumination, or temper tantrums, secondary gains usually provide the following cushion:

1. They allow the client to procrastinate and put off action. As long as clients have distracted us (and themselves) to focus on their favorite method of acting out, they do not have to take risks that are part of growth and change.
2. They aid the client in avoiding responsibility. "It's not my fault" and "I can't help it" are favorite laments of difficult clients who externalize problems. Because they blame oth-

ers for their suffering and seek to punish perceived enemies, they never have to look at their own role in creating
their suffering.

3. They help the client to maintain the status quo. As long as
    we look at the past, there is no opportunity to examine the
    present or future. The client remains safe and secure in a
    familiar existence (however miserable it might be), rather
    than having to do all the hard work that is involved in
    changing lifelong patterns.

One client who had remained impervious to every effort
aimed at confronting his need to destroy all his intimate relationships finally started to come around after generating a list of
his favorite payoffs:

- "I get to feel sorry for myself that I'm so alone. It is other
  people's fault that they don't understand me."
- "I get lots of sympathy from others; they feel sorry for me."
- "I prefer to call myself 'complex' rather than 'difficult.' I like
  being so different from your other clients. That way you
  really have to pay attention to me."
- "As long as I can drive someone away before he or she gets
  too close, I don't have to grow up and learn to carry on more
  mature, adult relationships. I am able to remain selfish and
  indulgent."
- "I get a lot of mileage out of the excuse that I have this
  problem — *that* is why I am not more successful in my life. I
  am afraid that once I resolve this I might have to face the fact
  that I can't reach my goals. This way, at least, I can pretend I
  could have what I want if only I tried."
- "I like the idea that I am destroying my relationships on *my*
  terms, before anyone has the chance to reject me. As long as I
  am in control of the way things end, it doesn't hurt half as
  much as it would otherwise."

Confronting these ploys and forcing clients to identify
the games they are playing in order to avoid change is an
important step in creating more self-responsibility. Secondary

gains work best only when clients are not aware of what they are
doing; once these self-defeating behaviors become explicit, it is
much harder for clients to engage in them without laughing at
themselves. When the confrontation strategy is combined with
attempts to alter the systemic forces that are reinforcing the
secondary gains, many types of client resistance can be significantly reduced.

Homeostasis and the Meanings of Resistance

We in the helping professions are quite fond of borrowing
instructive concepts from the sciences and adapting them to
explain complex psychological phenomena. Maybe we are attracted to these concrete physical realities because the subject of
our own study is so abstract and elusive. Perhaps we are imitating Freud, who liked to "neurologize" psychotherapy. Maybe we
are frustrated doctors who envy those who are able to fix problems with a pill, a scalpel, or a laser beam. Or maybe there is just
a lot of intuitive sense in assuming that human behavior, both
internal and external, obeys laws similar to those of the physical
world.

     One of the more common ways we tend to conceptualize
the behavior of difficult clients is with the process of homeostasis, the body's strong determination to maintain equilibrium
throughout every system. Turn up the heat and the sweat glands
will kick in to cool the surface temperature of the skin. Invade
any part of the body's environment in such a way as to disrupt
the precisely calibrated temperature, pressure, and fluid balance, and defenses will work to repel perceived threats and
restore a stable cellular state.

     We often observe this same process in some clients who
will attempt to thwart our goodwill, as well as their own efforts to
make needed changes, in order to maintain the homeostatic
balance of even a dysfunctional organism. According to this
functional model of client obstruction, most forms of client
resistance and difficulty are efforts to avoid change that may
threaten existing conditions.

     People tend to become difficult when they are expected

or required to change something they are already doing. "Unless people are immediately persuaded by overwhelming evidence that a change in their behavior is necessary or beneficial, such as responding to a fire by exiting from a building, they will resist change in the status quo" (Anderson and Stewart, 1983a).

Clients play games to keep us from getting too close, to protect themselves from perceived attacks. Of course, clients do not participate in this process consciously, any more than they deliberately order their sweat glands to activate; the responses are automatic and therefore need to be recalibrated — the essential process of psychotherapy.

The homeostasis model allows us to view difficult clients in such a way that we do not take their behavior personally, nor are we shocked when they use manipulative games to sabotage progress. We fully expect almost all clients to be difficult on some level, and when they are not, we are pleasantly surprised. (Some practitioners would even insist that *apparent* cooperation is, in itself, a sneaky form of resistance, but that is another story.)

Lest we get carried away with the metaphor of homeostasis, we should note that some writers offer the compelling argument that human behavior is not subject to the same laws as biochemical or intercellular events. Haley (1989), for one, believes the whole debate about client resistance is ridiculous: clients want to change; they just do not know how. Nevertheless, the family therapists have been most passionately committed to the homeostasis metaphor in explaining family dynamics of power and control.

It may be sheer egocentricity on our part to assume that human beings are exempt from the laws of the universe that apply to everything else. Eastern religions, Native Americans, even physicists have been saying for some time that *all* events and actions, however localized, are connected and influenced by energy in other parts of the universe. This is the root of the most basic theorem in quantum mechanics (Zukav, 1979).

My assumption throughout this book is that when clients are difficult it is because they are trying desperately to maintain homeostasis in their lives. Through their behavior they are trying to get along as well as they can and keep their lives on as even a keel as possible. If that effort means that the therapist must be inconvenienced or aggravated along the way, so be it.

Most people in general, most clients in particular, and difficult clients most of all are trying their best to get through hard times by resorting to the strategies that have worked for them before, however dysfunctional these may be. They seek to control as much of their environment as possible and are in turn influenced by the events and people who populate their world. They are not deliberately trying to make our lives miserable nor do they stay up late at night plotting ways to get to us; they just want to be understood.

Difficult clients are difficult precisely because they are not always aware of what they are doing. Our job is to help them in this endeavor of self-revelation and personal change without being made to suffer ourselves during the process. To accomplish this mission requires us to have a thorough understanding of the exact circumstances and variables that make some people so challenging to work with. This knowledge allows us to increase our sensitivity to what clients are experiencing and permits us to respond to them compassionately and effectively.

CHAPTER TWO

. *Profiles*
of Difficult Clients

The clients whom therapists consider difficult to treat generally fall into one of two groups — those who are chronically mentally ill and those who have personality disorders. These are, of course, the client populations with the most severe disturbances, the most long-standing patterns of dysfunction, the worst prognoses for improvement, and the most irritating styles of interaction. They are usually people who have been incapable of establishing, maintaining, and nurturing healthy relationships with others. They tend toward one of two poles; either they are passive, nonresponsive, apathetic, and withdrawn or they are aggressive, manipulative, impulsive, and vengeful. In virtually all instances, they have been the way they are for a long time, and they appear, at least on some level, determined to stay that way.

Although some writers have argued that there are no difficult clients (Stieger, 1967; Altshul, 1977), only difficult therapists, Wong (1983) conducted a survey of prominent clinicians across the country to learn their views on the subject. Among these senior therapists there was a consensus regarding those most challenging to treat. Some obvious diagnostic categories immediately surfaced: borderline, paranoid, and antisocial personalities, for example. Narcissistic disorders also rose to the top of the list along with clients who are potentially violent or suicidal. Finally, among the most frequently mentioned as difficult to treat were drug and alcohol addicts, the chronically mentally ill, clients who are part of severely pathological family

15

systems, and those hospital patients labeled "gomers" ("Get out of *my* emergency *room!*").

Usually elderly patients who crave attention, gomers are a heterogeneous population evenly distributed among races, sexes, and classes. What they have in common is irreversible mental deterioration, complex symptomatic patterns, an inability to resume normal adult roles, and no place to go after they are discharged from the hospital (Leiderman and Grisso, 1985).

"Gomerism" is not just a charactistic of clients, however; it represents a degree of cynicism and frustration on the part of the helper. The caregiver feels helpless and must face the limits of his or her abilities. The lonely, elderly client may even understand that there is little that can be done for him, but he feels that a little attention would be nice.

In a factor analytic study of how therapists react internally to the behavior of difficult clients, Colson and others (1986) found that among the severely disturbed population, the suicidal-depressed client evoked the strongest reactions of all. Staff members suffered most as a result of their contact with severely depressed clients who elicited a multiplicity of discrepant feelings, responding more strongly to these clients than to hospitalized borderlines or schizophrenics. On the one hand, we feel tremendous resolve to save the client's life, to rescue him or her from despair. On the other hand, we feel immobilized, frustrated, fearful, and impotent. Many of these same feelings are also elicited by difficult clients who are not so much resistant as they are uncomfortable to work with, such as victims or perpetrators of incest (McElroy and McElroy, 1991) and torture victims (Pope and Garcia-Peltoniemi, 1991).

We could certainly add several other candidates to this list, including some of those we will discuss throughout the book—seductive, dependent, manipulative, controlling, boring, or belligerent clients. Unfortunately, after we complete such a compendium of categories we are left with a population of clients who are perfectly well behaved, cooperative, motivated, and especially, grateful for our modest efforts.

Although it is true that nearly all diagnostic categories

offer their own unique challenges, what makes clients difficult in therapy has less to do with their presenting problems or symptomology than with the style in which they respond to their troubles (Dowd, Milne, and Wise, 1991). Not all drug addicts or obsessive-compulsives or chronically depressed clients are especially difficult in therapy. In fact, some of our greatest satisfaction in this work comes from our interactions with those people who have quite severe disturbances.

Imagine two clients, Fran and Sasha, who are both labeled *borderline* — that miscellaneous diagnostic category used to describe people who appear extraordinarily unstable in their affect and relationships, and who are prone to self-destructive acts. Fran, however, is considerably more devious in the ways she acts out. It is as if she has a rare variety of viral infection that continually changes its form in response to any treatment introduced into the body. Whereas Sasha is somewhat predictable in her "borderlinish" ways and can be counted on to respond to vigorous limit setting, Fran has not reacted the same way twice to *any* thereapeutic intervention. Fran appears more functional in the world — she has friends and a good job, unlike Sasha — but she is much more difficult for anyone to be around. Sasha is soft-spoken; Fran is shrill. Sasha tends to blame herself when things go wrong; Fran blames you: "And unless you find a way to straighten out this mess you created, I just might sue you. Just kidding. Ha. Ha."

Sasha has not improved significantly faster than Fran in therapy, but most clinicians would have an easier time working with her because her style is not as overtly obstructive to the process and the alliance. It may be, however, that ultimately she will be harder to reach because she keeps so much to herself. With Fran you think you know where she stands every moment, but the process with Fran will also be more of a struggle. Thus, clients are difficult not only because of their type of presenting complaints and the severity and intensity of the symptoms, but also because of their individual interactive styles.

Many practitioners quite enjoy working with more severely disturbed clients, not because it is the mandate of their agency or because of a masochistic streak but because they thrive on the challenge of working with people who need their help the most. Such professionals report that it is not necessarily the disorder that makes treatment difficult, whether clients are schizophrenic, sex offenders, borderline, or cross-addicted substance abusers; rather, it is the unique way individual clients manifest their symptoms, express themselves, and respond to interventions.

Assessment of Client Difficulty

Any attempt to capture the tendency to resist change in a single definition of client difficulty has two immediate problems. First, as such a conception reflects what the therapist believes is resistant or obstructive, it omits interpersonal and environmental factors that may be playing a part. Second, it assumes that being difficult is a dichotomous construct that is either present or not present (Jahn and Lichstein, 1980).

Most of us understand that the question is not whether a client is difficult but the degree and intensity with which treatment problems are operative in the therapy situation. This consideration takes into account not only the client's unique personality characteristics (which may predispose him to be abrasive), but also such questions as who is working behind the scene to sabotage progress? In what ways are we exacerbating difficulties in the relationship? What is it about the client's support system, environment, or phenomenological world that is making things difficult?

The problem of reliable assessment is made even more challenging because of the intrinsically subjective nature of this process. A half-dozen therapists who are all presented with the identical client are going to experience and interpret the situation in different ways. As an illustration, imagine that a new client walks into your office and asks:

"May I know what your qualifications and training are before I begin?"

As you think about this client's question, and formulate your response, consider how a sample of therapists might interpret this initial query:

Therapist A: *Not another one of these cases again. He's going to be a tough one.*

Therapist B: *Sounds like a reasonable place to start. I wouldn't trust anyone with my life either unless I knew they were well trained.*

Therapist C: *He seems to have a need to control things from the outset. I will have to monitor that closely.*

Therapist D: *He seems very frightened by this unfamiliar situation and is giving himself time to get used to things.*

Therapist E: *As long as he can keep the focus on me he can successfully avoid dealing with his own issues.*

Therapist F: *Interesting that he would begin with that question. I wonder what that means?*

Any of these assessments could be accurate. The client could very well be quite demanding to work with, but it is just as possible that he is asking a reasonable question under the circumstances. Depending on a myriad of accompanying cues — nonverbal, contextual, the referral situation — a therapist may draw a number of conclusions: that the client seems difficult (Therapists A, C, or E), that the client's question is entirely appropriate (Therapists B or D), or that judgment should be withheld until further data are available (Therapist F). The last choice is probably the most desirable posture to adopt, given the therapist's neutrality and receptivity to whatever might be occurring; it is also the most difficult.

During initial encounters with clients we often feel anxious ourselves — trying to make a good impression, trying to figure out what is going on, deciding whether we can help this person, wondering how we can be of greatest assistance demonstrating our compassion and understanding. This internal stress is augmented by the direct pressure applied by the client who is testing us, checking us out, deciding whether this is the right place to get help. Further, he wants answers: what do we see is the problem? Have we worked with this kind of situation before?

How long will it take? What will he have to do? The primary challenge is to keep our own apprehensions and performance anxieties in check long enough to get a complete and objective reading of all the nuances contained in the way the client presents himself.

Some therapists conclude that almost all their clients are difficult; others hardly ever consider them so. I have mentioned that the psychoanalyst expects to see resistance in every client, sees this as normal and natural, and waits patiently for its manifestations to appear. The problem-solving therapist, on the other hand, views resistance as a label of convenience applied by practitioners who are frustrated because they do not know what else to do for the client. Client resistance, however, is an altogether different creature from client difficulty.

Resistance to change may indeed be a natural process for anyone letting go of old patterns and replacing them with new, more effective ways of functioning, but difficult clients are those who tend to resist in particularly annoying ways. We are dealing, then, with a continuum of obstruction to the therapeutic process, a level of self-defeating behavior by the client, and a degree of frustration in the therapist.

We may be uncertain of where to place the client statement that began this example on a continuum of difficulty—whether it is an appropriate question, a normal hesitance, a sign of abrasiveness, or somewhere in between—but we would have little doubt about a question posed by another client:

"What gives you the right to pry into other people's lives? Did they teach you to ask stupid questions in graduate school, or were you always so nosy?"

In this case, there would be little disagreement among Therapists A through F (and all the way through the alphabet) that this client has a chip on her shoulder. Regardless of the reason underlying her hostility, whether it masks deep hurt or shallow sensitivity, this is a person who will likely test the patience of even the most tolerant of clinicians.

Consesus on What Makes a Client Difficult

It is important to stress once again that some writers have argued persuasively that there are no difficult clients, only difficult therapists. Lazarus and Fay (1982) have called resistance merely a rationalization by practitioners who will not accept responsibility for their treatment failures. Although offered as a criticism of those clinicians who blame their clients every time something fails to work in therapy, this premise goes to the other extreme. Obviously treatment failures are the responsibility of *both* partners in the relationship (Golden, 1983; Kottler and Blau, 1989).

Yes, therapists *do* make mistakes and misjudgments. Yes, the way we operate, our degree of expertise and personality, our skills and style do indeed influence greatly the outcome of what occurs in therapy. Yes, there are "difficult" therapists who, because of their rigidity, are unable to help some clients and then project the blame onto them for being so inflexible. But there are also clients who display certain characteristics or behaviors that make them difficult to reach, regardless of the practitioner's level of competence. Based on research conducted by several authors (Stern, 1984; Ritchie, 1986; Robbins, Beck, Mueller, and Mizener, 1988; Leszcz, 1989) as well as my own interviews with practitioners in the field, I identify and discuss below the kinds of clients who are often described as being most difficult.

Clients with Physiological Disorders

Clients who have neurological problems or other chronic diseases that impair their ability to focus, listen, and communicate are included in the category of physiological disorders. Donald is a vigorous man in his early fifties, at least he was until he was struck down by a stroke that wiped out his right hemisphere. In addition to paralysis on his left side, he has a number of cognitive deficits that are difficult to assess because he does not want anyone to know what he cannot do. It is clear, however, that he repeats himself and has trouble focusing his attention.

Donald is intensely motivated to change some things about his life, but he misses a number of appointments because he becomes confused about the day and time he is to come. Home visits are arranged temporarily to ensure some continuity in the effort to help him come to terms with his disabilities, his conflicted family relationships, and the financial hardships brought on by the illness. In these sessions it becomes evident that he cannot concentrate for more than a few minutes at a time. What he seems to want is an audience who will listen to the sad story of his life that he will tell again and again.

Clients with Hidden Agendas

Some people come to therapy with motives they have no intention of revealing. Sandor says that he is depressed and cannot sleep at night. This has never happened to him before; it all started with the trouble he has been having at work. His boss claims that he has not been doing his job correctly and filed a reprimand with management. Could you please help him with this problem of depression? Oh, and by the way, maybe you could talk to his lawyer who wants to know about the psychological effects of this unjust action on his mental health. How long must he come in order for you to write this letter?

Clients Who Ignore Appropriate Boundaries

Because of feelings of entitlement or a lack of awareness about rules, these clients invade our personal domain. "What's the big deal if I leave my children in your waiting room while I run a few errands? I mean, hardly anyone ever comes in. I'm sorry if they got a little loud, but if you didn't want them to write on the walls, maybe you shouldn't leave those pens in here where anyone can get to them. Next time I come you should put those things away."

Clients Who Refuse Responsibility

Some clients are perpetually negative, critical, and demanding, always blaming others for their problems. "I can't believe how stupid those teachers are at my son's school. No wonder he has trouble; who wouldn't with those idiots in charge? And that means that I have to clean up the mess that they create. It's the same thing over and over again. I was telling you before about the people at work.... Hey, are you listening to me? Well, if you are, why did you look up at the clock.... What do you mean, our time is up? What kind of crap is that? You are just like those people I was telling you about; all you care about is yourself.... All right, I'll leave. But next time I expect you to do more than just sit on your butt and tell me that *I* have to change. Listen, buster, other people have got a lot of things *they* have to do differently if they think that I'm going to change."

Clients with an Argumentative Attitude

Certain clients enjoy verbal combat as a form of entertainment or a test of will. Onie is an elder on the Indian reservation's council. The nature of her work requires her to be able to compromise with others to take care of necessary business, but she is always at odds with everyone. She seems to take delight in stirring things up, provoking fights with the other tribal leaders, usually sabotaging whatever program is being developed.

In therapy she is similarly provocative. She challenges with a frightening ferocity everything that is offered. Onie says she genuinely likes the therapist and respects what he is trying to do to help her, but she disagrees with almost everything he says. Whenever the therapist attempts to agree with something Onie says, she will change her position and take the opposite point of view.

Clients with a Fear of Intimacy

Clients who desperately crave being close to others but are terrified of being vulnerable have a fear of intimacy. Crane has been rejected throughout his life, first by his parents who were alcoholics, next by his older sisters who considered him a burden they had to take care of, and finally by childhood friends who treated him like a leper (or so he recalls). He is close to nobody right now, except for you, of course, his therapist. Oddly, you do not feel close to him at all.

When you try to get close to him, or invite him to share something personal with you, he finds some way to push you away. At times, he will be sarcastic or ridiculing or withholding.

During those rare instances when some minimal degree of intimacy does begin to develop, he will "forget" to come to his next appointment. If by some miracle you do manage to bridge the distance between you, you fear he will flee. You recall that you are the fourth therapist he has seen in as many years.

Mismatch of Client and Therapist

The client presents issues or a personal style that is not generally responsive to what the therapist does and the way the therapist does it. Maurie is angry. He looks angry. He acts angry. In the very first encounter he makes it quite clear he has a problem with anger.

Maurie has suffered silently for many years at the hands of an abusive spouse. His wife is a state-certified schizophrenic; therefore, he has found it difficult to hold her accountable for her crazy behavior. If he is not angry with her, he is certainly angry with himself for putting up with her abuse for so long. He wants help expressing his anger.

I suggest to him that perhaps an even more desirable goal would be to harness the energy of his anger in more productive directions. He becomes angry with me because I am contradicting him. It is apparent to both of us that something is not clicking between us; some dynamic irritant is impeding our making contact.

Countertransference issues

Some clients bring intense issues to therapy that the client and therapist cannot fully work through. Only after I referred Maurie to a colleague, at his request (and my relief), did I begin to explore what in our interaction was so irritating. I had already been alerted years ago to monitor myself carefully whenever I worked with clients who were struggling with fears of death or fears of failure, but my response to Maurie seemed to be something new.

I eventually reached the conclusion that I have problems dealing with anger — my own as well as that of other people who are in the throes of an outburst. I reflected over the years at how often I had tried to talk people out of being angry; if that did not work, I had concentrated on other areas that were more comfortable for me.

Clients as Countertransference Objects

Certain clients remind us of others we have struggled with in the past. My first grade teacher called herself "Eagle Eye Silver" because she claimed she could read our minds and see *everything* we were doing. Once when her back was turned I tested her and put gum on my nose. She saw me through the back of her head and made me stand in front of the class for the rest of the morning with the gum still perched on my nose. I have had a problem with authority figures ever since.

When the grey-haired lady first walked into my office, I felt there was indeed some redemption in life. She was better than a first grade teacher — she was an elementary school *principal*. She carried herself with an air of great authority, even royalty. Worse yet, she addressed me as "young man." It was payback time.

Fortunately, I was under supervision at the time and my supervisor quickly helped me realize that this case of a difficult client was, in actuality, a therapist who was being difficult.

Impatient Clients

Some clients persist with unrealistic expectations regarding what therapy can do, how it works, and how long it takes. Sung was an engineering student who came to the counseling center because of an inability to concentrate on his studies. He missed his family who lived very far away, he had very few friends, and he was experiencing a number of problems adjusting to a new culture and climate. His one solace was in the purity of solving engineering problems: with the right tools and resources at his disposal, he felt that he could build or fix almost anything.

Sung had similar expectations for how therapy would operate. He would tell the therapist what the problem was and then this expert problem solver would design the best remedy.

Sung was adamant that this procedure not take longer than one
or two meetings. Also, the nature of his pain was such that he
insisted he could survive for only a few days without giving up
completely.

Inarticulate Clients

Clients who lack verbal skills or the capacity to describe what
they think and feel are often reported by therapists as being
especially challenging to help.

Therapist: What can I do for you?

Client: I don't know.

Therapist: You don't know why you are here?

Client: Yes. I mean no. I mean I know why I am here—I want
help and stuff—but I don't know what is wrong or what you can
do.

Therapist: Tell me something about yourself.

Client: There is not much to tell. I've lived here all my life. I
work just down the street. What is it that you want to know?

Therapist: Why don't you start with how you are feeling right
now?

Client: I'm not feeling anything at all.

Literal, or Concrete, Clients

Some people are unable to tolerate ambiguity and lack the
capacity for abstract reasoning. Stephen is an accountant—and
a good one, he is quick to explain. He has a clipboard on his lap
and in his breast pocket he has an assortment of different color
pens. Right now he is taking notes on what is being said and
highlighting something important in yellow. He reads from his
paper: "So what you are saying is that you are my consultant, sort
of like my mental accountant, ha ha, but I have to do most of the

work? I assume you will be giving me reading assignments and homework to do?"

Empty Clients

Some clients lack the capacity for self-reflection and have no interest in self-awareness. "I would certainly like to accomodate you, but the truth of the matter is that I don't really think about this stuff at all between sessions."

Clients Who Feel Hopeless

Among the most difficult of clients are those who are utterly despondent, seriously suicidal, and without the slightest hope that anything will ever be any better. Karyn is diagnosed with major depression that has been unresponsive to a half-dozen different medications. She cries constantly, great sobs of excruciating anguish, and looks at you with eyes that plead: "Please do something! How can you sit there and see me literally dying inside and not do anything?"

Compliant Clients

There are clients who pretend to cooperate with therapy by being overly solicitous and complimentary, but they do not ever change. Frieda has been appearing at her appointments for years. In fact, she has been at the agency longer than most of the staff, having seen four different therapists who have now moved on to other jobs. Although each of the clinicians followed a somewhat different therapeutic approach, the progress notes are remarkably similar: Frieda is a quite pleasant and cooperative client. She will do whatever the therapist asks and seems grateful for whatever assistance is offered. However, after many years and four therapists she is still living in a dysfunctional marriage, still working at the same dead-end job, and still seeing the same friends who ridicule her. But she sure looks forward to her weekly sessions!

Clients Who Attack the Therapist

Some clients seek to intimidate and control the relationship by
attacking the therapist's credibility, or even physical health.
"Look, I have explained to you what I need you to do. I want you
to call my wife and tell her to come home. She trusts you. In fact,
you are probably the one who put the idea in her head to leave in
the first place. Either you straighten out this mess that *you*
created, or I'm going to straighten you out. I know where you live.
And if you don't hear from me real soon, you will be hearing
from the state licensing board and my attorney."

Clients with Little Impulse Control

Clients lacking impulse control may be the most difficult of all.
These are people who have a hair-trigger temper and are prone
to violent outbursts; also in this category are often substance
abusers. Nate has four convictions for driving under the influence of alcohol and other miscellaneous substances. He has
been referred to therapy by the court as an alternative to serving
jail time and has been ordered to attend sessions until *you*, the
therapist, release him.

In additon to his chronic alcohol abuse, he also has a
history of losing his temper and getting into fights. The last
episode, the one that led him to your office, occurred on an
expressway when Nate believed he was cut off by someone
driving into his lane. He forced the person off the road, kicked
in his window, yanked him out of the car, and "persuaded" him to
apologize. Nate explains, "It was no big deal; I wasn't really going
to hurt the guy; I just wanted to teach him a lesson."

A review of the categories that therapists report as most
difficult to treat shows that the most dominant characteristic of
difficult clients seems to be their demanding behavior. Regardless of their diagnosis (paranoid, narcissistic, or borderline),
regardless of their primary traits (stubborn, manipulative, or
complaining), regardless of their behavior (rejecting help, failing to cooperate, acting dangerously), difficult clients feel entitled to more than their fair share of attention. In several studies

of what makes clients most difficult to their therapists, the most recurring themes are centered around the demand for extra time and attention (Rosenbaum, Horowitz, and Wilner, 1986; Robbins, Beck, Mueller, and Mizener, 1988).

A second theme equal in importance to the demanding nature of difficult clients is their need for control. Any client can become resistant when experiencing a sense of helplessness and seek to restore a sense of personal power by attempting to control the therapy and the therapist. The truly difficult client, however, is one who is not only situationally resistant but characterologically reactant as well (Brehm and Brehm, 1981). Such an individual responds to threat (which is perceived to be everywhere) by attempting to dominate and control all encounters in his or her life (Dowd and Seibel, 1990).

A third factor that easily distinguishes difficult from more cooperative clients is the nature of their defensive organization. Higher-order defenses like repression, intellectualization, and rationalization are relatively easy to deal with compared with the more primitive mechanisms described by Kernberg (1984) as splitting—which involves the actual dissociation of unacceptable impulses often seen in borderline personalities. These defenses are quite effective at protecting the disturbed client from intrapsychic conflict, but they have side effects that reduce the client's flexibility and adaptability.

A fourth theme is the tendency of difficult clients to externalize problems. These are people who wage war against the human race. They are in such pain that they have become vengeful and retaliatory for past injustices that were inflicted upon them. "Rather than the problem being lodged in themselves, in such a way that it might be possible to reach and help them, it becomes lodged in the outside world. It is 'other people' who are seen as disliking them, preventing them from living their lives, making them worried and anxious, and depriving them of their rights" (Davis, 1984, p. 30). Thus they devote all their energy and attention to righting perceived injustices, complaining about how unfairly they are being treated, and guarding against being hurt by attacking those to whom they are closest.

We can therefore conclude that most therapists agree about which clients are the most difficult. They tend to demand more from us than we are willing or able to give. They fight us every step of the way for control and attempt to manipulate us to do their bidding. They do not admit they have the same problems we think they have. And when they do acknowledge that they have some deficits, they refuse to do what we want them to do to resolve them.

We might then justifiably wonder: if this is only a *partial* list of what therapists experience as their most difficult clients, is there anyone left to treat who may be described as cooperative?

The Ideal Client

You are waiting in your office for your next client, a new referral about whom you know nothing. You hear the door open and someone enters the waiting area. Whom do you hope it will be? Construct an image of your ideal client, the one perfectly suited for the way you prefer to work. Is it a man or a woman, boy or girl? Is the client old, young, or middle aged? What does he or she look like? What does this person do for a living? What is the presenting complaint?

My client is definitely a she. She is in her forties, about my age, attractive, but not distracting. She is in good shape phys-ically. She is a movie producer. No, make that a photographer (more reliable in showing up for appointments). She is self-assured and poised, though she is not afraid to show her vul-nerability. She has come to therapy not because of any debilitat-ing problem but for growth and self-understanding. She wants to learn about herself, and while she is already quite effective in her life, she would like to become even more so.

My gosh, this exercise is revolting! This is the last person on earth who needs my help, and yet she is my ideal client. When I examine my attitudes more closely, however, I realize that I get considerably less satisfaction from this type of "easy" work than from working with so-called difficult clients who force me to go beyond what I already know and can do.

Most professionals can do quite easily what I just did:

create a portrait of their ideal client. The perfect client is trusting and disclosing, has realistic and positive expectations for
what therapy can do, has acute rather than chronic problems,
and is willing to accept major responsibility for progress in
sessions (Stiles, Shapiro, and Elliot, 1986). When asked to compare the easiest client in their caseload with their most difficult,
therapists were able to distinguish consistently among several
characteristics: their ideal clients were more attractive, less
pathological, and had a better prognosis for improving than did
their difficult clients. They were also less likely to be labeled a
personality disorder. Overriding every other consideration, including the therapist's level of experience and theoretical orientation, was the universal conclusion that the best clients are
highly likable and have good relationship skills (Merbaum and
Butcher, 1982).

In a review of client characteristics most often associated
with positive outcomes, Sexton and Whiston (1990) concluded
that the best candidates for therapy (at least in terms of measure-
ment criteria used in empirical research) tend to be those who
are more intelligent, better educated, members of higher socioeconomic groups, Caucasian, emotionally healthy, and experiencing acute problems. The authors also refuted a number of
myths regarding client characteristics. For example, the sex of
the client is unrelated to outcome (Jones and Zoppel, 1982) as is
age (Luborsky, Crits-Christoph, Mintz, and Auerbach, 1988) or
race when the client is in the upper socioeconomic stratum
(Jones, 1982).

The clients who are usually most desirable, whom psychi-
atrists, psychologists, family therapists, social workers, and
counselors compete for in the marketplace, fit a definite profile.
They are bright, vibrant, and interesting people. They are professionals. They are reasonably healthy, have no underlying
personality disorder, and present symptomology that is easy to
treat. They are highly motivated to change, yet are patient
enough to wait for results. They have a great capacity for developing insight, can tolerate ambiguity, and have a high threshold
for dealing with uncertainty. They are verbally expressive, creative thinkers who present vivid material rich in detail and

symbolism. They are socially skilled and responsible. They show up on time, pay their bills promptly, and offer to pay for cancellations. They would never call therapists at home or bother us between sessions unless they had a genuine emergency. They are appropriately deferential toward and respectful of our position. They are also very grateful for our help.

A discussion of cultural issues is also in order here, for if some therapists were to make a list of clients they would rather not work with, these people would likely be poor, disadvantaged, and members of minority groups. These clients are generally perceived to have poor motivation to change, to be members of dysfunctional families likely to sabotage treatment, and to present disorders that are generally not amenable to psychotherapy—child abuse, alcohol and substance abuse, abject poverty, and chronic hopelessness (Larke, 1985). I should note, however, that many of us in the field prefer to work with people who are disadvantaged or culturally different because we are forced to stretch our values and skills to reach those who need us the most; often such clients are not difficult so much as they are different and thus more challenging than people who are most similar to us in background and life experiences.

Although we would be quick to point out that it is not racism, cultural insensitivity, or biases that lead many of us to prefer a young, attractive, verbal, and intelligent clientele, this would be a feeble protest, indeed. The truth is that, more often than not, difficult clients are difficult because they are not like us. They operate under rules and values different from ours. Often, they have not been prepared to get the most from a therapeutic experience. They may be mistrustful of authority and reluctant to talk about what is bothering them.

It is easier to communicate with someone with whom we share the same background, language, and customs. The degree to which these life experiences differ determines the amount of time and energy we must invest in finding common ground.

It is ironic that the people who most need the services of an advocate or confidante are those who are least likely to get one, and to keep one for any length of time. Clients are difficult not only because of what they do and how they do it but also because of how they are perceived and labeled by their therapists.

CHAPTER THREE

Calling Clients Names

Traditionally, in medicine, education, and the social sciences, when we do not understand something very well we give it a fancy label. It seems that if we can name a complex phenomenon, we can harness it. Thus diagnostic systems based on the medical model equate complex psychological processes with discrete categories. In theory, this is a wonderful idea; in practice, however, difficult clients are often shuffled into boxes called "borderline," "narcissistic," and "histrionic," even though they often fit the criteria of all or none of them (Kroll, 1988).

Our diagnostic systems are also unacceptably unreliable. They stigmatize people for life and substitute their uniqueness and individuality for labels that are both ambiguous and confusing (Boy, 1989). They also emphasize, disproportionately, what is wrong with people—their psychopathology rather than their resources and strengths (Kottler and Brown, 1992).

Difficult clients have been given a number of different descriptors: character disordered (Leszcz, 1989), stressful (Medeiros and Prochaska, 1988), bogeyman-like (O'Connor and Hoorwitz, 1984), obnoxious (Martin, 1975), hateful (Groves, 1978), help-rejecting (Lipsitt, 1970), manipulative (Hamilton, Decker, and Rumbaut, 1986), impossible (Davis, 1984), entitled (Boulanger, 1988), and abrasive (Greenberg, 1984) as well as the more benign labels of reluctant (Dyer and Vriend, 1973), resistant (Hartman and Reynolds, 1987), and unmotivated (West, 1975).

The major thrust of most literature on this subject is that

some clients, for a variety of reasons that may or may not be their fault, have a need to *enact* while their therapists have a need to *act* (Fiore, 1988). Therein lies the struggle. We feel a strong drive to do something, to fix what we find broken, whereas the difficult client feels compelled to behave in ways that are beyond our comprehension. He or she operates under different rules from those we are used to. Whether these are forms of resistance is beside the point; these unusual ways of acting in therapy (to use neutral language) are disorienting and often frustrating as we try to make sense of and respond to clients' behaviors without escalating their intensity.

Although labeling our problem clients provides us with some relief initially (sort of like making up an explanation for a mysterious sound in the middle of the night so we can go back to sleep), ultimately these labels can prevent us from seeing the people we help as unique individuals. Once we start thinking of our clients as borderlines, hypochodriacs, or narcissists, we sometimes sacrifice much of our compassion and caring. These labels do not quite elicit the same sympathy as other medical terms such as cerebral palsy or multiple sclerosis.

If we are to be of much use to clients who are already mistrustful and cautious, who already feel weird and unfairly judged by others, we should not confuse the labels we insert on treatment plans or insurance forms with the actual people we are seeing. It is often in anger and exasperation that we use psychiatric labels to refer to clients in our own minds or when we talk to colleagues: "You wouldn't believe the borderline I saw today . . . ," "I've got this obsessive . . . ," "Time to gear up and see Mr. Narcissism and Mrs. Hysteria . . ."

The cynicism implied in these statements illustrates the disdain (and fear) that we sometimes feel in response to clients who give us a hard time. The first step to being able truly to help them is to regain the caring, compassion, and empathy that we once felt while protecting ourselves from further abuse. Sometimes we can accomplish this by substituting more behaviorally based labels that do not reduce the whole person to a dysfunctional entity. Thus, if we say or think that a client is engaging in "borderlinish" or "narcissistic" behavior, we describe what might be occurring while we still recognize that this phenomenon could be situational and certainly is not the sum total of what this person is like. Even the *Diagnostic and Statistical Manual* of the American Psychiatric Association (1987) is moving away from labeling people and is instead, in its subsequent revisions, describing disorders.

It is a sign of maturity in our profession that we are ready to confront the difficult client; more and more, books, workshops, symposia, panel discussions, and special journal issues are appearing on the subject. In a parallel process, increasing attention is being directed toward the therapist's own countertransference reactions to difficult clients and his or her contributions to the conflicts (Slakter, 1987; Wolstein, 1988; Tansey and Burke, 1989; McElroy and McElroy, 1991; Natterson, 1991).

Feiner (1982) views the broadened attention to difficult clients and their impact on therapists as a healthy attempt to extend our influence to those who need us the most but who do not conform to the rules we consider sacred. The main problem, however, is that by confronting the difficult client as an issue, we negate a particular person's autonomy and uniqueness. We take people we consider hard to deal with, even a little frightening, and we use labels to smother the life out of them.

Sometimes Ignorance Can Help

Not everyone is a suitable candidate for psychotherapy. Some clients do not work well with particular therapists but would do just fine with others. Other clients cannot respond to what anyone does to try to help them. They are either unwilling or unable to make substantial changes in their lives. These forms of resistance are so virulent they could defeat Carl Rogers, Albert Ellis, Sigmund Freud, and Virginia Satir before lunch and still have time for Milton Erickson for a little afternoon diversion. These clients, in short, are difficult people to be around.

We are speaking of those who fit mostly in the personality disorder categories of the *Diagnostic and Statistical Manual* (American Psychiatric Association, 1987). It is just this classification, however, that sometimes gets us in trouble, even though we find it helpful to diagnose accurately the disorder a particular client is manifesting. The labeling process helps us to get a handle, or at least a starting point, on what we are dealing with — the etiology, symptom clusters, prognosis, and the like. It is also very comforting to see in black and white a description of what we are encountering in the office.

But these labels occasionally do us, and our clients, a disservice. Early in my career a young man came to see me complaining of irresistible urges to dress up in his wife's underwear and run out in the street for all his neighbors to see. His compulsion had escalated to the point that now he would sit by the door wearing a favorite negligee, just on the verge of bolting out the door. In my naivete and inexperience I simply offered the explanation that all of us do things we are ashamed of. So what? But it is the *guilt* that destroys us.

He seemed especially relieved to hear that, and I could see he felt much better. Before I saw him the next week I met with my supervisor who expressed astonishment at my innocence and stupidity. The client was clearly exhibiting a problem of impulse control and sexual deviance; it would be very difficult to treat and take years to resolve successfully. I was suitably chastised and adequately prepared for next time in which I would take a thorough history and begin the lengthy process of whatever is involved in working with sexual deviates.

The client entered my office with a bright smile on his face and a hearty handshake. "Thanks for your help. You were certainly right. When I left you I decided it was the shame and guilt that were eating me up. I decided to tell my best friend about my compulsion, and rather than fleeing from me he told me his own kinky preferences. Then when I got home, I tearfully confessed to my wife, convinced she would want to institutionalize me, or at least divorce me. But to my astonishment, she asked me to dress up in her underclothes and we had the wildest sex of our lives! Thanks a lot. I feel just great. And no more impulses to run outside."

It would be easy to say that obviously this was not a true sexual deviate (because by definition he could not be cured in a single session), but I would like to think (and please indulge me for the moment) that it was my inexperience, ignorance, and lack of sophistication that allowed me to label this case not an "impulse disorder" but a "man-who-does-strange-things-and-feels-guilty-because-he-can't-accept-himself." I have never forgotten the lesson of this case (nor did my supervisor who wanted to transfer me to someone else). Many times since then I have worked with other so-called impulse disorders, personality disorders, and the like, and while a part of my brain automatically supplies a label, I stubbornly refuse to use it in my thinking about the case.

Diagnostic labels depress me. Once I read how morbid the prognosis is for a particular label, I lose my hope and faith that I can be helpful. (I also do not feel so bad when the client fails to improve.) Many of the clients we will discuss in this book are frustrating, even infuriating, to work with. They easily provoke our anger and lead us to compromise our compassion. They get under our skin and sometimes even try to hurt us deliberately, to knock us off our high horse. Therefore, some form of counteraction is needed to keep us from losing our composure and our caring. I find it helpful in talking about and working with difficult clients to remind myself, constantly, that this is a human being in pain who is doing the best he or she can.

Clients Are Not the Enemy and Therapy Is Not War

Some practitioners think of their difficult clients as lethal, dangerous, ferocious barracudas who engage us in a contest of wills. In his book *Fishing for Barracuda*, Bergman (1985, p. 3) describes this point of view, noting that clients do their best to defeat mental health professionals any way they can: "Once I learn from the initial telephone conversation about this impressive history of treatment failure, I immediately begin thinking in my 'resistance mode' and seeing the family differently from the way I would see a less resistant family."

Bergman (1985) measures the degree of client difficulty by several factors: (1) the client's previous history in defeating other therapists, (2) the chronicity of the present symptoms, (3) the level to which the underlying issue is covert and hidden,

(4) the number of other helpers involved In the case, and (5) the context in which the referral was made. He claims that he can easily determine whether he is dealing with a "barracuda" in the very first telephone contact with the client. Those who call from phone booths, ask questions about his credentials, communicate that they feel little anxiety, or believe someone other than themselves is the source of their problems are immediately diagnosed as resistant and needing unusual forms of treatment.

Concluding after only one brief phone conversation that a client will be difficult sets into motion a series of actions that are irrevocable. Yet there is no dishonor for a client in being resistant, no reason to be called names just because he or she wishes to avoid pain. As Breuer and Freud (1893) originally conceived their term in *Studies of Hysteria*, resistance was meant to describe the client's attempt to avoid real or imagined pain. Milman and Goldman (1987) recount the startling event in which Freud first stumbled on what could be causing his twenty-four-year-old client, Fraulein Elizabeth von R., to be unable or unwilling to remember certain thoughts and memories from her past. After repeatedly admonishing her to continue her associations, and still feeling frustrated in his efforts to enlist Elizabeth's cooperation, Freud excitedly concluded: "A new understanding seemed to open before my eyes when it occurred to me that this must no doubt be the same psychical force that had played a part in the generating of the hysterical symptoms and had at that time prevented the pathogenic idea from becoming conscious" (Breuer and Freud, 1893, p. 268).

Freud, of course, spent the rest of his life searching for why certain clients resist and become difficult, discovering in the process the heart of his theories of repression, defense mechanisms, and transference. Understanding what makes clients uncooperative thus became the cornerstone of all psychoanalytic thought.

Subsequent generations of analysts attempted to expand Freud's notions on resistance; these included such writers as Wilhelm Reich, Heinz Kohut, Robert Langs, Jacques Lacan, James Masterson, Anna Freud, Peter Giovacchini, and Otto Kernberg. The principal value of this attention to the subject, regardless of whether the clinician is sympathetic to psycho-dynamic theory, is the central premise that a client's obstructive behavior should be respected as a source of valuable information about what clients fear, what they are avoiding, and what this warding off means.

Difficult clients are frightened. Their behavior, which we call resistance, is normally something that we try to prevent or circumvent—an enemy to be defeated. These people are certainly not ferocious barracudas seeking to eat us alive. Difficult clients are often just people with problems that are more complex than those we usually confront, and with an interactive style that is different from what we might prefer. Calling them names only disguises the reality that resistant clients are attempting to tell us about their pain, even if their method of communication is sometimes indirect and annoying.

Chapter Four

In the Eye
of the Beholder

In spite of what we sometimes believe, clients do not deliberately try to make our lives miserable. From their own perspective, they are just trying to fumble through life doing what works best for them. They are attempting to keep the fragile threads of stability and security in place.

"No sudden movements please. Just understand that I am trying, I am *really* trying in my own way, to cooperate with you. I know you are only trying to help me. And I am not being difficult on purpose. But I just can't be who you want me to be and do what you want me to do. At least not yet. I'm tired of living up to everyone else's expectations. Can't you just humor me for a little while longer? I don't mean to be a pest."

This soliloquy represents the absolute truth of what is happening as understood by many difficult clients. They may have some awareness that they are behaving in ways that make it hard for others to get close to them, but they are not sure what those ways are. Further, it is absolutely terrifying to them to imagine an existence without the means for keeping people at a distance.

Resistance to change and defensiveness against threaten-ing stimuli are a way of life. They buy us time to build new cognitive structures that will accommodate strange and wonder-ful ideas. They give us breathing room to get used to foreign and often disorienting perspectives. They are adaptive mechanisms that are part of every organismic system. They help prepare us to

40

formulate a response to something we have not experienced before.

This moment, and every moment, our defense systems are operating inside our brains. Our very first inclination, after being presented with a new idea, is to find ways to discount or disqualify it. If we accept some novel idea as true, then we have a lot of work ahead of us trying to figure out ways to incorporate this new information and clean out all the obsolete plans we have been relying on for a long time.

I first learned to do therapy during the encounter movement when the focus of most interventions involved the expression and stimulation of affect among clients. Most everything I did revolved around helping people get in touch with and express how they feel. Emotions are the heart of human existence, the source of all pleasure and pain. Help people to understand and express how they feel and the rest of life changes will naturally follow.

I thought this was a lovely way to operate as a therapist. And it worked quite well.

The first time I heard Albert Ellis introduce the idea that disordered thinking was the source of psychological suffering I remember being incensed. How dare he spout such nonsense that threatened to undermine everything I understood about human change! I delighted in finding ways to make fun of this brash New Yorker and his absurdly logical system. In time, however, my rancor lost some of its force as I slowly found ways that I could blend cognitive therapy ideas into my own style of practice. I have undergone a similar process just about every one of the several hundred times I have been exposed to other novel ideas that threaten my comfortable professional orientation. Of course, what I am doing is exactly what the difficult client does on a larger scale: buying time until he or she can feel comfortable enough to venture out into the unknown.

Therapist and Client Expectations

When a client walks through the door, we often have a long list of preconceptions and predictions about what will occur, what the

client will do and say, and how we will respond. The difference
between clients we like and those we dislike is essentially based
on their willingness to subscribe to the rules and values we have
established. All therapists have certain expectations regarding
what they consider most appropriate in their clients' behavior.
These include some of the following:

- The client will be deferential and impressed with our general persona.
- The client will clearly and concisely tell us what is wrong and
  what we can do to help.
- The client will be reasonably lucid and orderly in his or her
  presentation.
- The client will occasionally pause in the narrative, allowing
  us to interject our perceptions, and then confirm that we are
  on the same wavelength.
- The client will have realistic expectations for what we can
  and cannot do for them.
- The client will express gratitude for our desire to help and
  express confidence in our abilities.

     The strength with which therapists endorse these rules is
directly related to how annoyed they become when clients do
not act as they are expected to (Fremont and Anderson, 1988).
These premises, of course, neglect the most basic rule in the
therapeutic contract: the client's main job is to be who he or she
is. "He cannot do otherwise. When he conveys his sense of futility
and impotent rage, if these are salient issues for him, he is then
doing his 'job'" (Fiore, 1988, p. 91).
     The most common problems that arise in the therapeutic
relationship come not only when the client does not live up to
the therapist's expectations but when the reverse is true as well.
Most clients eventually are disappointed by their therapists;
difficult clients are the most diappointed of all. They have their
own unrealistic expectations for us, expecting us to fulfill the
following:

- To know everything and be able to do anything
- To have limitless patience

- To be servants who are paid to suffer all the indignities that they wish they could have inflicted on others
- To have secrets that permit us to remove all their pain without their having to do much at all
- To clear our schedules and our personal lives so that we can spend all our free time thinking about them and be available for them in case they should want to talk
- To be not the least inconvenienced if they should forget an appointment, or be upset if they fail to pay their bills

It was Freud ([1915] 1957) who first spoke at great length about the unconscious need of clients to elevate their therapists to the position of omnipotent parents who can protect and rescue them from distress. It is also inevitable that one day they will discover that this "ideal parent" is not perfect after all. They realize we make mistakes. We do not know everything. And sometimes they can even sense our impatience or boredom or frustration. When they do begin to lash out, it is most often by indirect means, punishing us because we have let them down, because we don't say or do enough. They come late or forget to come at all. They refuse to comply with basic requests or seem to regress out of pure spite (Strean, 1985).

Many of the problems encountered in therapy arise because one or both partners feels disappointed in the performance of the other. The therapist is troubled because the client is not following the usual rules of conduct. The client is upset because the therapist is not as loving, tolerant, wise, and magical as he or she had expected. The principal work, then, is for both participants in this process to come to terms with what each of them requires from the other without either one feeling that he or she is compromising safety or integrity.

Wherever You Go...There You Are!

In a guidebook on Latin America, Franz (1990) laments that most of his competition offers the prospective traveler an endless list of itineraries, recommendations for where to stay, what to eat or buy, what to see and take pictures of, and how to feel. It is Franz's belief, however, that traveling in foreign lands should be an adventure, filled with spontaneous opportunities and individual possibilities, depending on one's mood, resources, and goals. Rather than trying to get to a certain place in a particular order, wherever you go, you are already there.

Psychotherapy is very much like a journey that has several popular itineraries. Although most people tend to proceed in a reasonably predictable path from describing their symptoms to stating their goals to exploring their background to developing some understanding of how their problems started to translating these insights into action, there are also wide individual differences as to other ways this process can occur. One can certainly see Latin America without stopping at all the universally sanctioned tourist spots.

I have mentioned how we create expectations for our travels with clients and structure programmed itineraries, as much for ourselves as for them. We are more comfortable when we have an idea of where we are headed. Difficult clients are those who deviate from what we expect.

Enter Marigold, a woman in her forties. *Marigold? What kind of name is that?*

Before she even sits down, she walks around the perimeter of the office, carefully inspecting the books, diplomas, the lay of the land. *What is she doing? Doesn't she see me waiting over here?*

Without warning, she swivels on her heels like a soldier on parade, and points a finger in my direction. *Oh my gosh, I knew I shouldn't have taken this case!*

"So Doc, how are they hanging?" *Hanging? She's asking me how my testicles are hanging? I can't believe this.*

"Excuse me? How are *what* hanging?

"Why, these pictures on the wall. How do you get them to hang so perfectly in alignment with one another? Are you one of those obsessive-compulsive types?" *Well, she has ME pegged in the first two minutes, and all I know about her is that this is going to be trouble.*

"Why don't you come over here, have a seat, and tell me what I can do for you?"

"You mean it's not all right if I stand over here? And why don't you tell me about you first?"

Looking at this dialogue from one perspective, there is no doubt we have a difficult client on our hands, especially if we compare her conduct to what we typically see and normally expect. But if we suspend, temporarily, that part of ourselves that feels threatened by her unusual approach to being a client, we can meet her with a more open mind. On one level this interaction is fascinating in terms of what it reveals. On another level, it is downright amusing. On still another, perhaps the fairest word to describe this client might be *challenging*. The term *difficult*, after all, can sometimes mean that the client is not following the itinerary that we had in mind. Langs (1989, p. 3) therefore cautions therapists to approach every session "without desire, memory, or understanding." It is only after we have emptied ourselves of preconceptions that we may view and interact with the client from a fresh perspective that invites new insights.

When Therapists Hate Their Clients

One therapist, a veteran of two decades in the trenches, was heard to say to her colleagues who had been commiserating about their caseloads over coffee:

"I've cut my practice down to five clients. And I hate them all."

Everybody laughed uproariously.

However embarrassed some of us are about our genuine feelings, it is a reality of professional practice that we hate some of our clients (Winnecott, 1949; Epstein, 1979). They do not pay us enough to put up with the obstacles they run us through, the games they play with our heads, the obstructive, vindictive, manipulative ploys that we inadvertently find ourselves caught up in. I suppose if we thought about it, we would have to be crazy *not* to dislike someone who places additional and unnecessary burdens on our lives and who evokes fear, aversion, guilt, and inadequacy in us because of his or her ability and interest in being dependent, self-destructive, and controlling (Groves, 1978).

   This perspective on difficult clients views them more as a function of the therapist's frustration tolerance than of their own behavior. Even Freud was said to have become so irritated on occasion with his more resistant clients that he would kick the couch they were lying on (Singer, 1985).

   When we reach the limits of what we know or can do, when we feel confused or blocked by a situation that is beyond our understanding or abilities, an easy way out is to blame the client. Looked at structurally, difficult clients are not problems in themselves, but are more often problems for others, especially the therapist (Kitzler and Lay, 1984). It is therefore crucial when we attempt to unravel the dynamics of what is going on with an especially challenging case that we look first to ourselves and to what we may be doing to make clients difficult.

PART TWO

When the Therapist Is Difficult

CHAPTER FIVE

When Therapists
Sabotage Themselves

My most difficult client is a man about my age who initially presented many of the characteristics that I prize most in people I work with. He is fairly bright, verbal and articulate, sensitive, and apparently motivated to work on himself. About the only thing that would make me feel ill at ease is that he is significantly smarter than I am—and knows it. He is very psychologically sophisticated and has been in therapy before, several times in fact, so he knows exactly what is expected. He can talk the jargon and understands the concepts of therapy quite well.

This person is in a professional position in which he is used to getting his way and has been quite skilled throughout his life in accomplishing this goal. Because he is so articulate and persuasive, he has rarely met with any serious resistance to following his own agendas. Further, he has *extremely* unrealistic expectations for himself, perfectionistic notions that he could never be enough, never do enough. What makes him especially difficult for me to work with is that he uses his knowledge as a way to avoid real changes in his life, all the time employing his verbal skills to keep me satisfied. I find immensely frustrating the extent to which he uses his intellect to run circles around me.

One of his most pervasive qualities is his impatience. He demands instant results in his life—from himself, and I suspect from others—although he denies this vehemently. I sense his disappointment in me when I am not quite as brilliant or inventive or perceptive as he thinks I ought to be. I feel tremendous pressure to reach beyond what I am capable of understanding and doing; while I appreciate this challenge to grow and stretch myself, the constant performance anxiety takes its toll

This guy also pushes my buttons constantly. Almost against my will I start to feel defensive or threatened in response to things he does. Even when I know what he is up to, I still feel powerless to stop myself from reacting negatively. It is as if he can read my mind.

And he can.

My most difficult client is *me*.

Looking Inward

In Part One we noted that "being difficult" is a judgment by one person in a position of authority about another person's failure to meet expectations. It is a label of convenience selected on the basis of one's individual subjective impressions. Therefore, we cannot consider clients to be difficult without examining our own role in formulating that label.

Much of what we experience from working with these clients comes not only from their behavior but from our own self-critical attitudes and wishful thinking (Medeiros and Prochaska, 1988). Client difficulty is not "out there," it is "in here," inside each of us where we observe, perceive, define, organize, construct, and analyze our experiences of other people. Mahrer (1984, p. 70) describes the origin of his own feelings when he encounters someone he considers abrasive: "I feel it in me. It is the experiencing of abrasiveness here in me. If someone were to ask me where it is, I would point to me, to my way of being, to feelings and experiencings in me."

Perceiving Clients Subjectively

Reporting the case of Anna O., Freud wrote about one of the first instances of a therapist's own unresolved issues making a client appear difficult to work with. Anna O. was actually a client of Joseph Breuer, Freud's collaborator in *Studies on Hysteria*. Breuer, it seems, had a tremendous fear that Anna O. might develop erotic feelings toward him. He prematurely ended their treatment together because of *his* feelings toward her, compounded by his wife's jealousy of Anna (Feiner, 1982). The interesting observation is that Breuer perceived Anna as the impediment to their therapeutic progress; he did not acknowledge his own role in creating the impasse.

Whether a client is difficult or not often depends on the therapist's perceptions as well as the client's behavior (Roth, 1990). Consider that regardless of setting or theoretical orientation, half the clients who come for a first session do not return. The prevailing wisdom has been that these are treatment failures, dropouts, or resistant clients. Because we did something wrong or were unable to build an alliance or could not sufficiently motivate the client, or because the client is so defensive and problematic, he or she elected not to return.

Then a researcher decided to investigate the reasons clients do not return after a single treatment session. Much to his surprise, Talmon (1990) discovered that in his own practice 78 percent of the clients he had seen for a single session reported improvement! In another study of two other practitioners, 88 percent of the single-session clients felt they had made definite progress. Whether or not these figures are inflated, they demonstrate quite clearly that different perceptions of the same clinical event are possible.

Because the participants in the therapeutic process are coequal in their subjectivity, the use of interpretation as an intervention is loaded with the clinician's own values, perceptions, personal feelings, and subjective impressions (Natterson, 1991). Therapists who are looking for evidence of resistance in their clients will find it. Shades of the Hawthorne Effect and the Pygmalion Effect! If you anticipate that a client will be difficult, he or she will probably live up to your expectations.

I recently listened to a tape of the first interview between an intern and a client I had referred to him. I had initially interviewed the client, but as she had no health insurance and could not afford even a minimal fee, I suggested she work with another therapist I was supervising. She readily agreed as she was quite motivated to make some changes in her life.

The first interview between the client and the intern

began with the same cadence and rhythm that I remembered from my experience: she asked a number of rapid-fire questions. What were his qualifications? How long had he been in the field? What was his theoretical orientation? Could he see her during the evenings? When she had asked me these questions, I believed the woman was quite anxious and was giving herself some time to get used to the situation. I had therefore patiently addressed each query and then we began a delightful and productive dialogue.

I listened aghast, however, as quite another scenario unfolded from the identical beginning script. When the client asked the therapist about his therapeutic style, he became evasive, putting the focus back on her. "Why did she want to know?" he asked curtly. And anyway, before he could answer such questions, he would need to know more about her.

Just as she was about to ask another question, the therapist interrupted: "You seem to have a number of questions for me. But if you don't mind, I would like to ask you a few things first."

The client became progressively more stubborn and reticent as the interview progressed. In fact, she became downright hostile—the prototype of a difficult client—demanding, controlling, shrill, and uncooperative. As the therapist shut off the recorder, he shook his head and commented: "What a bitch, huh?" My experience with her had been quite different because my interpretion of her initial behavior was so unlike the intern's interpretation.

Encouraging Clients to Be Difficult

"At about the time I decided to quit doing therapy and go into business, I noticed *all* my clients seemed to be difficult." So spoke a burned-out professional.

It is true that therapists who feel depleted, who have lost their passion and excitement for their work, and who are tired, bored, and indifferent to what they are doing are going to encounter more clients who appear uncooperative and resistant than are those practitioners who truly love doing therapy. The depleted therapist views certain behaviors as annoying while the energized practitioner sees them as challenging. The former calls uncooperative clients "a pain in the ass" whereas the latter resonates with their pain. The burned-out clinician is impatient, frustrated, and overly demanding that clients do exactly what he expects. Any deviations from the program are labeled resistant and are dealt with accordingly.

Often the depleted therapist is actually the one who helps launch the client in a career of being difficult. Caroline walks in feeling hurt, rejected, and abused by her ex-husband. She longs for understanding, even attention from someone, especially a man. She is needy and vulnerable, and this condition becomes immediately evident as she attempts to engage her therapist in some personal interaction. She desperately wants him to see her as a person, not as an object, a client who is just paying money for his time.

The therapist is exquisitely sensitive to Caroline's neediness — or to anyone's for that matter. He is making child support payments that are more than he can afford. He is seeing many more clients than he feels comfortable with but he needs the extra money. Everyone seems to want a piece of him — his exwife, his children, and the thirty-some clients whom he has begun to fantasize as leeches clinging to his body, draining his life blood. And then Caroline walks in.

The therapist puts on a mask of compassion, pretending to care. His disdain and revulsion for this dependent woman, another leech, inadvertently seep through. Caroline can sense that he does not like her; she has vast experience reading men who act as though they care about her but only tolerate her presence.

"And here is another one. I can't believe I'm paying this jerk and he still doesn't have the courtesy to be considerate. Look at him, trying not to yawn. This is humiliating. Who the hell does he think he is?"

Caroline tries harder to win her therapist's approval. As she becomes even more contrite, deferential, and clinging, the therapist withdraws further.

"Why do these people find ME? Look at her — hanging on every word I say. I suppose I should confront this dependency stuff or she will never let go."

He does so. Caroline explodes. For the first time in her life, she tells somebody, a male somebody, to go screw himself. She storms out of the office in tears.

The therapist shakes his head. He can't wait to tell a colleague about this latest wacko. He wonders why they always end up on *his* doorstep.

Two years pass before Caroline builds the confidence to see another therapist. This time it is a woman. But before Caroline even begins, she lets the new therapist know her terms and expectations. The therapist sighs to herself: *"Another difficult client."*

Feeling Threatened

One of the premises of this book is that clients' negative responses to therapy are not necessarily results of their resistance or tendency to be difficult. Often they are defending themselves against perceived attacks by clinicians who have been insensitive or clumsy in their interpretation or confrontation (Strupp, 1989).

Contrast, for example, how two therapists might offer different responses to the following client statement:

Client: I'm not sure that I am ready to get into that yet.
Therapist A: I notice you seem very defensive when I probe in that area.
Therapist B: You're not sure that you can trust me yet and I can understand how you would prefer to wait until we get to know each other a little better.

Although we cannot necessarily conclude that one response is more effective than the other, it seems clear that the more provocative intervention of Therapist A is likely to spark entrenched resistance in the client. As so often occurs, *we* become the catalyst for creating monsters of our clients by not respecting their pace or needs at a given moment in time. We may feel as though we are only trying to be helpful, but the clients feel that we are trying to nail them to the wall. The only possible responses a client can make to such a perceived attack are a strategic withdrawal, an unrestrained retreat, or a vehement counterattack.

In the *strategic withdrawal*, clients tell themselves that therapy is apparently not a very safe place. They begin to feel that any vulnerability they expose will be exploited, any weakness they show will be jumped on. They fail to see that we are only trying to identify their self-defeating behaviors and increase their awareness of their dysfunctional patterns. Instead, they devise ways to get through the sessions without sustaining too much damage. They throw up a smoke screen to cover their retreat, using rambling, distractions, overcompliance, anything to buy enough time to bow out without getting shot in the back.

An *unrestrained retreat* is a considerably more direct response to perceived attack: "Goodbye. I'm not coming back. But I will be sure to call you when I am ready." The message is clear that therapy does not feel safe to the client and it is time to leave the scene.

The *vehement counterattack* may actually be the healthiest response of all, even if the therapist must expend considerable trouble to neutralize it. The client feels hurt, rejected, and belittled; like most wounded creatures, he or she is a formidable foe when cornered. Either as a reflex action or a deliberate choice to do battle, the wounded client begins a war of attrition. He or she has now determined that we are indeed like other sadistic authorities who have wielded unrestrained power in the past. But since we are being paid to be helpful, we are certainly fair game from whom the client will exact retribution. Payback is a bitch.

Difficult clients threaten us in ways we would prefer to ignore and avoid. They challenge our expertise (*"I'm too perceptive for him and he just can't handle it"*). They test our patience (*"She just doesn't seem to have the motivation it takes to get anything out of therapy"*). They threaten our very sense of competence as professionals (*"Who is HE to talk about being a fraud?"*). It is for these very reasons that we prefer to keep potential failures at a distance, disown them whenever possible, and blame the

client as being difficult whenever we feel threatened (Kottler and
Blau, 1989).

Making Excuses

Certain qualities predispose a therapist to encounter more than
his or her fair share of difficult clients. Smith and Steindler
(1983, p. 110) believe that clinicians who are most vulnerable are
those who have developed "therapeutic zeal"—"a kind of mis-
guided conviction that they must provide treatment literally at
all costs."

This idealism, unrealistic expectations, and search for
perfectionism lead the therapist to experience much disappointment. Clients are not sufficiently grateful for all the effort
that has been expended on them. They fail to live up to the
therapist's expectations for where they should be. Further, the
therapist feels disappointed in his or her own performance
when a client is not cooperating: "I must be doing something
wrong." "If only I were more skilled/intelligent/creative, surely I
could solve this problem."

His analysis of resistance in therapy led Ellis (1985) to
believe that the most difficult client of all is the therapist, especially when he or she stubbornly holds onto beliefs such as the
following:

- "I must be successful with all my clients all the time."
- "When things don't progress in therapy the way I believe they
  should, it's because of my essential incompetence."
- "My clients must cooperate with me at all times, and love and
  appreciate everything I do for them."
- "Therapy should flow smoothly and easily and I should enjoy
  every minute of it."

These internal assumptions operate in those therapists
who are most prone to the deleterious effects of working with
difficult clients. Such clinicians assume too much responsibility
for therapy outcomes, believing they are at fault when the client's
problems are not resolved positively. One successful defense

against the temptation to accept responsibility for negative results is to take the opposite tack: blame the client for being difficult.

Therapists generally make two types of excuses to account for the client's obstructiveness: one is the tendency for the therapist to be a perfectionist and to blame herself when therapy does not proceed according to plan. The second is to be defensive and disown any responsibility for negative outcomes. These extreme points of view are shown below by a description of the internal dialogue of the Perfectionistic Therapist and the Defensive Therapist in response to several difficult client behaviors.

> Client: I'm sorry I missed my last appointment.
>
> Perfectionistic Therapist: *If only I could be more engaging and firmer in setting limits, this kind of thing wouldn't happen to me.*
>
> Defensive Therapist: *I'm obviously getting close to something that the client cannot handle.*

> Client: I really don't appreciate what you just said.
>
> Perfectionistic Therapist: *Oops. I really blew that one. Why can't I be more patient? I can't seem to find the right way to get through.*
>
> Defensive Therapist: *He's just trying to distract me from the point I made. Boy, has he got a thin skin!*

> Client: I think one day I'll just decide to kill myself.
>
> Perfectionistic Therapist: *After all this time I still haven't been able to reach him. There must be something else I can do.*
>
> Defensive Therapist: *Hey, that's his choice. If that is what he decides to do, I can't do much to prevent it.*

> Client: You're a fraud. You just sit there each week pretending you know what you're doing, but you don't have any earthly idea how to help me.

Perfectionistic Therapist: *Got me!*

Defensive Therapist: *It's not MY job to fix his problem. He is just angry because I'm so calm and composed when things get a little bumpy.*

———————

Client: I don't know how I will survive when you go on vacation.

Perfectionistic Therapist: *Maybe I shouldn't be away so long. I seemed to have allowed too much dependency to develop, and now I'm cutting him off abruptly.*

Defensive Therapist: *He is just playing mind games with me. He will do just fine. And if he has a hard time with me away, it will be a good lesson for him not to become so dependent on me in the future.*

———————

Client: I've decided not to come back.

Perfectionistic Therapist: *Where did I fail? I thought I did everything right. Yet here is another one I lost because I just can't adapt quickly enough. Maybe if I offered to lower my fee . . .*

Defensive Therapist: *It's probably for the best. She is just not ready to change. Now, who can I put into that time slot?*

At the heart of any answers we might formulate in response to the client statements listed above are our own inclinations toward being perfectionistic or defensive. Our core issues remain ever-sensitive to the buttons that are triggered by work in sessions every day. The more difficult and challenging the client, the more we must resort to our own self-protective defenses.

Centered between these two perspectives is a position that allows us to be realistic about what we can and cannot do. On the one hand, it is important not to fall victim to the client's attempts to draw us into a dysfunctional system; maintaining emotional distance is helpful in this regard, as is having reasonable expectations for our clients and ourselves. Yet hiding behind a thick mask of clinical detachment is ultimately not useful, either. It makes us appear withholding and cold to people who so strongly crave a little caring and cuts us off from our personal issues that are ignited by therapeutic interactions. If we are not willing to admit the extent to which we are affected by certain kinds of clients and incidents, we can never attempt to loosen their stranglehold.

CHAPTER SIX

Talking to the Winds

Feelings of futility and frustration have been companions of therapists ever since our craft was first invented, although Freud dealt little with this subject. In his later work (Freud, [1915] 1957), he did eventually admit some of his negative feelings that cropped up during sessions with clients: "At no point in one's analytic work does one suffer more from the oppressive feeling that all one's efforts have been in vain and from suspicion that one is 'talking to the winds' than when one is trying to persuade a female patient to abandon her wish for a penis" (p. 270). Although we may not recall the last time we had a female client who wanted a penis, most of us can relate to the feeling of "talking to the winds" with those who are uncooperative.

In one of the first documented cases of the profound effect a difficult client can have on a therapist, Sigmund Freud and Carl Jung commiserated with one another over their mutual exasperation with a client named Otto Gross (McGuire, 1974). Gross, it seems, was causing Freud some degree of frustration and anxiety because of his severe narcissistic pathology, a situation aggravated by Freud's own self-admitted "egoism" and feelings of countertransference. Freud found a way to pawn his patient off on Jung for the summer. With great optimism, Jung proceeded to treat Gross, only to find that all his empathy, good intentions, and brilliant interpretations were virtually useless; the patient hooked him as well. In a letter dated June 19, 1908, Jung complained to Freud about Herr Gross: "He is now living under the delusion that I have cured him and has already

60

written me a letter overflowing with gratitude. . . . For me this experience is one of the harshest of my life." Jung then expressed his sincere desire, tinged with guilt, that although he would not wish to inflict this patient on anyone else, not the least back to Freud who originally referred him, he had had quite enough of him — and so pronounced him cured (Liebenberg, 1990).

When Clients Push Our Buttons

Clients seem much more difficult to us when we are feeling dissatisfied with some aspect of our personal and professional lives. One therapist recently described to me quite poignantly the effects one particular case had on him during a time in his career when he was suffering from burnout.

> My most difficult client was not challenging be-cause of his diagnosis or his treatment require-ments. He wasn't very interesting or colorful or dynamic. What made this case so trying for me was the emotional reactions that I developed in re-sponse to working with him.
>
> I was working as a therapist in a mental health center where I had been for the past four years. I was frazzled. I was burned out. I was emo-tionally exhausted. I had no sense of personal ac-complishment. And I was depersonalizing every-thing and dehumanizing my clients, or I should say "patients" since about 90 percent of my caseload were chronically mentally ill. My job was primarily case management, putting out fires for over ninety patients in my caseload. That's an important job, but not the job I wanted to do.
>
> This particular client was a 70-year-old black male just released from the Mississippi State Hospi-tal after a stay of fifty years. He had been there all his adult life, since he had first been diagnosed as schizophrenic. He seemed to respond to gestures better than words, so I motioned for him to follow

me to my office, which he proceeded to do in the sporadic shuffle that is so frequent among patients who have been on psychotropic medication for long periods.

I tried to talk to him, but really didn't put much effort into it. He was like so many other patients I had seen — mute and dead to the world. To every question I asked, he responded with a grunt. So I set him up in a boarding house and arranged to see him again in three months. Then I proceeded to fill out the thirty-three different forms that were required to process his case.

I had spent a total of twenty minutes with the guy, and the only thing I knew about him was that he had cut out the backs of his shoes — a brand new pair of shoes with the heels missing. I had several other no-shows and cancellations that morning so I had plenty of time to think about this man, and there was something about him that was bugging me. Something about him or his name seemed familiar to me, but I figured maybe he had killed somebody or escaped from the state hospital at one time and his name or face had been in the papers.

I was leafing through his file when it finally hit me: he had the same name and was born on almost the same day as my grandfather, who had died seven months before. And I had not yet fully worked this through. I was the strong person in my family and I had to take care of everybody else, never giving myself time to grieve.

So then I became absorbed in his records, and the more I read, the more indignant and disgusted I became. At age twenty he had been seen by a doctor for some brief psychotic episode, and by a series of mishaps and incompetencies that are typical of state hospital systems, this man had been condemned to a life in a warehouse doing the "Thorazine shuffle." Four months after his original admission, they wanted to release him, but because his family didn't want him and there was no place else for him to go, they just put him on a shelf and forgot about him. Another iatrogenic psychosis, created by the doctor.

I was furious at the mental health system for how they had victimized this man, and then I realized that I had done the same thing. I, too, had refused to treat him as a person; he was just another schizophrenic, another hopeless case. I was no better than everything I despised.

I then started to run this guilt trip on myself. I started to become obsessed with his case. I decided I was going to cure him. I got him in to see the psychiatrist the next day and insisted we change his medication. I started to see the man three to four times per week. We went for walks. I bought him a new pair of shoes without the backs cut out of them. I even altered my own shoes to resemble his.

We sat on the porch and I tried to talk to him. I used everything that I knew how to do. After four months I never got the slightest response from him, or even an indication that he knew I was there, before he died in his sleep.

Of course, I now realize that I wasn't so much trying to treat him as I was myself. But then I think that most of the clients I find difficult are those who plug into my own issues. I also realized that I was going up against my limits, and that is something that I don't take very easily. For five to six months after this experience I was an emotional wreck. If I had been burned out before I met this man, by this time I was toast. I needed a month's leave of absence to recover.

Taking Matters Personally

Therapists enjoy helping people and expect in return some degree of appreciation. When clients respond instead with hostility, disrespect, or indifference, it is difficult for the therapist not to take these reactions personally. In the case of the hospitalized schizophrenic described in the previous section, the therapist became emotionally overinvolved, not only because his own personal issues were intertwined with those of his patient but because he needed and demanded some success from his treatment. He could not save his own grandfather, but he was determined to make this patient's life a little easier, regardless of whether the man wanted or was able to respond to the therapist's intervention.

In many similar situations, we often feel frustrated, insecure, and hopeless when the client does not respond as we wish. We communicate our dissatisfaction directly or through withdrawal. In response, the client feels even more rejected and devalued, and the resistant behavior intensifies. Thus the endless spiral of hurt and retaliation continues until each participant views the other as uncooperative.

In a study of patients who were generally resistant to medical intervention and noncompliant with treatment recommendations, Martin (1979) found several common characteristics. These patients tended to conform less to suggestions and to show less deference to doctors than did the general population. They used denial as a defense against acknowledging their problems. They also manifested high degrees of anxiety.

Although the subjects of these studies were patients with tuberculosis and diabetes, those suffering from other chronic illnesses, and patients with unusually difficult dental problems, results can be instructive for therapists. The most common characteristic of all these resistant patients is "the fundamental importance of anxiety in determining individual reactions to illness, to preventive campaigns and to treatment situations" (Martin, 1979, p. 5).

Deep down inside, the difficult client is a very anxious person who is trying to cope with a painful and vulnerable existence. This observation is so obvious and such a basic part of therapeutic lore that we hardly ever mention it. However, we must not forget that the difficult client is just trying to get along as well as he or she can. When this client attacks us, withdraws from us, plays games with us, our first instinctive reaction is take the gesture personally: "Why are you making *my* life so unnecessarily difficult?" It is only after stepping back from the situation that we eventually realize: "No, you are not doing this to me; you are doing it to yourself. I am the designated target for your wrath. I am the one person you feel safe enough with to let all the demons out. Lucky me."

Similarities Between Difficult Clients and Their Therapists

As much as we may dread or even despise certain clients because of traits or behaviors that we find especially annoying, we may be more like these individuals than we would care to admit. In a comparison of the most common characteristics of physicians and features of their most difficult patients, Ford (1981) discovered a fascinating but disturbing parallel. Most doctors would identify those patients who consistently give them the most trouble as the ones with chronic somatizing disorders who have made illness a way of life. These are patients with chronic pain who relish a sick role, or chronic complainers about symptoms that the doctor can do nothing for. They are the patients with hysterical or hypochondriacal tendencies, the malingerers, and those with factitious disorders, disability claims, or conversion reactions.

All these patients share some common features, a finding that is hardly surprising. For example, somatizing patients often come from childhood homes that left them with unmet dependency needs. They often have had experiences with illness or death as children. They exhibit marked depression, excessive use of medication, and emotional constriction. The surprise came when Ford (1981) compared these qualities to the most common characteristics of the doctors and found that doctors and patients exhibited many of the same characteristics.

There are other ways that difficult patients and their doctors are often linked. The patient is hypochondriacal; the doctor is counterphobic in regard to disease and death. The patient exhibits blatant dependency needs; the doctor develops a reaction formation to defend against dependency wishes. The patient has a desire for protection while the doctor entertains fantasies of omnipotence. After reviewing this pattern, Ford (1981, p. 255) concludes: "Because of the psychological similarities shared with physicians, somatizing patients have the capacity to tap into the physician's own intrapsychic conflicts."

It would be interesting to extrapolate Ford's findings to the therapeutic encounter: what are the similarities between ourselves and those clients we despise the most? What are the common features of difficult clients and our own backgrounds, personalities, and unresolved issues?

Therapists often come from homes characterized by a high level of conflict, just as their clients do. We also share a number of other qualities such as the ability to influence others, a highly developed sensitivity to what others are feeling, overreactions to themes of dependency, and a need for power and control in relationships. This comparison leads us to the inescapable conclusion that the clients with whom we have the most trouble are those who are like us in ways we find most distasteful; but in a positive light, our own emotional reactions to our clients can give us the most valuable clues for how to treat them.

Who Gets to You and Why

Because difficult clients are often defined in terms of their effects on their therapists—their ability to induce anger, irritation, anxiety, or oversolicitousness—it is important for us to look at our own arousal potential. Which kinds of clients, diagnoses, behavior patterns, and interactions do you consistently find upsetting? At the very least, even if you cannot agree that your own biases, perceptions, and issues make clients difficult, you must certainly acknowledge the interactive effect of both client and therapist contributions to the problem.

When we encounter obstructions to progress in therapy, the *first* place we should look is toward ourselves:

- What am I doing to create or exacerbate problems in the therapeutic alliance? *Isn't it interesting that I talk to this client so differently on the phone than in person? I seem to feel some need when he is in my space to let him know firmly who is in charge.*

- What unresolved personal issues are being triggered by the conflict I am experiencing? *I am definitely not doing enough for this lady. No, maybe I am trying to do too much for her, and am taking too much responsibility for how this turns out. No, I mean, I don't know what I am trying to do. I get frustrated and confused when I don't know where I stand with someone, whether she likes me, whether she thinks I am doing a good job. This woman gives me no clues so I end up being caustic and sarcastic with her to provoke some reaction, and then I don't like what I get.*

- Who does the client remind me of? *My Uncle Matt. Definitely Matt. They both have the same manipulative way that they get other people to eat out of their hands. I remember all those times Matt sweet-talked me into. . .*

- In what ways am I acting out my frustration and impatience with the client's progress? *She just asked me when we can re-schedule her next appointment since she can't seem to make it here on time in the mornings. Why did I give her such a hard time? I am not usually so inflexible about things like that.*

- What expectations am I demanding of this client? *This guy is really hurting because his father is in the hospital. I tell him about my own father, that I know how he feels, and he blows me off as if I am a servant who has spoken out of line. Come to think of it, maybe my disclosure was inappropriate.*

- What needs of mine are not being met in this relationship? *I expect — no, demand — that people show me a degree of gratitude when I put myself out to help them. Even though I am paid to deliver a professional service, I do this type of work primarily for the kick I get in seeing others grow. OK, it even makes me feel powerful to think that I helped in some way. When a client doesn't acknowledge that my efforts have been appreciated, I start to feel cheated.*

You may think of other questions as you try to figure out why a certain client is disturbing to you, or why you are being considerably less effective than you could be: what information am I missing that would help me understand better what is happening? In what ways have I mismanaged this case? How have I been unduly manipulative and controlling? How are my operating assumptions getting in the way of my understanding and dealing with the client? And probably the most important self-query of all: what is keeping me from being more caring and compassionate with this person?

By going through this checklist of questions when we find ourselves having trouble with a case, we are able to identify our role in exacerbating the problems before we heap accusations on the client that he or she is being obstructive, resistant, and uncooperative. When clients are difficult, it is usually for one of two reasons: (1) they are not feeling accepted or understood by the therapist, or (2) they are fearful of allowing the therapist to get too close. In either of these scenarios, the therapist's own feelings of anger and frustration as well as his or her ongoing personal issues become a fulcrum by which resistance can be understood and worked through.

CHAPTER SEVEN

Games Therapists Play

When a client is difficult, this condition is often a function not only of client characteristics and behavior but also of therapist qualities and issues as well as interactive effects between the partners in the relationship. The client takes a particular stance that the therapist then interprets in a number of ways — "frightened," "defensive," or perhaps "controlling" or "difficult." The therapist responds in some way based on the meaning she assigns to the client's behavior. The client, in turn, senses or observes the way the therapist feels about him. That perception influences the client's next move in this complicated interaction. Before long, the therapist is convinced that the client is "being difficult," but sometimes this behavior is a legitimate response to the therapist's unresolved issues, as illustrated in the following case.

Marilyn and Nathan were on the verge of divorce. Nathan, contrite and apologetic, expressed his willingness to do anything in his power to save their marriage. Marilyn was filled with rage toward this man, who for over twenty years had demanded that she stay home and put her own career on hold. For her to realize how resentful she had felt all these years represented tremendous progress for her.

In our third session together Marilyn felt ready to tell her husband how she felt, yet the more passionate she became in expressing her rage, the more objective, aloof, and infuriatingly logical Nathan became. In response to all her outbursts, he simply shrugged and said softly: "We can't change the past, dear.

69

Why don't we talk about what we can do now Instead of rehashing this stuff over and over?" His attitude generated more anger in Marilyn. Clearly, she was being difficult.

Or at least that is what I thought at the time.

I took the position that we could not settle this problem until they were both calm enough to talk to each other like rational adults. *(They reminded me of my parents when they used to fight and my feelings of helplessness to stop them.)*

Every time Marilyn's rage would boil, I would attempt to divert her, to calm her down. *(I have real problems dealing with anger. I don't allow myself to feel angry very often and whenever anyone is angry with me, I withdraw and pout.)*

Marilyn felt that I did not like her. She told me she did not feel safe, that her husband and I were ganging up on her, treating her like a child. *(I felt attacked, as though she were questioning my competence. Now I was really convinced she was a most difficult client.)*

I attempted to reassure her that I *did* like her and I was not siding with her husband against her. *(I lied. By this time I was strongly identifying with her husband whom I felt sorry for. In spite of my best efforts to appear neutral, I definitely had strong feelings about who the real problem was.)*

After this fateful session, I was able to step back from the scene and reflect on what was going on inside me that led me to dislike this woman so much. Yes, she was forceful. Yes, she made a lot of noise. Yes, her style of expressing herself was different from what I am used to. But here was a person doing her absolute best to work on herself, to change a codependent relationship. And all I could think of was that she was being difficult.

Horseradish! *I* was being difficult because of my inability or unwillingness to accept the way she needed to express herself. I had to face the chronic problem I have in denying my own anger. Overidentifying with client problems is certainly one of the most common ways in which we make therapeutic encounters more trying than they have to be, and contact with disruptive family situations such as the one between Nathan and Marilyn are among the most disturbing of all.

Favorite Games

Too often therapists play games with themselves and with other people. There are several that I have observed in my own behavior and the behavior of colleagues whom I have interviewed, supervised, and observed. These are described below.

1. I worked hard to get where I am and you should show great deference and respect for what I know and who I am. It is not necessarily arrogance and narcissism that leads us to believe we are important; society pays homage to members of our profession. We are the sanctioned healers and gurus, duly deputized by the legislature to provide sanctuary for the walking wounded. We have worked very hard to get where we are. We have paid our dues in a multitude of ways—through personal sacrifices, by subjecting ourselves to rigorous training, and in devoting our lives to the pursuit of knowledge. It is really not difficult for us to believe that we are indeed very special.

Have you ever noticed the way some therapists will hold court at a social gathering, fielding questions, offering definitive answers to life's most perplexing problems with a voice of authority? When a therpaist talks, people listen. They assume we have a special pipeline to truth.

It is easy to see how we come to expect, even demand, that clients pay tribute to us. We may act like folksy, easygoing people, but cross the line of respect and watch us flare. It is all right not to address us by title but only after you ask our permission.

Interrupt us while we are talking and we will easily relinquish the floor. What you have to say, dear client, is eminently important and should be heard. We will even make that very point aloud. But inside we feel uneasy and unfinished. Next time, we may not back down so easily.

Make fun of what we do or tell a "shrink" joke and we will laugh at the absurdity of our profession. But inside we feel hurt and offended.

This first game that many therapists play (those like myself who are unfinished in our need for validation) sets up a competitive arena in which clients who are already suspicious of authority are given permission to be themselves, yet they are often punished by the therapist's withdrawal if they cross an imaginary line.

  2. I am omnipotent and omniscient. I have magical powers that allow me to read your mind and predict the future. Our power to be influential is based, in part, on our ability to set ourselves up as models whom clients find attractive, mysterious, and trustworthy. We rely on a variety of mechanisms to instill this sense of confidence. We appear to see things that are invisible to mere mortals. We reflect underlying feelings and interpret messages that previously have been buried. We predict that certain things will happen; most of the time they occur just as we said they would. Even when things do not unfold exactly as we predicted they would, we always have a reasonable explanation prepared.

  Like any good magician, we have a number of tricks that make us masters of illusion. And we get mad when perceptive but ornery clients seek to destroy our attempts at "sleight of mind." I have a small clock perfectly positioned on a table next to my "client chair" that allows me to monitor time unobtrusively. My clients are usually quite impressed with the way I always seem to know exactly when the session is over — without ever looking at my watch.

  One client, who began our very first session by announcing that he considered all members of my profession to be "money-grubbing frauds," always found a way to block my view of the clock. Some days he would "accidentally" push the tissue box in front of it. Other times he would toss his keys or sunglasses on the table and knock it askew. One time, he even had the audacity to turn it away deliberately and then challenged me to say something. I did, of course. Something suitably caustic and censuring like "You seem to have a need to control every little thing in your environment." I was very proud of putting him back in his place and decided that at the very next opportunity, I would demonstrate my magical powers in other ways. Nevertheless, he was never much impressed. So we went around and around, competing to see who could be more difficult.

  3. I am impervious to any attempts you make to get to me. I am thoroughly objective and detached. While I care for you, you are only a client, not part of my life. I like this one a lot. This is when we put on the "Freud mask" and appear thoroughly unflappable. This is when we pretend we really are not shocked or hurt or disappointed or angry or frustrated or anxious — even though deep inside us is a seething cauldron of emotional activity. The difficult client is, of course, exquisitely tuned to these feelings and knows that he is getting to us. We pretend to be impervious to these assaults and act as though when the client walks out the door she is out of our lives. This behavior only makes the client more determined to make us cry inside. Then, naturally, we become even more aloof and withholding. And so the dance continues.

4. *I am everything that you should strive to be. Look at me — how calm, self-assured, and in control I appear. You could be like this, too, if only you would listen and follow my advice.* In spite of our claim that therapists are value-free, nonjudgmental, and accepting of different cultures, backgrounds, and life philosophies, we all have our preferences regarding the best way to operate. This means that although we start with the announcement that we will help the client reach whatever stated goals she feels are important, we have our own agenda of alternatives that we consider far preferable. We do not, of course, let the client know this explicitly, but often she is highly suspicious that we are trying to talk her out of her agenda in favor of our own. The following are examples of this game.

"You want me to see both you and your husband so that I can convince him to be more attentive to household responsibilities? Well, that certainly sounds like an important issue to explore between you." READ: *Come on, lady! If that's what it takes to get you both in here, fine. Then we can really get to the heart of the matter — examining your interactive patterns.*

"You would like me to talk to your son who has been causing a lot of problems since your divorce? I wonder if I might meet with you first to get some background information?" READ: *I would rather work with you. Besides, it is probably YOUR problems that your son is drawing attention to.*

"That is an excellent idea — to talk to your boss about your dissatisfaction with your job. And if that doesn't work, maybe we can think of some other alternatives." READ: *How many times do I have to tell you: unless you go back to school and finish your degree you are going to be stuck in that dead-end job forever!*

"You say you are ready to stop therapy for awhile and try things on your own? I see no immediate objection. Why don't we talk about that just a bit to explore the ramifications of your decision." READ: *You have got to be kidding! There is no way I am letting you out of here right now, given the impetuous way you run away from relationships once they start to become intimate.*

Reframing problems and formulating our own diagnostic impressions apart from client self-perceptions is what we are being paid for. This becomes a game when we know the client is not ready to accept our interpretations and we try to appease him with something else more palatable. The client senses what we are up to, and so becomes "difficult" in an attempt to get us to admit our ploy. When we innocently deny any such effort, the client becomes even more mistrustful and escalates the battle of wills.

5. *I am very good at what I do and I have helped a lot of people. If therapy isn't going the way it should, it's YOUR fault.* There is a game plan that we memorized in graduate school. It goes something like this: our job is to be a good listener, the client's role is to be a good talker — to say whatever is on her mind, to be straightforward and truthful, to be thorough in her descriptions. Without such cooperation, we can hardly be expected to be very helpful. An analogy of this noncooperation is that of a patient who complains to his doctor of excruciating pain. When the doctor asks where it hurts, the patient smiles enigmatically and replies: "That is for *you* to figure out."

We therefore expect, if not demand, that the client provide a degree of cooperation so we can work our wondrous healing magic. If therapy does not proceed as expected, or if the client's condition worsens rather than improves, the *first* place we think of placing blame is squarely on the client's shoulders:

"I'm doing the same thing with you that I am doing with everyone else, and *they* are getting better. So it must be you."

This reasoning obviously ignores the reality that if we insist on applying a similar strategy to all our clients a few become angry because they believe we are not treating them like individuals. Sometimes they are right, as shown in the following example:

Tricia and Danielle are both suffering from the aftermath of a sticky divorce. They are both depressed and have self-esteem problems. I treat them both with a dose of caring and support. I challenge them to put the past behind them and to venture out into the world again. I am positive I am doing essentially the same things with both of them. Tricia rapidly improves while Danielle slowly deteriorates further. She is being difficult.

At times Danielle becomes seductive. I gently reassure her while interpreting what she is up to. She pouts and becomes worse — to punish me, I think egocentrically, because I did not respond to her the way she wanted. I analyze meticulously every aspect of *her* behavior to find the source of her resistance. She claims that I am disappointed in her. I lie and say no. She does not believe me and worsens still more.

Months go by before I stop and consider *my* role in this mess. What am I doing to sabotage the treatment? In a moment of frustration I blurt out this very question. And to my surprise, she gives me a very coherent answer. Danielle feels that I am angry with her because she cannot or will not be the way I want her to be. She got enough of that crap from her husband. She does not mean to be so difficult, but I rub her the wrong way when she senses my disappointment in her progress. Isn't it all right if she moves at her own pace, she wonders?

Conflicts of Power

The therapeutic relationship is not only a type of partnership; it is also a confrontation between two persons representing different goals and values, and in many cases, different genders, races, ages, education, cultures, religions, and socioeconomic backgrounds (Mens-Verhulst, 1991). Conflicts of power are thus at the root of most difficult relationships.

The games that clients play to maintain some degree of control are compounded by those of their therapists, who are also trying to establish dominance and also inadvertently acting out unresolved personal issues. Every time clients speak, we relate to what they are saying, not only as a helper but also as a person. When these roles conflict, the result exacerbates any resistance or defensiveness that the client may be feeling.

Take, for example, the need many of us feel for control and power. Many of us gravitated toward this field because we like to be in charge of relationships in our lives. We may hate, even more than most people, the feeling of having others pull the strings. For this reason we selected a profession that not only allows us to establish ground rules for our working relationships but one that also equips us with the skills to control, to a large extent, our personal relationships. We tend to be more articulate and to be better debaters than others we know. We have made a life study of how people behave and why they act the way they do. We understand motives and human phenomena that are un-known outside our field. We are acutely sensitive to moods and are able to perceive things operating that are invisible to most others. In short, we are the olympic athletes of interpersonal relationships. We are armed to the teeth with understandings, techniques, interventions, and maneuvers that allow us to con-trol relationships far more than others who have not had our training. And we enjoy this power a lot.

Enter a client who is used to exercising control over others, someone who also enjoys wielding power in relation-ships. Such persons, mortally wounded in earlier life because they were once at the mercy of another who betrayed their trust, object vigorously to the idea that someone else (even a paid professional) would exercise any power over them. They see the books and diplomas on the wall that advertise our ability to see inside them, and they feel threatened. They notice how deftly we guide the interaction and manage the session, and they feel envious. They sense our need to be in control and they feel intimidated. And once threatened, they declare war.

PART THREE

Some Very Difficult Clients

CHAPTER EIGHT

In Case
I Decide to Kill Myself

It is true that therapists can create difficult clients or certainly train them to be more obstinate than they are normally inclined to be. Some people, however, come to us with their manipulative skills already well honed. At times these clients, described by Kernberg (1984) as "malignant narcissists," take sadomasochistic pleasure in triumphing over the therapist, even if it means engaging in essentially self-defeating acts. They experience a tremendous sense of power over being able to block their progress in therapy, all the while complaining bitterly of their disappointment in the way things are going. Kernberg (1984) describes one such client who repeatedly burned her arms and then hid the festering wounds under long sleeves while she reported how splendidly her life was going. What power she, and other clients like her, feel at being both victim and victimizer, able to reduce an omnipotent authority figure to an impotent and frustrated mortal!

Clients can use more benign styles of manipulation when they are committed to having their way, no matter how determined we are to follow our own agenda. Gladys began her story precisely as she crossed the threshold of my office. Out came a torrent of frustration and anger, mostly directed toward her husband who never listened to her. After forty years of marriage, Gladys and her husband had reached an uneasy truce, partitioning their home and lives into separate worlds.

Gladys spoke continuously and incessantly throughout that first session and beyond. Although I am usually quite good at ending a session precisely at the appointed time, with this particular woman, none of my usual cues made a dent in her monologue. I interrupted and politely informed her our time was up, asking when she would like to schedule her next appointment. She carried on as if I were not in the room. I stood up and walked to the door—surely a clear signal it was time to leave—but Gladys resolutely remained on the couch, continuing her litany of complaints.

I looked at this aging, forlorn, little grandmother camped out in my office, my heart aching for her. It seemed as though this was the first time in years that she had had anyone to hear her—and I had stopped listening some time earlier as I plotted ways to pry her off the couch and move on to my next client who had now been kept waiting for twenty minutes.

The problem of ending our sessions became the primary struggle of the first stage of our relationship. I tried closing the session a half-hour after we began. I would even leave the room and call to her from the hallway: "I think it's time to leave." All to no avail. The best I could do was wait for her to run down of her own accord like a wind-up toy whose energy is finally depleted. One day, in exasperation, I confided to her how abused and frustrated I felt. Her innocent response was, "Why didn't you just tell me?"

Initially, the sessions went by quickly. Gladys had many things to say, and apparently, nobody to say them to. All I had to do was sit back and let her go. She talked with great feeling about the people in her life, about her past, and about the impotence she felt to alter her marriage.

At first, I ventured a few tentative probes and questions, but since she had her own agenda to follow, I decided to wait her out before I attempted to intervene. Little did I ever imagine I would end up waiting for two years! For over 100 hours, she talked, and I listened. Any attempt I made to alter this routine was met with the same stubborn resistance she had shown earlier when I had tried unsuccessfully to end her sessions on time. Clearly she felt she was getting her money's worth and seemed delighted by the progress she was making. And indeed, her home life did improve and she became less depressed.

But what was my role in all of this? Every time I tried to say something to her — supportive, reflective, or interpretive — she would stop for a moment, regard me as she would any distraction, and then say: "Where was I? Oh yes. . . ." continuing on with her monologue. Gladys would have been perfectly content if I had not uttered a single word in any session, but my own self-respect (and sense of challenge) urged me to insert a few feeble comments during those rare times when Gladys would draw a breath.

After rehearsing for hours in my mind, I finally decided one day to confront her about this sorry state of affairs. I felt completely useless. I wondered whether I even needed to attend the session at all. Maybe she could just borrow my office and leave a check when she was done. I told her these things. Bluntly. Decisively. Clearly.

Gladys faced me fully. She frowned as she considered what I said. Immediately I felt remorseful. This sweet little old lady is getting just what *she* wants out of therapy; who am I to argue with her? She nodded her head. Once. Twice. Acknowledging she heard me. And then she continued right on with what she had been saying before I had interrupted her! Oh, there was a barely perceptible change in the cadence of her monologues after that; with an obvious show of great self-discipline, she would once, sometimes twice during a session, grind to a sudden halt and look at me expectantly as if to say: "OK, smartass, throw in your two cents if you think you have anything to add."

The strange thing is that I liked Gladys a heck of a lot. I *enjoyed* listening to her even as I resented not being allowed to respond to her (just as her husband felt shut out). Yet there are few clients with whom I have ever worked so hard. I became a therapist because I *like* to talk; I like to be actively engaged in animated conversation, to share and exchange ideas. But Gladys seemed to know what she needed, and that was an audience — one she could pay not to interrupt her.

Gladys represents those clients who come to therapy with their own skewed plan for what they want from us. It makes little difference to them how we prefer to work best, or what we think they need. They will interview a dozen prospects, if necessary, to find a cooperative therapist whom they can manipulate to do their bidding.

Styles of Manipulative Behavior

Manipulation can be defined as "deliberately influencing or controlling the behavior of others to one's own advantage by using charm, persuasion, seduction, deceit, guilt, induction, or coercion" (Hamilton, Decker, and Rumbaut, 1986, p. 191). The term is almost always used to describe the client's attempt to control the relationship; if the therapist tries the same thing, it is called "artful management of client behavior."

For this reason Hamilton and his coauthors prefer to speak of "manipulative behavior" rather than "manipulative clients," since they are talking not so much about a stable disorder as a situational strategy to gain control. This conception also helps us to focus on aspects of the client that need to be altered rather than considering the client an enemy who is challenging our turf.

Clients can be manipulative in many different ways, both directly and indirectly, consciously and unconsciously. In the direct mode they will attempt to set the conditions of therapy, solicit promises, or ask for reassurances; in the indirect style, which is even more difficult to recognize and manage, they can be very creative. Murphy and Guze (1960) have described some of the more common forms of manipulation. I have summarized these below with representative examples:

> *Unreasonable Demands:* "I'm sorry to bother you at home, but I can't sleep. Isn't there something that you can do to help me?"
>
> *Controlling the Conditions of Therapy:* "You never told me I had to give twenty-four hours' notice to cancel an appointment if I didn't feel well. I thought you meant only if I didn't want to come back. And I *do* want to schedule another appointment, that is, if you intend to be reasonable about this misunderstanding."

Soliciting Promises: "You said I could call you if I felt worse. I was wondering if my headache could be part of my symptoms also?"

Special Attention: "I know you don't usually work on Wednesday evenings, but just this once couldn't you see me?"

Self-deprecation: "I don't know why you are so nice to a person like me. I really don't deserve such attention."

Expressing Dissatisfaction: "And I thought you were different from all those other doctors I've seen. But you can be so cruel."

Threatening Self-Destructive Behavior: "I'll probably be all right this week. But in case I do decide to kill myself, I want to thank you for everything you tried to do to help."

One Case Among so Many

Many of these examples of manipulative behavior make up the repertoire of the most dreaded of clients, the most difficult people to deal with because of their tendencies to resort to extreme measures to bend us to do their bidding. I am speaking, of course, about the Borderline.

The beginning usually seems innocent enough. In one case, Maybelle asked me if I would read a brief letter she had written me during the previous week. "Now?" I asked. "No," she said sweetly. "You can read it later."

We began our second session and Maybelle continued the narrative from the first time we met. She recited some of the more despicable experiences she suffered at the hands of parents who were both wretched: neglect, verbal abuse, overtones of sexual molestation, endless mind games. She looked so incredibly vulnerable I could hardly stop myself from reassuring her over and over that everything would be all right, that she had come to the right place and I would help her.

Soon after Maybelle left, I unfolded the two-page letter. In the writing she essentially demonstrated how well she had been listening during our first session. She repeated the themes we had discussed, even quoted me verbatim in places. I was impressed and a little flattered. I was further moved by the pain she was living with and the intense desire she had to live a normal existence, once and for all free of her parents' poisonous influence. I jotted a few notes to her in the margin and mailed the letter back to her.

Just prior to the next session, our third, she handed me another letter—this one quite bulky. I began to get the first glimmers that things were not all they appeared. But by then I was hooked.

The phone calls during the week began soon thereafter. At first, they seemed harmless enough. Might she reschedule her appointment? She lost her reminder card; was her appointment at 3:00 or 4:00?

Over the course of a few months the calls escalated until I began to expect them at regular intervals. I had not, as yet, had the heart to cut her off; I was, after all, the only close relationship in her life. And she did seem to be improving.

It was a colleague who first cued me or at least labeled what might be going on. Furthermore, this friend gave me the permission I felt I needed to start setting limits with her. At the very next session, I informed Maybelle I would no longer accept her calls during the week unless she had a genuine emergency (what an invitation to disaster!). It was then that the calls at home began.

I picked up the phone very late one evening to hear the sounds of sobbing on the other end of the line—gut-wrenching, pitiful sobs. I knew instantly who it was. After many fruitless minutes of trying to calm her down, my own voice took on some of the hysteria she had been demonstrating. *I just know she is going to kill herself. And it's all my fault because I cruelly rejected her just like her parents* (she may even have spoken those very lines).

Just when my own patience reached the limit, Maybelle miraculously regained control. She thanked me profusely for being there when she needed me the most. I probably saved her life, she repeated over and over. When I hung up the phone, I felt as though I was still dangling on the end of the line.

She was most cooperative during the following sessions, a model client — grateful, eager, and fully in control of herself. In much the same way a person in the eye of a hurricane tells himself that maybe the storm is over — after all, everything seems calm — I blithely proceeded along, intensely proud of myself and progress we were making.

When the calls at home began in earnest, I should have been better prepared to expect them. They were, after all, the next logical step. But by then I was in way over my head. Desperate to find some way to extricate myself from her manipulative ploys, I suggested that a psychiatric consultation might be in order. Wails of protest: "You're just trying to get rid of me." *Right you are*, I thought, but said instead: "We need to check out the possibility of medication for your depression."

The psychiatrist was most sympathetic. To me, not to her. "Yes, you've got yourself a full-fledged borderline all right. I'd be careful if I were you."

"Borderline" sounds so dismal, so hopeless and frightening. It conjures up images of someone walking a thin line he or she can never quite cross, postponing the inevitable fall into the abyss below. Yet Maybelle made unsteady but consistent progress over several years, eventually stabilizing herself in a good job and support system up to the time I moved out of state.

A year later, her letter found me:

> Let me tell you: I am in big-time trouble and things don't seem to be getting better. I am very withdrawn. I haven't shown up to work or called them. I am drinking a lot and taking all kinds of different drugs. I stay in my room, will not answer the phone, and have no contact with my family or friends. Things are going downhill very quickly and I have no desire to do anything to stop myself.
>
> I have been irritable and I have raging outbursts for no reason. I wake up screaming in the middle of the night. I am injuring myself in the hope that I might do some damage or make the right cut so I can bleed to death. I don't know what

is happening to me or what to do about it. I have all
but given up.

I feel like some strange person has control
over my body and there is nothing that I can do to
stop it from destroying me. You would not believe
that I am the same person who you worked with for
two years and did so well.

Please send me some magical words to help
me think more clearly and get back on track or I
know I will never live to see my twenty-fifth birthday
next week. Take care, and maybe you will hear from
me again.

The depth and intensity of Maybelle's pain are so profound I can hardly read her words without feeling scalded. She is
not deliberately trying to cause me anguish or punish me for
deserting her; that is just part of the "natural" way in which she
functions. She has learned to survive, however tenuously, by
drawing people in and then keeping them where she wants
them.

What I find so remarkable about Maybelle and her
strange behavior is that almost every therapist I have ever met—
whether working in a university counseling center, mental
health center, hospital, private practice, rehabilitation center,
crisis center, or school—has had a similar case. Some therapists
thrive on the challenge of dueling with manipulative clients like
Maybelle. Others of us lose a part of ourselves in each exchange,
lick our wounds, and jump back into the arena for more. One
thing is clear to me: the pathologically manipulative borderline
is the ultimate test for any therapist's compassion, skills, and
expertise.

Greater Risks and the Ultimate Challenge

The emotional strains we suffer as a result of interaction with
severely disturbed clients is not the only hazard of our work;
even greater are the legal risks. Filled with so much rage and
schooled in sophisticated methods of manipulation, some cli-

willing to inflict as much damage as possible on those who are close to them. Therapists often become targets of retribution in the court system, not only because they commit some professional transgression but because a difficult client wants to get even with them for some imagined offense.

Even when clients refuse to pay their bills or fail to cooperate with treatment, we become liable for malpractice suits if we attempt to terminate the relationship without ensuring that they receive continued care (Vandecreek, Knapp, and Herzog, 1987). Some clients may feel abandoned at the slightest provocation, and those who wish to inflict the greatest damage can initiate nuisance legal action. Given the climate of the times, in which insurance companies prefer to settle claims as quickly as possible, we may never have a chance to tell our side of the story.

Practicing our profession with the people who need our services the most presents real obstacles and dangers. An analogous issue is being debated by surgeons, deciding when and if they should jeopardize their safety by conducting elective operations on patients with auto immune deficiency syndrome (AIDS). The main differences are that our most difficult and manipulative clients are suffering spiritually, not physically. And although we cannot become infected by their disease, we can and do become affected by their toxic behavior.

The manipulative client described in this chapter and the controlling client discussed in the next chapter present the practitioner with the ultimate professional challenges and also the greatest satisfaction. Working with severely disturbed and/or resistant clients requires incredible patience, high frustration tolerance, realistic expectations, excellent diagnostic and clinical skills, and the guidance and support of a group of experienced colleagues and supervisors. Such clients may change more slowly than we would prefer. They may test us in devious ways. They may get under our skins and force us to look at our own unresolved issues. But they also need us the most. And when, sometimes after years of hard work, they do lead more productive and satisfying lives, we realize that there are few accomplishments about which we can feel more proud.

CHAPTER NINE

I'm Coming Back
Until You Fix Me

Her first action when she walked into the office, even before she sat down, was to turn the clock around so she could not see its face. "I can't look at that thing staring at me all the time. It makes me nervous. I would just sit here counting the minutes."

Next, she told me her rules: she was willing to pay only a certain amount; she would pay her bills only after receiving her insurance reimbursements; I was not to talk to her husband under any circumstances; the only time she was available for appointments was Wednesday or Thursday at 5:00. Was that satisfactory?

"Why can't I talk to your husband?" I was so stunned it was the only thing I could think of to say.

"Because he doesn't know I'm here—he would never let me come if he knew. That's another thing: you can't ever call me at home, I won't even give you my home number. And you should send the bills to my office address."

The situation did get better after this initial encounter. I decided not to challenge her. (She reminded me of a bully in my third grade class and I was afraid she might beat me up.) I exercised supreme tolerance and patience, which for me is especially difficult—I have my own problems related to not being in control. But I decided to wait her out. Maybe I was feeling unusually secure that week.

Sometime between the second and third appointment I received a message from my answering service to call her. I waited until my next break, a few hours later, and called her back.

"Hello."

"Hi. This is Jeffrey Kottler returning your call."

"Is this how long it usually takes you to get back to someone?"

"Excuse me?"

"I said, does it always take you so long to return a phone call?"

"This was my first break," I said more meekly than I would have preferred.

"Well, this isn't acceptable at all. What if this had been an emergency?"

"Obviously it isn't an emergency. What can I do for you?"

"I just wanted to know if we could change our appointment from Wednesday to Thursday?" This next week only, she was quick to inform me.

"I'm sorry but I have no other times available." I didn't feel very accommodating.

"If you can't make a simple change, maybe I should find somebody else who can be more flexible." *Flexible? She's accusing me of not being flexible? This woman cannot even deal with the fact that I hung a new picture in my office—she noticed immediately—and she's telling me that I am rigid? Talk about projection!*

So, I said: "Maybe you should."

I felt immediately sorry afterward. I knew she was only testing me, yet I felt helpless to respond the way I wanted. At that moment I just wanted to be rid of her.

And she accommodated me by hanging up.

A few days later she called back and left a message. I returned her phone call immediately, even with someone else in the waiting room. Neither one of us mentioned the previous incident, but in our own ways we each apologized—she by calling back, I by complying with her cry for prompt attention.

After several months, most of her demands gradually eased. One day I forgot to turn the clock around as she had trained me to do. I realized this partway through the hour, but I

did not want to draw her attention to that stupid clock. I was
escorting her out the door when she touched me on the shoulder
and smiled, "What? You didn't think I noticed? I guess I'm
getting a little better, huh?"

I could have hugged her.

Some Clients' Need for Control

Controlling clients feel entitled to special treatment. As children
they threw temper tantrums to get what they wanted; as adults
they find more sophisticated ways to perpetuate their feelings of
omnipotence (Boulanger, 1988). They become needy, whiny,
demanding, or pathetic—whatever it takes to maintain control
of their relationships.

Brehm and Brehm (1981) believe the need for control is
based principally on a perceived lack of freedom. When people
feel a loss of power in other arenas of their lives, they become
especially determined to maintain as much control as possible
in the therapy situation. In the absence of internal power, they
try to wield as much external control as possible in an effort to
restore the illusion of freedom.

Labeled *reactance theory* by Brehm and Brehm, this motivation to control can be quite healthy in small doses as it helps to
promote a degree of autonomy. Dowd and Seibel (1990) further
distinguish between situational and characterological reactance. In the latter condition, which is most typical of difficult
clients, control, coercion, and manipulation become a way of
life. In situational reactance, which the authors equate with
what we most often think of as resistance, the client is attempting
to defend against temporary helplessness.

There are other benefits of control as well. In discussing
the dynamics of controlling clients, Fiore (1988) describes some
of the more primitive defenses these people use to help them
maintain intimate contact without losing control, externalize
conflicts to keep them at a safe distance, and use the therapist as
a container for frightening impulses. In the most common of
these defenses, protective identification, the client is able to
disown unacceptable feelings, dump them onto the therapist,

and then enjoy vicariously what he or she is renouncing. Fiore (1988, p. 99) gives an example of how the controlling client would describe this process:

> When I get close to somebody I start dumping all this negative stuff on them. Even though I know it's my stuff, sometimes I think they're doing it to me. Sometimes it shifts back and forth so much I lose track of who is doing what to whom. Then I really start feeling crazy. Now you can point this out to me, and I can know it intellectually, but it doesn't seem to make any difference. One of the things that really bugs people about me is that I am so controlling. That's because when I dump this stuff out there, it feels like the other guy is out to get me so I really have to stay in control of things.

The challenge of therapy, then, is how to tolerate the client's need to act out the controlling scenario, to contain its effects, without suffering undue hardships. The secret to being a successful "container," according to experts on this subject such as Winnecott (1960), Bion (1977), and Kernberg (1980), is to maintain an empathic attitude while defining the parameters of the "holding environment" until the client no longer requires the defenses. This is some challenge indeed: to absorb the brunt of a client's controlling efforts without becoming frustrated in the process!

The Seductive Variation

One of the most challenging clients is the one who attempts to control us through seductive behavior. Conventional wisdom maintains that sexually provocative behavior represents the client's attempt to disown underlying feelings of anger, fear, and emptiness by controlling the therapist. Clients who sexualize relationships do so to avoid true intimacy, to keep others under their spell, and to feel desired by others. They are never able to feel satiated in their attempts to win attention and devotion (Shochet, Levin, Lowen, and Lisansky, 1976).

Close to 90 percent of practicing therapists say they feel sexually attracted to some clients (Pope, Keith Spiegel, and Tabachnick, 1986), and the majority (64%) feel guilty, anxious, and confused by these feelings. Although these reactions do not necessarily involve a client who is trying to control us and can often be the result of our own unresolved issues, seduction is a relatively common and effective way some individuals use to try to get under a therapist's skin. Many of us feel temptations that we know would have dangerous and detrimental results for the welfare of clients if we acted on them; nevertheless they are distracting and can make us feel almost as vulnerable as the person we are trying to help. Of course, the situation is even more difficult when the controlling client is doing everything within his or her power to be seductive, especially when the therapist finds that person especially attractive.

Maria is one of the most beautiful women I have ever seen — and she isn't wearing any underwear. At least I don't *think* she has anything on under that tight, sheer dress. Incredible as it may seem, I have hardly looked at her (after my first astonished glance).

My legs are crossed. My armpits are wet. I'm doing my best to look cool and detached. It isn't working.

Maria, however, is quite enjoying herself. As she tells me why she is here, she has slipped her shoes off so she can tuck her legs underneath her. Her already short dress rides further up her thighs. I am panicked. Where can I look now? Everywhere seems dangerous. I fixate on her eyes, and that is when I notice her smug smile. Why did it take me so long to notice that she is doing this on purpose? I breathe a little easier. But I don't dare uncross my legs.

Maria informs me that she has been in therapy before. Actually she has seen four different therapists in as many years. Why, I ask her innocently, has she then landed in my lap. . . er, office? She has nowhere else to turn. She feels lost, abandoned, completely alone. It all started when her boyfriend abruptly ended their relationship. Her boyfriend, you see, was also her previous therapist.

I become indignant, enraged. How could a professional in whom this vulnerable woman bestowed her trust, take advantage of her? How, indeed! And then she tells me that he was not the first. Two of her other former therapists also became intimate with her (the third was female). I see. I *do* see. I am next.

I understand that her faith in men in general, and men therapists in particular, has been compromised. In fact, she cannot like members of my sex and profession very much at all. I tell her this and then suggest *very carefully* that it seems as though she is even being seductive with me — the dress and her actions. I explain that if I am to help her at all we must both agree to keep the barriers of this relationship intact. (I realize that I am talking as much to myself as to her.)

Maria smiles sweetly and innocently, but I see a flash of anger that passes so fast I am not sure it was not my imagination. Then her indignation explodes. How *dare* I suggest that she is nothing more than a whore! But I didn't mean . . . I am just like all the men she has ever known. She spits out the accusation that I want to sleep with her, just like all the rest before me. (She got me on *that* one, anyway.)

"Look," I tell her patiently, "I want to help you. I really do. But you just told me you ended up in bed with all your previous male therapists. I'm male. I'm a therapist. Don't you think there is a pattern evident here?"

Maria never came back after that first session. And, boy, was *I* relieved! What if she had gotten me on a bad day, when I was mad at my wife or when I forgot to cross my legs? What if, in spite of my best intentions, I lost control?

Well, Maria is still out there in the world and I'm certain she is still trying to seduce as many male therapists as she can — unless someone has finally been able to reach her. Because I decided to confront her about the games I sensed she was playing, and because I desperately wanted to protect myself, Maria bolted. She could not feel that she had sufficient control if she was not allowed to be seductive.

Although she is a dramatic illustration, Maria is not representative of most seductive clients, who generally operate with greater subtlety. An example occurred while I was acting as a coleader of a group and one of the members was obviously attracted to my partner. The member would do everything he could think of to capture her attention or to receive the slightest acknowledgment from her that she liked him. His most successful seductive ploy was to belittle himself and complain that he would never have a good relationship with a woman. This remark was an invitation for the female members of the group to jump in and reassure him that he was attractive, but only my partner's comments would spark a reaction. He would gush to her about how grateful he was for her support. Everyone else reacted with exasperation, and it was that very phenomenon that my coleader pointed out to him. "Why don't you check out what other members are reacting to in that last exchange with me?"

Unlike Maria, this man was able to acknowledge his attempts to control female authority figures by being seductive. He eventually developed some real insight into why this controlling behavior had worked so well while he was living in a household with three sisters. He further responded positively to the female group members who shared with him their feelings about his controlling games. In spite of his ability to understand what he was doing, he required forceful confrontation within a very supportive context to alter his seductive behavior.

The Need to Be Forceful

Greenberg (1984) describes an extreme case of a controlling client who neither respected nor valued other people's rights. She was consistently unpleasant and irritating. When placed in a therapy group, she successfully alienated most of the other members by interrupting them constantly. Most often, whatever she said was phrased as a complaint or a criticism. She told others how contemptible she found them and would not hesitate, at a moment's notice, to lambaste someone into submission. She became the focal point of the group's energy and the vortex from which all conflict radiated.

Yet Greenberg maintains that in spite of this client's attempt to control other people's behavior, it was *his* problem rather than hers that needed to be worked on first. He views controlling abrasive clients as presenting opportunities for him to become more flexible. He even sees possible benefits for other group members in the constructive dialogue that can ensue when the abrasive member challenges the existing group cohesion.

Having led a number of groups with such participants in attendance, I am not altogether certain I agree that the potential benefits of including someone with a high need for control and dominance outweighs the risks.

I had been running one therapy group quite smoothly over a period of many months when I added a new participant. I believed that Dorothy could gain some valuable insight from hearing how others perceived her. This assumption certainly had some merit; however, I did not anticipate the extent to which she could pollute the trust and intimacy levels that had long been established among the other group members.

At first I was delighted with how members pulled together to confront this "alien" in their midst. It did not take Dorothy long to get her bearings, identify the leaders and weak links, and go to work instating herself as the President-for-Life. Some rumblings of discontent, some feeble protests regarding Dorothy's style were heard, but such rebellions were ruthlessly stamped out. And where was I during this coup d'etat? Dorothy had found a way to neutralize me as well; she recruited support for the idea that the group members could never learn to become independent from therapy if I was always doing the rescuing. She had a point. So I backed off to see what would unfold.

Because they no longer felt safe expressing their dissatisfactions, fearing that they would be stomped on by Dorothy or one of the "storm troopers" she had trained, several members dropped out of the group. Before I realized what was going on, I was left with a nucleus of Dorothy and a few others who had fallen under her spell. We continued the group for some time afterward, but the levels of trust and intimacy were never the same.

Some clients, such as Dorothy, feel that if they cannot be completely in control they will cease to exist. Therefore they will do everything within their power to keep things on their terms. And they are lifelong experts at getting others to do their bidding. Based on this realization, Boulanger (1988) recommends that a strict therapeutic contract be negotiated in advance with these clients, especially with regard to time considerations. If rules are firmly established about the handling of cancellations, missed or late appointments, and length of session, clients do not have to be confronted directly.

I agree thoroughly with this premise. Unfortunately, however, I am something less than a strict disciplinarian in enforcing rules. Because I act rebelliously myself whenever I get the chance, I secretly admire others who challenge existing rules and see how much they can get away with. Also, in order for me to feel competent, I need for almost every one of my clients to like me. Obviously, controlling clients have a field day with me.

In the end, I choose the easier of two paths, all the while hearing the admonitions of former supervisors: "Don't do it! You can't let them take over or they will eat you alive!"

I have had a hard time seeing a client as the enemy, as a person who needs to be "managed" or wrestled into submission. I prefer instead to give people the benefit of the doubt. I can allow a client to control the sessions (and me) within certain limits and for a certain period of time. I have not found it untenable to give a client free rein until he or she has crossed a line of unacceptability. My greatest concern was the fear that I would lose a client by being too demanding. I was in awe of colleagues who could get their clients to jump through hoops if that was what they wanted, much less get them to pay for missed appointments. My approach is that if I ignore the problem, maybe it will work itself out. Much to my surprise, in the majority of cases this is exactly what happens. Only when that tactic does not work will I resort to more forceful means.

Preventive Actions

The best antidote for clients who have a history of poisoning their intimate relationships is a dose of preventive limit setting. Smith and Steindler (1983) suggest that by being sensitive to the signals clients send, we can anticipate the directions in which they may act out. We can then establish firm boundaries before matters escalate to uncomfortable levels.

Imagine, for example, that any of the following incidents occurs during an initial interview:

- The client asks if you are married.
- The client comments that you seem so much nicer than any of the other therapists she has seen.
- The client directs you to close the curtains so the lighting in the room will be more muted.
- The client talks nonstop during the whole hour without responding to any of the few questions you ask.
- The client takes issue in an especially vehement manner with several things you say.
- You have a hard time getting the client to leave when the session is over.

These behaviors do not necessarily signal that trouble is around the corner, but they do alert us to be vigilant and to expect the unexpected. Assuming that we do not create a self-fulfilling prophecy by reading more danger than is necessary into relatively benign messages, accurately predicting problem areas that may develop can help us to prepare effective responses.

Ashley talks about problems she has had with previous therapists. "Can you believe how rigid some people can be? I mean I wasn't all *that* late most of the time, but this one doctor absolutely insisted that he would not see me any longer than the scheduled hour, even if he didn't have anyone else waiting immediately after me. That's why I like you so much. It wasn't my fault that traffic was so bad today and I really appreciate your letting me stay this extra time."

Warning bells are clanging like crazy. She is practically giving us her plan to test the limits of what she can get away with. And the therapist has already stepped into the trap, but not too far; he still has the opportunity to alter the norms that are being established. This action may be the most important key for helping controlling clients: to intervene *before* behavior has gotten out of hand.

It is important for clients to feel some degree of control in a situation that can be quite threatening. Extremely vulnerable people attempt to exercise even more control than is either necessary or helpful; it is our job to help them slowly relinquish this control without losing their dignity. This therapeutic task requires a delicate blend of tolerance for individual differences, on the one hand, and firm limit setting when things become chaotic, on the other. The controlling client eventually learns one of our most sacred premises: that being in control is much more an internal rather than an external state; it represents a degree of confidence in the ability to function in difficult situations and yet know that stability can be maintained. Of course, this axiom is true as much for therapists who feel the need for total control as it is for their clients.

CHAPTER TEN

You Can't Make Me Talk

Harold is extremely depressed over the breakup of his eight-year marriage. His wife says that he is impossible to live with. She claims he is neglectful, abusive, insensitive, and hostile—not a nice person at all. But Harold begs to differ: "The bitch is just ungrateful. And after everything I did for her, too. She was nothing before she met me. I introduced her to a world that was beyond her reach. And this is how she pays me back—by walking out. I say fuck her!"

I find myself liking his wife already for having the courage to walk out on this jerk. Guilt seeps through before long and I remind myself that Harold is hurting. He probably is not always this obnoxious. At least that is what I thought before he turned on *me*.

Harold was immediately suspicious and cynical about therapy. He wanted me to know that he was here under protest— only hoping to convince his soon-to-be ex-wife that he was at least trying to change. He thought this whole profession was a sham, nothing more than a form of prostitution, and further-more, he let me know that he didn't care for me one bit!

I sputtered out some response that I appreciated his honesty and that I didn't take his attacks personally.

"You better take it personally, buddy, if you expect to get paid."

I let that one slip by and redirected things back to his miserable life. He had a long history of alienating the people in his life and claimed nobody he could call a friend. He felt completely alone. I felt bad about my cynicism and defensiveness, my need to ridicule him to diffuse his attacks. Clearly, the man was really in trouble, and in his own unique way, he was asking for my help.

The half-dozen hours that we talked together were almost nonstop struggles. Harold could be polite and cooperative one minute and incredibly hostile the next. He was seething with anger; and I was the target of his abuse. He never apologized. In his mind, I was being paid essentially to tolerate whatever abuse he felt like dishing out.

I tried to tell him how hard it was to be with him, how other people in his life must have felt the same way that I did. I explained that the pattern for all his relationships was getting people to reject him. He called me a fraud and stormed out of the office without rescheduling another appointment. His last words were that I could stick my final bill "where the sun doesn't shine." I was so glad to be rid of him I hardly cared.

Harold, and clients like him, are among the greatest challenges in our work—the hostile and aggressive person, the belligerent adolescent, and even the combative couple who turn their rage on one another. In all these cases, we are exposed to emotional upheaval in its most powerful and extreme manifestations—a cyclone of destructive energy directed toward anyone who happens to get in its path.

The Abrasive Client

Almost by definition, violent, aggressive, hostile clients who lash out at others have problems with impulse control. They feel entitled to special treatment that they believe they have been denied throughout their lives. They expect their therapists to make up for these perceived deprivations by providing instant relief of symptoms, and they become even more frustrated and angry when they are once again disappointed (Madden, 1977).

Alicia is an abrasive person who was able to penetrate the composure of a therapist who considered herself especially experienced and skilled at managing even the most belligerent and unpredictable of clients:

I really want to forget her, just forget her. It has been four years. But I don't think she is gone. I catch myself looking twice at small green compact cars even though I remember her saying she had to get rid of her car. I think I'll hear from her again down the road. Although I have invested volumes of myself in other suicidal patients, wanting them alive, wanting them whole, wanting them to see Life's Potential, I confess I would be relieved to read or hear of Alicia's death. This is not characteristic of me. I consider myself on the end of the scale as having the widest range of tolerance for annoying, irritating behavior of any therapist I know. Hallucinations in my office are not something with which I can't cope. I have never been attacked by a patient; I think I know how to gauge rage that well. Simpler levels of obnoxious behavior seem to me to be rather clear messages of the depth of a patient's misery and I am generally able to respond therapeutically.

Alicia was different [Brothers, 1984, p. 45].

What made Alicia so different for Brothers were her degrees of desperation and intensity, coupled with a rampant unpredictability and tendency to become verbally threatening. Even the answering service complained they would no longer take messages from her because she became so abusive. While Brothers took some degree of comfort in knowing that a half-dozen other professionals were also pulling their hair out in response to their contact with Alicia, she had to conclude that ultimately she had failed: "I terminated my end with Alicia, reluctantly on the one hand and with great relief on the other. Yet, I still wonder if there were a way, which I just didn't discover, that would have led to her center and to her eventual healing" (Brothers, 1984, p. 53).

Abject failures with these sorts of cases are quite common. Giovacchini (1989) described the discomfort he experienced while working with an aggressively intrusive client. The client

began initially by accusing him of incompetence because he
had failed to foresee a catastrophe that had occurred in the
client's life. Eventually, her rage escalated to the point that she
held him accountable for all the pain she had ever suffered. She
became progressively angrier and more accusatory over time.

As much as he tried to understand the origins of her rage
and to maintain his professional detachment, Giovacchini finally lost his temper and told her how it felt to be dumped on.
She then fled treatment.

With each of these cases the therapist is confronted with
someone who does not respect the usual rules of human contact
that are part of therapeutic engagement. These people are
abrasive, rubbing us (and others) the wrong way because of their
pervasive mistrust and hostility. Nowhere is this abrasiveness
more evident than in the hostile male client who, unfortunately,
sometimes ends up in our office against his will.

Taffel (1990) has made a study of men who sound familiar
to us, the man who is the prototype of Jackie Gleason's character
in *The Honeymooners* — irritable, moody, critical, demanding, hostile, a caged animal who paces relentlessly, stomping, snarling,
and sniping. He is certainly not the best candidate for therapy.
But sometimes such a man does seek help, or more likely, is
forced by his wife to get help under the threat that she will walk
out on him if he doesn't.

This man who appears so gruff and hostile is actually
masking a chronic depression, according to Taffel (1990, p. 51):
"Whether the men passively disappear into the woodwork or
shake the foundation of the house with their agitation, they
share one characteristic — they cannot regulate their own moods
or affective states and they depend on their partners and children to do so for them."

Cast in this light, hostile men are unable to articulate
what is bothering them and are completely unaware of their
feelings. Their behavior is in sharp contrast to that of many
hostile female clients (and also other men) who become deeply
and overtly angry precisely because they are so aware of their
feelings of resentment and helplessness. Taffel believes that if we
would give as much attention to underlying affective states in

hostile people as we do their power and self-esteem issues we could really help them deal with the feelings that are eating them alive.

This hypothesis, even if it is valid only half the time, has helped me to work with clients I find especially difficult. Hostile people frighten me — as they are supposed to. Yet once I get beyond the bluster I am able to home in on the hurt and pain that lies beneath the surface. To make that much noise one would have to be wounded deeply in some way.

I try not to see the hostile client as purposely attempting to manipulate and control; if I do, then *I* become angry. Almost against my will, I rise to the challenge of locking horns to protect the vulnerable and innocent against this big, bad monster. Alternatively, I try to look at the hostile client's underlying suffering, the desperate attempts to live up to an idealized image that is unreachable. Even if this assumption of hostility-as-masked-depression is not valid, the framework helps me to remain compassionate rather than threatened, empathic rather than defensive. Nowhere is this conceptual framework more helpful than when that most exotic, elusive, and challenging of all clients crashes through the door with a wail of defiance — the belligerent adolescent.

The Belligerent Adolescent

"Look you stupid ass, my mother made me come so I have to sit here, but you can't make me talk."

"I don't blame you for being angry when you are forced to do something you don't want to do."

He hunches deeper inside himself, crossing his arms. His scowl turns into a smirk.

"Look, this isn't exactly a lot of fun for me either. We seem to be stuck with each other for awhile. We might as well make the best of the situation. Why don't you tell me about why your mother thinks you should be here?"

"Fuck you."

"Your mother mentioned to me on the phone that unless

your grades improve dramatically in the next few weeks you won't graduate from high school."

He looks up for a moment in defiance and then shrugs. I shrug back, imitating his movements. At least we are communicating on some level.

"She also said that your friends are worried about you, too. What is your best friend's name? Ronnie, isn't it? (I deliberately mispronounce it.) Anyway, Ronnie called your mom to tell her that he was real concerned about how moody you have been lately."

"Lonnie."

"Excuse me?"

"Lonnie. His name is Lonnie. Can't you even get *that* right?"

"Thanks. Lonnie, then. So what *is* the story?"

He sinks so deeply into the couch I wonder if it will swallow him up. He is chewing on his nails now. His teeth peel off a curled strip of nail, which he casually drops off the end of the couch. He glances at me to see if I noticed.

"I want to help you. I don't work for your mother; I work for you. Neither she nor anyone else needs to know what we talk about — it's just between us. I don't expect you trust me; you don't even know me. But we have lots of time to get to know one another. Meanwhile, I have a problem that I need your help with."

He doesn't take the bait, nor even nibble. But I continue anyway.

"When this session is over, your mother is going to ask me how it went, what we talked about. What should I tell her?"

Another shrug, saying he doesn't care.

"What I intend to tell her, then, is nothing. Just that what goes on here is between you and me. And that things went fine. How does that sound?"

"Look, man, I already told you I don't want to be here and I don't want your help. You guys can make me come here and make me go to school, at least until I turn eighteen next month. But you can't make me talk."

And so the battle goes between the well-meaning therapist

and the surly adolescent who is hurting so much he can't ask for help. Jurich (1990) describes kids like this as the therapist's worst nightmare: defiant, obnoxious, a tough-ass who dares you to come close so he or she can eat you alive. "When they are not making our lives miserable *in* the treatment, they are making us feel worse by refusing have anything to do *with* the treatment" (Shay, 1987, p. 712).

But of course these children are hardly agents of the devil sent to torture us; they are acting out quite honestly what they genuinely feel inside. In speaking of the younger "hateful child," Brenner (1988, p. 188) describes his or her intensely negative energy: "Sometimes there is hardly a room that can contain them. They may use the walls to climb on, the window to jump from and the closets to hide in. Their attention span is short, and they are fast going in and out of drawers and closets, with jet speed. While they continuously look for assurance and love, they are acting out of pure fury and hate. They are hungry, and their continuous movements are, like scavengers, always searching for food in the environment. They appear to be an example of pure ID impulse."

Rebellious children feel such anger and hate that they inspire similar feelings in us. Often abandoned or neglected by one or both parents, they are on a single-minded mission to make surrogates pay the price for their perceived (or actual) abuse. Their acting out, however raw and impolite, is the form of communication with which they feel most comfortable.

The days of the teenager who would act out through being promiscuous, listening to rock and roll, and smoking pot are over. Now we must contend with adolescent belligerence in nuclear proportions. Because sexual acting out is not as safe any more, there is a backlog of repressed energy that finds itself expressed in acts of violence. Who could ever have imagined that inner-city elementary schools would have guards and metal detectors, that fourth and fifth graders would control the drug trade for particular territories, that children would be murdered for their Nike Air Jordans or their leather jackets?

Among the affluent population, belligerent teenagers drive their parents crazy not with drugs or social protest, as many of us did, but with racist or anti-Semitic posturing. For a generation of parents and therapists who grew up during the turbulent sixties, when a certain amount of rebelliousness was fashionable, we are now stunned by the extremes. There are kids who act out with automatic weapons, and then there are those who swear off all drugs and alcohol and rebel against their parents by becoming neo-Nazis or materialistic wheeler-dealers.

Dismissing the Hostile Client from Treatment

One obvious solution to the problems of treating belligerent adolescents is to get rid of them altogether and work with the parents instead. Quite often their behavior is the result of dysfunctional family structures in the first place, so it makes sense to see the people who experience the greatest difficulty and therefore should be most motivated to initiate change.

   Adolescents (or anyone else for that matter) cannot be made to do anything they firmly refuse to do. The teenager who has already become entrenched in a defensive position, who has reached a point of simmering hostility, is simply not going to be budged through a frontal confrontation. Some therapists suggest that rather than targeting the child directly in such cases, the therapy should concentrate on other family members who are more cooperative and motivated. Sometimes, dismissing the belligerent adolescent from treatment even has the paradoxical effect of piquing his or her interest. In several cases described by Anderson and Stewart (1983a), the problem children were asked specifically not to participate in the therapy with the result that they became much more cooperative in their efforts to make themselves understood.

   The rationale is clear: take somebody who is a world-class expert at rebellion and defiance and then ask him to do what he does best. Even if this isn't immediately effective in eliciting the sullen teenager's cooperation, you have at least eliminated the major impediment to the therapeutic process. The client is now facing the consequences of his belligerence—that is, he is not permitted to participate as an adult in the attempt to find a solution to the problem. If he decides to continue pouting he will at least not disrupt the therapy the way he has stirred up the family. Meanwhile, there is plenty of work that can be done with the parents to help them understand their child and deal with the conflicts more effectively.

It is also quite helpful for the child to get the clear message from his parents: "We want to help you. We will do anything within our power and resources to be of assistance. If you do not want our help, we have no alternative but to respect your choice. However, we have decided to get help for ourselves. And we have definitely decided to try doing some things differently. With the support and expertise of our therapist, we are optimistic that needed changes can be made."

A great number of the times that belligerent teenagers are dragged into treatment they are acting out the problems manifested in their parents' relationship. The message above lets the child know that the parents are getting help for themselves. It is no longer necessary for the child to act as a scapegoat or distractor.

Parents are often urged to come in for the first session on behalf of their child, ostensibly to provide needed background information. At least half the time, once we get into the family history and dynamics of the couple's relationship, we end up starting there first. If the parents are going to be at all effective in helping their child, they have to be reasonably cooperative with one another first. In an amazing number of times, when we start working on the marital relationship, the hostile child's behavior miraculously improves.

A plan devised by Roberts (1982) helps the parents of acting-out adolescents to create a more mature and satisfying relationship with their child. The change is accomplished through a sequential process beginning with the *preparatory phase*. The object of this stage of the therapeutic relationship is to instill positive expectations, raise morale, and recruit support. We are also gathering specific information regarding what the adolescent does and what effects such behavior has on others.

In the *rethinking phase* no effort is made to explore the marital relationship; rather, the focus is exclusively on the angry adolescent and the parents' relationship to him or her. Roberts (1982, pp. 20–21) has observed that "while a few families can meaningfully begin quickly to broaden the context of therapy to include their personal lives, the great majority are unable to, and premature termination is likely to occur if the therapist gets fooled into pushing such areas too soon."

The principal goals are thus to help the parents become more reflective about their child's behavior, to understand better what he or she is going through, and what is being communicated through the acting-out behaviors. Madanes (1990a) described the helpfulness of such awarenesses to the parents of a young girl who was especially difficult to deal with. The parents claimed they could tell immediately on awakening whether the girl was going to be in a good or a bad mood throughout the whole day.

"And if you believed it was going to be a bad day, how would you greet your daughter?" Madanes inquired.

"Well, we would usually go in her room and ask her to get ready for school. It was all business. We knew we were in for a fight."

"And what if you anticipated she was in a good mood?"

"Oh, then I would sing to her and play games."

The parents believed the child was dictating to them what life would be like; in fact, they were unconsciously cuing their child as to what *their* mood was, based on reading (or misreading) her behavior.

Understanding communication patterns and relationship structures is the bread and butter of the family therapist. In this specialized form of treatment, attention is concentrated primarily on the parental dyad in relationship to the hostile child. Efforts are made to strengthen the parental bond through joint problem solving. The therapist gives the couple permission to do what they need to do to protect and take care of themselves. Finally, rethinking is initiated in areas of defining responsibility—who is in charge of what, and what realistically is within their power to influence. The general emphasis is in training the parents to be more objective and less emotionally vulnerable to the whims of their irresponsible child.

This strategy proved to be especially helpful to the parents of Clem, a young man who had been dragged to therapy but refused to participate. The parents were at the end of their rope. Once they came in for sessions they sent a clear message to their son: "We may not be able to stop you or get you to act more civilized, but we're damned if we will let you control our lives anymore!"

Understanding why Clem was so difficult was quite an interesting exercise for the parents but less useful than their resolve to take better care of themselves. As happens so often in such cases, Clem considerably reduced his acting-out behavior once his parents stopped overreacting. Further, he seemed less angry when his parents began operating with cooler heads.

In the *directed action* phase, the meat (or "potatoes" for vegetarian readers) of therapy is accomplished. Insight and understanding are useless unless they are translated into action. This transition occurs when any number of strategic, structural, or behavioral interventions are implemented, depending on one's theoretical preferences. There is no doubt, however, that *some* action is required to alter the parents' responses to the belligerent adolescent. The action plan can run the gamut from being more supportive to kicking the young adult out of the house. In any case, the parents are likely to be more successful in their efforts than they would have been without their newfound alliance, their objective problem-solving attitude, and their detachment from the bonds to their child that previously held them immobile.

Neutralizing Hostility

According to Bowlby's "attachment theory" (1973), hostile clients are expressing their frustration toward authority figures who have been continuously nonresponsive. As the hostile activity is based on a lack of trust, the object of therapy is to work on establishing an affectionate attachment with the person who is rebellious.

In an unusual application of Bowlby's theory, Nelson (1984) suggests that the best way to treat disruptive and hostile adolescents is through abrupt shifts in emotion to create bonding and trust. Dysfunctional or inappropriate behavior is confronted for a few seconds, after which it is juxtaposed with support and affection. The "scolding" initially creates anxiety, followed by the reassurance that produces relief and eventually trust.

Hartman and Reynolds (1987) provide a partial list of resistant behaviors that should be confronted within this context, such as a client's showing disrespect to authority figures or becoming obstinate. According to the authors, these behaviors, and hundreds of others like them, should be confronted vigorously and then immediately followed by caring reassurance. This paradigm counters resistance by working on both process and content levels. It creates a safe atmosphere in which the therapist can let the child know that what he or she is doing is not acceptable, without breaching the trust that has been established between them.

When I read about models such as this I usually shake my head. Slowly. I think to myself: that's all very fine, and what the authors are saying surely sounds good on the drawing board, but what about when some kid is trying to take my head off? I smile as I try to imagine some belligerent adolescents I have known sitting still while I "juxtapose confrontation with caring." Most difficult clients I have worked with are difficult precisely because they see through attempts to control them or modify their behavior. Yes, they need firm boundaries, but not within the context of a game called "good cop, bad cop" where I alternate scolding with a sappy smile.

One of the major points we gleaned from Sigmund Freud, Erik Erikson, Jean Piaget, Lawrence Kohlberg, and the other developmental theorists is that adolescence is a time for testing limits. It is the period in which the half-adult–half-child seeks to exercise autonomy and to test himself in combat against established authorities. In fact, being resistant and rebellious is part of the job description of a teenager and a component of many relationships teens have with their parents and other authorities. Novelist Len Deighton once wryly observed that the universal conflicts between adolescents and their families is necessary for the very survival of the planet: if kids did not fight with their parents, they would never leave home. And then the world would end.

While adolescents may indeed be sullen, secretive, self-absorbed, and sometimes rude, most have not developed rebelliousness to an art form. A number of studies have indicated that adolescent belligerence is overstated and that most arguments that take place are over relatively inane issues — whether to take out the garbage and how one's hair should be cut (Gelman, 1990).

McHolland (1985) cautions that adolescent resistance must be looked at in terms of the system it serves; quite often the acting-out behaviors serve a protective function in the family. He also notes that in many cases the therapist, by her attitude, expectations, and labeling, can create resistance where little or none exists. McHolland, therefore, offers several guidelines for avoiding the manufacture or stimulation of adolescent hostility in the early sessions:

1. Establish general rapport before beginning any attempt to get into the presenting problems. Start with basic interests in music, sports, school, and other activities.
2. Keep the pace moving. Do not let silences last too long. Engage the client in interactions.
3. Do not interrupt the client while he or she is talking. Do not offer advice or judgments.
4. Use self-disclosure to build trust. Stay within appropriate boundaries while sharing one's own feelings and experiences.
5. Do not expect or demand that the client do something that he or she cannot do. Learn about present levels of functioning — cognitive, affective, interpersonal, verbal, and developmental — and stay within them.
6. Use humor whenever possible to diffuse tension. For example, one especially potent technique most adolescents cannot resist is to ask them: "Would you like to see me imitate

the way you look? Now, how would you like to imitate the way
I look to you?"
7.   Avoid taking sides with the adolescent or the parents.

    I find this last guideline the most challenging of all. If the
adolescent perceives we owe loyalty to her parents, there is no
way she will ever trust the relationship. And if the parents believe
we are too closely aligned with their child against them, they will
yank her out of treatment. I have often found it helpful to recruit
the child's assistance in this matter:
    "Look, I need your help with a problem. Your folks will
want to know what we talked about in this session. If I don't tell
them, they probably won't let you come back—and that means
they may find someone else you would like even less than you like
me. So let's agree on what is OK for me to say to them, and what
you would prefer that I not tell them."
    Even the most obstinate of adolescents can recognize a
good deal when he hears one. We are now coconspirators in a
plan to help him attain autonomy and maintain dignity, and to
do so without alienating other family members.

Confronting the Hostile Client

One of the most trying aspects of working with hostile clients is
that their anger often elicits anger in us as well. We feel abused
and attacked. No matter how much we reassure ourselves that
this hostility is part of the client's pathology, we find it hard not to
take the attacks personally—especially with clients who deliberately try to provoke us. These individuals are often exquisitely
sensitive to vulnerability. If attacking our competence fails to
strike a spark of indignation in us, they will try a host of other
ploys to elicit a reaction—make a lot of noise, complain to
others behind our backs, and even threaten physical violence.
We then seek to retaliate under the guise of confrontation
(Youngren, 1991).
    Fremont and Anderson (1986) analyzed the client behav-
iors that provoke anger and suggested that in dealing with these,
our first step should be to determine whether the anger or

frustration we feel is indeed appropriate or whether it is a function of our own personal issues. The authors recommend that we next examine the hostile incident to learn whether it reflects the problem that brought the client to get help in the first place or represents an interpersonal dynamic in us. Then, and only then, should therapists talk about the feelings they are experiencing, although fully 90 percent have some reservations about sharing these reactions aloud (Fremont and Anderson, 1986). The principal criterion for determining the appropriateness of voicing these reactions is the same one that should be used before any self-disclosure: will hearing what I am about to reveal be helpful for the client, or am I doing this just to meet my own needs?

We must be sure that we are not disclosing our feelings to let off steam, to inflate our own egos, to put the client down, or to strike back. If we genuinely desire to give feedback that can be helpful to the client, however, such interventions can be a tremendous turning point in treatment.

One reason that hostile clients employ their abusive style of communication is because they have been allowed to get away with it. Other people feel so intimidated by hostile clients that they will not challenge them, nor will they risk greater vulnerability by revealing how the hostile behavior has affected them. The therapist, however, is in an ideal position to force the hostile client to accept responsibility for the negative impact he or she has on others.

"I am sitting here thinking to myself that if I were not paid to listen to you, I would never put up with your antics. In fact, I am wondering if I am paid enough. No wonder your wife left, your children are afraid of you, and you have no friends. Why would anyone subject himself to your childish outbursts? Now, you can storm out of here if that is what you want to do; it's what you have done every other time somebody has tried to help you; but if you do leave, you are going to stay a very unhappy human being. I want to help you, but you make it very difficult for me to like you, to be with you."

A brilliant speech, I thought. But he did leave. And he did not come back. I reassured myself that even if he had stayed, I could not have helped him much, anyway. I did know that before I told him how I felt, I was absolutely positive I was doing it to help him (although I certainly felt some small satisfaction as well). If I had been more compassionate or softer, could he have heard me without feeling so threatened? I doubt it. Why should he give up a lifetime strategy of intimidation just because I did not like it?

There are other possible benefits of confronting hostile clients with the therapist's own feelings. For one, it helps them to distinguish between anger and hostility, to learn the benefits of expressing feelings without inflicting damage on others (Cahill, 1981). It also opens up avenues for exploring interpersonal conflicts in healthy ways and helps clients to learn they can have intense feelings and can express them with consideration for who is listening (Welpton, 1973).

Regardless of the preferred interventions, the hostile client must be taught that while it is indeed legitimate to feel hurt and angry, there are appropriate ways to express these feelings. The best place to practice these more effective ways of communicating is in the therapy itself, with the clinician taking the lead by modeling assertive responses in a compassionate and sensitive manner.

Chapter Eleven

I Don't Have a Problem—
He/She Does

My attention was first drawn to Mr. and Mrs. Ridley when I heard the commotion in the waiting room. I was just finishing a session when I heard a loud thump, followed by a series of smaller indistinct noises, and then a bloodcurdling scream. My client and I looked at one another — each daring the other to see what had happened. Since it *was* my office, it seemed only fair I should peek first. I cautiously cracked open the door, the client peering over my shoulder, and there to our surprise was an elderly couple in the midst of a violent fist fight.

Mr. Ridley was a slight, frail-looking man of seventy-eight. His wife, a stout and hearty woman of seventy-four, was trading punches with him as if they were in the same weight class. Their lips were curled back in a snarl, revealing their perfect white dentures. Each bellowed in exasperation with the other and tried to land a solid punch. Mr. Ridley was the first to notice us. He tried to regain his composure but it was difficult with his wife, her back to us, wagging her finger in his face, tweaking his nose, and calling him a gutless wonder. And then they were flailing at one another again, making a lot of noise but doing little damage.

Several minutes later I had them separated on opposite sides of the room. Their glares were so intense they were still landing punches with their eyes. They told their story of being married for over fifty years, a half-century of combat. Although they had grown accustomed to a certain level of conflict between them, lately the war had escalated. Mrs. Ridley said she became

115

enraged whenever her husband flirted with other women. Mr. Ridley, with a wink at me, innocently denied that he ever flirted. The couple had been forced to move frequently during the past few years because of complaints from their neighbors about their arguments. Finally, they were referred to me by their physician after they had a fist fight in his office.

Their problems seemed serious, yet I could not look at them without laughing. They were so cute. And beneath their surface bickering, they seemed to have great affection, even love for one another. When I told them this, they grumbled a bit, then grudgingly admitted it was true. And much to my surprise, they made solid progress within a short period of time. They learned to fight more fairly, to communicate more appropriately, even to share their love for each other. It was indeed a happy ending for them, but this encounter took a gigantic piece out of my own armor.

I hate seeing people being mean to one another. I hate it worse when I am trapped in a room with two people who are bickering and screaming, probing for weaknesses they can exploit, doing whatever they can to humiliate or even destroy one another. Maybe I am even more intolerant of couples who abuse one another than I ought to be. My parents divorced when I was a child; I grew up in a home where calling each other names, screaming, and slamming doors were normal modes of communication between parents. I am sure it is more than coincidence that I find myself so often acting as a referee to temper the blows of a heavyweight bout involving a married couple.

Why Couples Are Difficult

Difficult couples are even more challenging than individual resistant clients. They also drop out of therapy faster if things aren't going their way (Allgood and Crane, 1991).

Couples become difficult to work with for a number of reasons; being combative is only one of the most dramatically challenging scenarios we must confront in our line of work. Luther and Loev (1981) have identified other expressions of resistance in marital therapy, described below:

A fatalistic attitude. "We have always been like this, ever since we can remember. Even our respective parents treated one another the same way that we do. I don't know what you can do to help us; nothing else has worked."

Blaming the other. "Look, I'm here because my wife dragged me in. *She* is the one with the problem. My life is going just fine. If only she would stop complaining all the time."

Aligning with the therapist. "Look, I would like to do whatever I can to help you with my husband. He just hasn't been well for some time. Maybe we can both come up with something together; I've tried everything I can think of by myself."

One wants out, and the other does not. "My husband betrayed me. I don't trust him, and I never will again. He says he will do anything to save this marriage. I say it is too late. I'm here only so I can say I tried everything before I walk out for good."

Denial of progress. "She says that she has been initiating sex more often, but I don't see it that way."

Collusive distractions. "Our child is having problems in school again. If you don't mind, we would rather deal with that problem first."

As daunting as these forms of marital resistance are to confront, they pale in comparison to the weapons of the couple who express themselves primarily in the language of conflict, usually at high decibel levels. These are marriages not made in heaven; in the words of a character from a novel by Tom Robbins, "Mine was made in Hong Kong. By the same people who make those little rubber pork chops they sell in the pet department at K Mart" (Robbins, 1990, p. 6).

With combative couples, it takes not one difficult person but two individuals who exhibit a high degree of inflexibility and disturbance to create such poisonous interaction. The other qualities that make them so unique among the clientele who seek marital therapy are the intensity of their conflicts, the vested interest they both have in maintaining their argumentative behavior, the perverse enjoyment they seem to derive from the ritualized combat, and the degree of resistance they show to changing their dysfunctional patterns. People tend to resist

change in general because of a fear of the unknown; this situa
tion is made worse when a person's emotional security is at stake.
"Whatever the causes, the need for stability in families is so
strong that it is usually not the desire for change that leads
families to seek therapy, but rather it is the *failure* to accommo
date to change. Most families come to therapy in response to
changes which they do not like or have not adjusted to" (Anderson and Stewart, 1983a, p. 29).

Each member of the couple in conflict is reluctant to give
up something that is familiar for some other elusive goal that
could turn out much worse. The partners cling together in
destructive patterns in an effort to minimize further risks or
threats to their self-esteem. The possibility of change becomes
even more frightening than the prospect of spending an eter-
nity together locked in combat.

"I hate all this bickering," one spouse was heard to say, "but
it is really not as bad as it seems once you get used to it."

For once, his wife agrees: "I don't like this fighting all the
time, either, but it is all we know."

Of course, they are not telling the complete truth: on
some level, they *do* enjoy mixing it up with one another. It is the
way, maybe the only way, they have learned to express their
feelings and communicate their needs. It is also a wonderful
distraction that keeps them from ever having the time or the
opportunity to explore deeper into the core issues that each
partner keeps at a distance.

Fran and Stan had their routines down to split-second
timing. They were artists, even maestros, in their uncanny ability
to sense just when we were getting close to something significant; then one or the other would quickly start a fight to get us off
track. If Fran would forget the rules temporarily and start to
express some tenderness toward her husband, Stan would sneer
or ridicule her for being weak. If he on some rare occasion of
clarity (or insanity) would compliment Fran for something she
did that he appreciated, she would use that as a starting point to
berate him for not doing it himself.

Fran: What are you, an invalid? You can't make your own damn
lunch in the morning?

Stan: I was only trying to say thank. . .

Fran: Don't feed me that crap! You think I was born yesterday? You just want me to do it *every* morning.

Now we are really off and running. I find a way to get their attention so we can begin anew. Unknown to me, however, they have already signaled a new play.

Fran: Well, I'm glad you enjoyed your lunch. It was no big deal. I had to make mine anyway.

Stan: It was OK. You know I don't like. . .

I: Time out. It seems to me we were talking about the ways that each of you mistrusts the other's intentions. You were saying how each of you felt betrayed by your own parents and that you find it difficult to get close to anyone of the opposite sex.

Stan: Well, dear, you sure don't make it seem like it is all that hard for you to get close to those guys you work with.

Fran: Me? How about you? You're the one who had the affair!

Stan: How many times do I have to tell you? It wasn't an affair. She was just a friend. We talked sometimes. Besides that was six years ago!

I: Hold on a second. We were talking about trust issues between you, and now you are fighting again. What is going on?

Fran: He started it.

Stan: Right. I always start it, don't I? It's all my fault. Just forget it.

Interventions with Combative Couples

One way of untying the knot of conflict between combative couples is to help them express their feelings to one another without being abusive. Because the marital bond is the primary

intimate relationship for most adults, intense emotional reactions to one another are inevitable in a marriage.

Greenberg and Johnson (1988) have developed an emotionally focused therapy for couples that seeks to access primary
emotional experiences of each partner and then helps each one
communicate these feelings in ways that the other spouse can
hear and respond to. This is standard operating procedure in
many forms of marital therapy. Each partner is helped to express
the feelings that underlie the hostility, whether it is the fear of
abandonment, engulfment, or intimacy. In the case described
earlier, for example, Fran is encouraged to share with her husband the underlying feelings of mistrust and hurt that she
expresses through anger. Simultaneously, Stan is assisted in his
efforts to express his fear of losing his wife and how he covers up
his vulnerability by keeping her off balance.

More specifically, the authors propose a multistep program for diffusing the marital conflict, beginning with a delin-
eation of the salient issues. The therapist identifies and labels
the position each partner is taking in relation to the another.
The problem is then redefined in terms of emotional pain: "How
are your needs not being met by your partner? What pain are
you experiencing? In what ways do you feel vulnerable? What
are you afraid of? When you become so angry, what else are you
feeling inside?"

Next, the therapist attempts to sort out the interaction
cycle. Considered systemically in terms of communication patterns and interaction sequences, what vicious cycle has been
established? How is one partner aggravating the other, and in
turn, being reciprocally punished?

"I notice the following scenario unfolding between the
two of you: First, Carol, you ask your husband to be more open
with you. Then, Burt, you try to comply. You start to tell her what
things are like for you. While your voice sounds sincere, you
seem to have a smirk on your face that says 'I'll do this but I don't
like it.' This attitude develops at just about the same time that
you, Carol, start to get frustrated because Burt is so concrete in
his descriptions. You then interrupt Burt in the middle because
you don't think he is being responsive. And then Burt withdraws,

feeling hurt. He starts to snip at you. You snap back. And the next thing you know, it is World War III. I've seen this happen several times right here in this office."

It is at this point in the process that therapists tend to diverge in their next step with this couple. Greenberg and Johnson, as well as other experientially based practitioners, would help the couple to admit and express their feelings more sensitively and clearly while fostering greater acceptance of each other's positions. Instead of resorting to rage and combat when a partner feels neglected, rejected, or inspected, he or she can express needs and wants in caring, sensitive ways.

Several authors (Watzlawick, Weakland, and Fisch, 1974; Stuart, 1980; Madanes, 1981) would disagree that more direct and open communication is possible, or even desirable, with combative couples. Behaviorally oriented marital therapists would home in much more directly on those actions that are counterproductive and attempt to substitute for them more caring responses. Structural therapists might work to realign the power balance within the couple while strategic practitioners would be more concerned with disrupting the dysfunctional communication patterns. Others, such as Nichols (1989), prefer an even more pragmatic approach with polarized couples, concentrating on helping the partners to renew their commitment to one another, bridging misunderstandings between partners, and rebuilding the trust that has been ruptured.

The important point, however, is not that there are a dozen valid treatment strategies that may be helpful but that with violent, abusive couples it is necessary to do everything possible to disrupt their destructive patterns. This includes working with their unexpressed feelings *and* their irrational cognitive structures *and* their unresolved family-of-origin issues *and* their individual intrapsychic issues *and* their power struggles *and* any external situational factors that are compounding everything else.

Reducing all these interventions to their essence, Shay (1990) reminds us of the most basic therapeutic principle of all when working with discordant couples who fight a lot: EVERY-BODY WALKS OUT ALIVE. As I mentioned earlier, like many members of our profession, I came from a conflicted family. My parents fought constantly. I fell asleep many nights to the sounds of slamming doors or screaming voices. While I was unsuccessful at keeping my parents from divorcing, at age ten I decided I did not like being around people who were cruel to one another, and I did everything within my meager power to stop people from hurting one another.

As a marital therapist, if there is one thing I do well (and sometimes it is the only thing that I can do), it is to not permit couples to be abusive to one another in my office. They can fight, but the fight must be fair. They can argue, but only with respect. They can be as passionate, emotional, and expressive in their communications as they would like, as long as they do not jeopardize each other's physical or psychological safety.

Most couples are usually more polite and civilized in their behavior when a witness is present, especially one whose approval they are trying to win. There are occasions, however, when one or both partners cannot or will not control themselves, no matter who is present. They would just as easily rip into one another in a crowded restaurant or your office as they would in the privacy of their own living room.

Unless we can get the couple to behave themselves and find a therapeutic window in their intense conflict, little else we can do will be helpful. The object, then, in making sure everyone leaves the room alive is to do something to shift the level of interaction away from the battle. Shay recommends turning to the past as a way to restore calm—although some couples will use this intervention to renew their fight over some favorite issue that is good for a few licks. I tried this very technique with the elderly couple who began this chapter:

I: So tell me about how you met.

He: (Smiles inwardly) She picked me up in a bar.

She: You know that's not true! Why do you tell such lies?

He: Don't you know I'm kidding? Actually, I was really interested in her sister, but she wasn't available, so I went out with her instead.

I: (Trying to head off the argument I saw coming) You met one another when you were both quite young?

She: (Ignoring me) I could have married any young man I wanted. Lord knows why I picked this man who betrayed me . . .

He: I never betrayed you.

She: You did. Don't lie.

He: Did not.

She: What about that affair you had with your secretary?

He: Jesus! That was over thirty years ago! And we didn't have an affair. You just have an overactive imagination.

And then they were flailing at one another again.

When history fails, the next option Shay suggests is to try problem solving. This changes the emotional tenor of the interactions as the participants work together toward a mutual goal. With the couple above, we brainstormed ways to lower the decibel level of their screaming matches. They decided to try wearing surgical masks when they fought since it is harder to yell through those things (and besides, they look so silly wearing them). They bought the masks, but refused to wear them.

Whatever ingenious method is eventually stumbled on, explosive couples must be neutralized before they ever have the chance to listen or talk to one another, much less change the pattern of their interactions. Once they have agreed to abide by certain basic rules of human consideration—speaking in a more subdued tone of voice; not interrupting one another; refraining from abuse, accusations, or verbal violence—combative couples can then learn to communicate with one another more healthily. They need to find ways to express accumulated resentment without being abusive, and they must learn to be more responsible for what happens to them instead of blaming their partner.

Bergman (1985) finds it especially helpful to assign homework assignments to couples trying to devour one another. Each evening the couple is instructed to spend five minutes each telling one another the ways that they feel hurt. They are to use only the pronoun "I" throughout the exercise and to refrain from blaming the other, attacking, or becoming angry. While one partner speaks, the other listens quietly and finally responds with an apology to the effect that he or she has been unaware of the hurt, feels badly about it, and then asks for forgiveness. Although these assignments can be potentially problematic or even dangerous without adequate supervision, most of the difficulties can be circumvented by first having the couple practice the exercises in the sessions before trying them out at home. This strategy will probably work for only about half the couples who comply with the task, but half is certainly impressive. And the other half, who will not comply, can always be given the paradoxical assignment of arguing more often.

As frustrating as combative couples and other violent, abusive, and aggressive clients can be to work with, we often feel some appreciation for the passion with which they express themselves. They are people who are intensely committed to their beliefs, and while quite rigid and obstructive, they most definitely engage us thoroughly in their struggles. This is not the case with another kind of difficult client, discussed in the next chapter. This person seems to exhibit an almost opposite style— a definite lack of passion and energy.

CHAPTER TWELVE

I Already
Told You This Before?

The first thing you would notice about Sam is how eager he is to please. He smiles nervously, with a sickly sort of expression — as if I am the doctor about to inform him he has terminal cancer. There is reason for his pessimism: although twenty-five years of age, Sam has been in therapy most of his life. He was recently "fired" by his previous therapist who said there was nothing else he could do to help.

When I asked Sam what about him was so hopeless that even his therapist gave up, he shrugged meekly and said that reaction was not so unusual — everyone gets tired of him after awhile. Intrigued, of course, by this challenge, I was eager to discover what it was about this gentle young man that drove people away.

Sam had certainly been trained well by his previous therapist in the rules and etiquette of therapy; he attended sessions religiously and had no difficulty filling the time with a running complaint of who had rejected him and how he felt about it. He was most cooperative and seemed dedicated to doing whatever was necessary to turn things around. How could any professional have a hard time with someone who is so unhappy with his life and so determined to change?

Yes, his monologues on office politics were a bit tedious, and he did have a tendency to repeat himself. I could even understand how his voice, devoid of inflection, might begin to grate after a time. But how could I, or anyone else, desert a man who was trying so hard to change?

125

Five years elapsed before I realized that he was fundamentally no different from when I first met him. He was still complaining about the same things and still struggling with trying to make a single friend. He was still living with his parents and working in some dead-end job. And I had stopped listening to him in our sessions — the boredom and his passivity had become excruciating to tolerate. For every inventive or creative way I had tried to enliven our time together, Sam matched me with equal determination to follow his methodical formula of complaining monotonously. I might try confronting him, or acting out what he looked like to me, or even going for a walk outside, but the result was essentially the same.

It was clear to me that Sam would keep coming to my office as long as we both should live. When I asked him what he was getting out of our sessions (feeling my own need for reassurance and validation), Sam replied that he wasn't exactly sure, but therapy had always been a part of his life. I now understood what his previous therapists must have felt.

Unwilling to continue treatment in its currently impoverished form and stubbornly refusing to give up entirely, I decided to invite Sam to join an ongoing therapy group I was coleading. I hoped the feedback he would get from other group members might spark some deviation from his habitual patterns. I also thought it might be easier for me to tolerate Sam if his behavior was diluted with that of other, more vibrant people.

Perhaps I wanted to feel some comfort in knowing that I was not the only one who could barely tolerate Sam's company for more than a few minutes before feeling an uncontrollable urge to fall deeply asleep. If validation was what I wanted, I got it in the resounding chorus of unanimous opinion in that group. One by one, all the group members eventually communicated to Sam that he had exactly the same effect on them as well. When it became obvious that he was unable or unwilling to alter his style, a way of being that was so pervasive it seemed to stifle the whole group environment, several members dropped out. The group soon ended.

By this time Sam had attended a workshop offered by another therapist who had invited him to continue treatment with her, and I was more than a little relieved to offer him my best wishes. I think we ended on an optimistic note that maybe a female therapist would help him work through his intimacy problems with women. When several months later, I ran into this therapist and asked her how Sam was doing, she rolled her eyes to the sky and punched me in the arm. Hard.

The Boring Client and Bored Therapist

When therapists encounter something they do not like and cannot understand, the first thing they do is name it. *Alexithymia* is the term invented by Sifneos (1973a) to describe people who seem incapable of describing their internal states. Such people, who appear to us as extremely bland and devoid of any passion, seem to have some deficit in their brains that makes it difficult for them to process their experiences, differentiate their emotional states, and develop insight into their existence. They are similar to surgical patients who, after having their corpus callosums severed, cannot communicate how they feel. Their fantasies and dreams lack richness. They think in the most concrete ways; their communications are devoid of imagination (Miller, 1989).

Feiner (1982) describes the client who is so concrete he (and it usually is a "he") is unable to deal with inner or outer experiences in psychological terms. Most often, he has found a line of work (accounting, computers, engineering) that allows him to relate to the world in concrete, literal ways, accessing that overdeveloped part of his brain that processes information in linear sequences.

When emotions come into play, when he experiences interpersonal difficulties, his preferred cognitive style fails him. His wife, children, and few friends (except those just like him) find him maddening: "But dear, you *said* I should loosen up around company so I thought I would do these stretching exercises."

He enters therapy completely unprepared for how to proceed. Tell him what to do and he will follow your orders to the letter. Tell you about his feelings? What feelings?

He has organized his world carefully and put everything in its proper place. But feelings? They are a nuisance, an unpredictable variable. As long as he can concretely label something, he can find a place to put it. Therapy is an enigma to him. What should we talk about? Don't you have an agenda?

Detached from life, aloof from the world of flesh things, he can hide in a world of computers where nobody will hurt him or make fun of him or reject him. If the computer does not respond correctly, it is because of something that *he* did, something he can control.

He will become impatient with you, skeptical that therapy can work. You are as alien a creature to him as he is to you. You speak a foreign language: "What are you experiencing right now?" "How did you feel after she said that?" He looks at you quizzically, eager to please, and says what he thinks you want to hear.

In addition to this inability to respond appropriately to therapeutic interventions, boring clients also exhibit a number of other qualities described by Taylor (1984). Their speech patterns are devoid of affect and the use of metaphors, while their thinking is preoccupied with the minutiae of the external world, sometimes demonstrated by endless lists of symptomatic complaints. They are unable to recognize and describe how they are feeling. Their descriptions lack color, detail, depth, and life. In short, they seem unable to elaborate on what is going on inside them. According to psychoanalytic theory, boring clients have an arrested emotional development because of defective parent-child relationships and psychic trauma. They therefore remain in a regressed state in which a boring communication style creates protective barriers (Krystal, 1979).

Altshul (1977) attempts to address the question of what makes a client boring, and his surprising answer is that we should more accurately be asking what makes a therapist feel bored. Although he acknowledges that there are indeed some people who may be more stimulating to work with than others, Altshul submits most confidently that *all* experiences of boredom in therapy are the result of the clinician's malignant countertransference neurosis. This most often takes the form of narcissistic depletion in which the therapist's need for absorption and expectations for entertainment lead him or her to feel deprived and resentful when the client does not provide stimulation that is missing in the therapist's personal life.

There is certainly some merit to this thesis. We do tend to withdraw from those clients who do not meet our expectations. And we do have varying propensities for becoming bored, depending on whatever is going on (or not going on) outside the office. I would also mention, however, that certain clients have the capacity to drive most any therapist up the wall regardless of how patient and ego-gratified he or she might be. Some clients speak in monotones that become difficult to listen to. Others repeat themselves constantly. Often, they seem to work at developing this quality as an art form:

". . . So where was I? Oh yeah. I was telling you about why I prefer to change shampoo products every few weeks. I find it makes my hair more manageable. Did I tell you about the time I was in the shower and I ran out of shampoo altogether? I did? Oh. Well, anyway. . ."

Sometimes such clients seem impervious to gentle or even forceful suggestions that they might use their therapy sessions more constructively by dealing with issues in their life besides their hair-washing rituals. Nevertheless, Altshul (1977) does offer us one key to working with anyone we find boring, either as an occasional episode or a prolonged and chronic case. The first place to start should always be to ask ourselves what is significant about this client or her issues that lead us to withdraw. In what points in the session does my attention wander the most?

I think back to Sam, the young man I discussed earlier. It is certainly true that a number of other therapists (and many non-therapists) complained about how boring he was to listen to, but I exacerbated the problem in a number of ways. During the first year I worked with him, I very much looked forward to our sessions. I liked him. I felt sorry for him. I badly wanted to help him.

But Sam disappointed me. He did not move as quickly as I needed him to. Aspects of my personal life had begun to feel stale and predictable. I wanted, even needed, more diversion. I turned to Sam, and a few of my other clients, to supply the entertainment that I was missing.

I am also aware of how infuriated I felt by his helplessness and passivity. My most recurrent fantasy about him was one in which I was allowed to become Sam for a single day. During the time I lived in his body I would do everything he was reluctant to try: I would make new friends, ask several women out on dates, look for another job, move into my own apartment. I figured that in twenty-four hours I could easily turn his life around.

And if that is so, why could I not do it for myself when I was his age? At that time I felt almost as helpless as he did. And I hated reliving my own ineptitude, recalling my adolescent geekiness, watching Sam struggle so, and feeling powerless to do anything to change his life. Yes, I became bored with him. I lost interest in him because he would not follow my plan for him. I punished him by withdrawing. I protected myself from his painful issues by tuning him out. He stopped being Sam to me; he became "that boring client."

Working with the Chronically Boring Client

If it is indeed mostly the client rather than the therapist who is the problem (and such a determination is difficult considering the interactive nature of this phenomenon), confronting the issue in therapy can be a major turning point. While this did not prove to be the case with Sam, other examples show that bringing the client's responsibility into the open can be quite useful.

Valerie spent hour after hour complaining that her husband ignored her and her friends did not seem to care about her. Even her children became impatient with her when she tried to talk to them. I knew exactly what they were going through. In fact, I felt immensely relieved every time she related the incident of another person who tuned her out; at least I knew I had company.

I invited Valerie to explore just what she might be doing to turn so many people off. Eventually, she gathered enough courage to ask me how I felt and whether I had any idea what others might be feeling. I took a deep breath and was just about to let her know that I felt much the same way when I had a flash of inspiration. I pulled out a tape player and suggested we record the last half of the session so that she could listen to herself to find some cues. I promised her that if she drew a blank, I would be happy to help at that point.

Fortunately, she was at her absolute best (or worst) during the interval we taped. Valerie began our very next session with the question: "Am I really this boring all the time?"

I looked at her sheepishly and nodded.

What Valerie finally noticed about herself in listening to the tape was that she exhibited many of the characteristics of people often described as boring—most notably a blunted communication style. She was able to learn about the ways her pattern of communication created barriers to intimacy with others, and she was able to realize what many experts consider crucial to changing this behavior—the defensive functions her boring style served (Langs, 1978; Taylor, 1984). When this strategy is combined with gradually increasing the client's tolerance for affect, she can eventually learn to show more variety in her interactions, especially to include the world of feelings, fantasies, and symbolic images (Krystal, 1982).

One operant in our work with clients who show restricted communication styles is our attempt to make up for the lack of stimulation provided by the client by creating our own. We often give ourselves permission to be more lively, dramatic, and engaged in an attempt to draw the client out of a shell as well as to keep ourselves awake. The following dialogue shows one possibility for helping a boring client to experiment with being more dynamic and lively in his communication style:

Therapist: Sorry I yawned just a moment ago. Sometimes it is hard for me to focus on what you are saying.

Client: That's all right.

Therapist: That's all right? It is all right with you if I fell asleep while you are talking?

Client: No, I mean that. . . I just mean I'm used to it.

Therapist: I noticed that you seemed taken aback just a moment ago when I implied that you were sometimes boring to listen to.

Client: Well, yes, it did surprise me. I didn't expect that from you.

Therapist: Go on.

Client: No, that's all.

Therapist: That's all? There seems to be quite a bit more that you would like to say.

Client: Not really.

Therapist: You know, for just a moment I saw a flicker of life in you. Your eyes smoldered. I really started to perk up. I thought, aha, there is some energy! But now you are dead again. So polite. So constricted. You are looking at me with that corpse-like expression. What is going inside you?

Client: I don't know. Nothing much. I'm just listening.

Therapist: This time I don't buy that. You seem angry. I called you a name. I told you that I found you boring. And you are going to tell me that's all right with you?

Client: Maybe I'm a bit perturbed with you. I thought you liked me. You told me you liked me.

Therapist: It is because I care so much about you that I am willing to be utterly truthful with you. But it is hard to get close to you when you don't tell me what is going on inside.

Client: Well, I do feel hurt. A little anyway.

Therapist: And angry?

Client: Yes, that too.

Therapist: Say it.

Client: I'm angry.

Therapist: That's the best you can do? No, don't look that way. Look at me.

Client: I *am* angry. And I *do* feel hurt. And I'm scared. I don't know if I can trust you if you think I'm boring. It just seems so hopeless!

Therapist: Thank you. Thank you for finally telling me some of what you feel. What was that like for you?

And so continues the dialogue, slowly, laboriously, haltingly playing itself out as the client struggles with trying to express himself in ways that he has never been able (or willing) to before. Obviously this kind of interaction is not right for everyone. It does illustrate, however, the importance of not colluding with the client and his dysfunctional behavior while helping him to access his affective dimensions. It also shows how within the context of a trusting relationship it is not only possible but desirable to use self-disclosure as the primary bridge by which to confront his most obvious problem. Most of his other issues related to poor self-esteem, depression, and isolation would vastly improve if he were able to enliven the way in which he relates to the world.

The Challenge to Stay Attentive

Morrant (1984) has stated that the reason some clients come to us in the first place is because they are so boring that they cannot find anyone else to listen to them. When we consider that the therapeutic situation itself is even predisposed to be boring, considering that everything is deliberately structured to remain the same — the room, the regularly scheduled appointments, the seating arrangement, the rituals for beginning and ending — the therapist is constantly challenged to remain attentive and responsive (Esman, 1979).

About the only things that change in therapy are what the client brings to the session and how we decide to react to what we have experienced. If a particular client is repetitious or limited in the stimuli that he or she presents, the clinician is tested to maintain requisite mental activity and focused concentration in order to remain interested and respond empathically.

Clients who are most restricted, inhibited, and monotonous in their communication styles are precisely those individuals who most need the very best that we can give. They believe themselves to be essentially unlovable and use their boringness as a defense against being hurt. That is why our essential mission, beyond all else, is to teach such people that they are indeed worthy of love and caring.

In order truly to love such clients who make themselves unlovable, we must separate our own narcissistic demands for stimulation from what the client is prepared to offer. To do this requires us to make a number of cognitive adjustments by which we challenge ourselves to stay attentive — much the same way that all meditative activities are practiced. Csikszentmihalyi (1990) prescribes the antidote to boredom which he calls *flow*, the optimal experience of life in which the mind is stretched to its limits in one's voluntary effort to accomplish something worthwhile.

In the context of therapy, clinicians practice flow when we are able to immerse ourselves totally in the experience of what is occurring and focus our concentration on the innumerable nuances that are visible only during an altered state of consciousness:

"What is he saying? . . . Where have I been? . . . What triggered this lapse? . . . Got to concentrate. . . . Take a deep breath. . . . Focus. Focus. . . . What am I missing? . . . Look! There! His eyes. . . . Look at his eyes. The way he breathes. His face is flushed. . . . Why is my heart beating so hard? . . . Gosh, I never noticed his eyes before. . . . Wait, I am starting to leave again. Got to stay here and stop drifting. . . . I am inside him now. . . . I think I can really feel it. . . . How could I have ever been bored? . . . There is so much to hear, to see, to say, to sense, to feel . . ."

Boredom is a state of mind, not of circumstances. The boring client ceases to be tedious once we are able to invest even more energy and concentration in our interaction. It is from such encounters that we learn to stretch our own limits of patience, concentration, creativity — and compassion.

CHAPTER THIRTEEN

Yes, No,
Maybe, I Don't Know

Among people who are not easy to work with because of their passivity and reluctance to change are those who are overly compliant. These clients are often considered difficult by their therapists as much for their interpersonal style (which may be boring and repetitive) as for their patterns of resistance. They can stay in therapy for years and years, dutifully attending sessions, performing like trained animals to do whatever we want—but only in the sessions. Outside the office, they remain just as passive and impervious to change as ever. They drive us to begin wondering whether *anyone* we are seeing is really changing anything; maybe they are all just talking a good game.

Passive, clinging, dependent clients are often unaware of their effect on their helpers. They are needy and lonely, often to excess; they perceive their doctors and therapists as an inexhaustible supply of support (Groves, 1978). They want complete and total devotion, no matter how repetitive they become and how unwilling they are to do anything to change. In fact, they do not seem to want to change at all; they like things just fine the way they are. They get to complain a lot about how helpless they feel. They can blame others for what is not working. And they can come to us week after week, tell us the same things, and know we have to listen.

Clients Who Pretend to Change Without Changing

Bonnie is just about the sweetest, kindest, most cooperative, and gentlest person I have ever had the pleasure to work with. She is

135

attractive, articulate, and sincere. Over a period of several years she has attended her sessions religiously and always greets me with a radiant smile as I meet her at the door. Furthermore, she feels tremendously grateful for the help I have offered her and expresses unrestrained satisfaction at the progress she has made over the years. Yet Bonnie is among the most difficult clients I have ever worked with.

How, you may justifiably wonder, can such a lovely human being be such an unremitting source of frustration? What more could any therapist ask for? She is dedicated to her growth and is so responsive in her sessions she could offer workshops to other clients on the etiquette of being an ideal prospect. Yet in spite of her smiles and contriteness, her apparent willingness to do anything to further the cause of her therapy, she harbors an especially virulent form of self-destruction resistant to any antidote I have yet devised.

All the time I have known Bonnie she has been involved in a relationship with a man she claims to love. This connection has been the source of much of her anguish—and mine as well. While not abusive in the strict sense of the word, her on-again, off-again fiancé Michael is, nevertheless, not a very nice person. He does not like women very much; although he cares for Bonnie more than anyone he has been involved with, you would never know it by observing him. Yet, he cannot seem to help himself; he has never been able to bond successfully in any intimate relationship. As hard as he tries, and sometimes he *does* try to work through his blocks to getting close to Bonnie, he ends up driving her away. Also as a footnote: he has no intention of *ever* getting into therapy himself.

Over the years, Bonnie and Michael have been engaged twice, and disengaged as many times. Just when Bonnie has finally seemed to cleanse him out of her system, she invites him back into her life to start the cycle again.

Because I have seen Bonnie over many years, she has had the opportunity to experience several different modes of treatment as I have evolved as a practitioner. We have worked together both existentially and psychodynamically, developing insights into the reasons she stays stuck in such a destructive relationship. She can vividly see how she is duplicating the same dance played out by her parents. I tried a more cognitive/behavioral approach for awhile, cuing her to think differently about her situation. And as with most of the interventions I employed, she responded brilliantly during our sessions only to contradict everything she learned by doing just the opposite in her life. "Yes, I know he is no good for me. I really do understand this relationship will never give me what I want. But I just can't let him go, try as I might."

Clearly this case was perfect for trying some paradoxical maneuvers. I encouraged her to see Michael *more* often, and every time she complained about his latest crime of insensitivity, I defended him. I could recite quite a list of the dozen other things we attempted together and with each one Bonnie would initially respond quite well. It was only later she would reluctantly confide she was up to her old tricks again. At the end of my rope, at one point, I suggested she stop therapy for awhile and she readily complied with that as well.

A year later she returned again, doubly committed to break free once and for all. This time I made a rule that I would see her only if she agreed not to discuss Michael. We could talk about anything other than him. We tried that for awhile, and things went quite well, if only because of our conspiracy not to discuss what she most obviously needed to deal with.

I have talked about this case with many colleagues. Everyone has suggestions, and I am sure a few have occurred to you as well. Bonnie is more than content to come to therapy forever. She likes it. And she is also quite clear that there are some parts of her life she has no interest in changing. And *that* is what is so hard for me to accept and live with — to work with clients who want to talk, but not to change.

Working with the Passive Resister

The codependent model is one that would commonly be applied to Bonnie's case. There are serious problems, however, with a theory that is intended to empower helpless, passive women but instead makes all those behaviors and characteristics associated with the feminine appear to be pathological. Walters (1990) is concerned with using a medical term such as *addiction* to describe adults who choose certain patterns or kinds of relationships in their lives. By subscribing to a codependency model we reinforce the idea that the client is not responsible for her behavior, that she was born or made into "a woman who loves too much," a "woman who loves men who hate women," or who has a "doormat syndrome," or any number of other euphemisms that explain the disease invading the "codependent psyche."

Walters (1990, p. 57) suggests the best way to fight back: "In our work as therapists we can't change the larger society, but we *can* help people to feel less oppressed in their lives by knowing that they are not just passively reacting to events, but are actors whose performance will be largely shaped by the way they *understand* the drama they are enacting."

I would go further and say that while understanding these codependent patterns is certainly important, it is often not enough. Passive resisters who appear to be motivated and cooperative but never change their behavior in any fundamental way require more direct intervention. And when a frontal assault does not work (as in the case of Bonnie), more indirect means are often helpful (Lazarus and Fay, 1982). Symptom prescription, for example, is sometimes effective; with this technique we are asking the client to do what he or she is already doing but with a small change in its context or sequence (Watzlawick, Weakland, and Fisch, 1974).

Madanes (1990a) recommends prescribing the symptoms for certain couples who attend sessions regularly, purport to want to change their ways, but continue to be critical of one another. She directs them to set aside a prescribed time each evening to criticize one another without responding or defending their positions (similar to the strategy I mentioned in Chapter Eleven in the context of combative couples). Although these paradoxical interventions are sometimes just as futile as the more direct strategies, at least they give us something to break up the monotony of doing the same things over and over.

The Lonely Client

A special case of passivity occurs with those clients who feel so vulnerable and lonely, so needy and dependent, that they appear immovable. They are indifferent to most of what is happening around them, and although they suffer from depression and melancholia, it is their utter alienation and estrangement from the human race that are most significant.

It is often hard to factor out which part of a client's distress is loneliness and which is depression, just as it is difficult to determine conclusively whether a mood disorder is biologically or situationally precipitated. We may even one day discover that there is a genetic or biochemical component to loneliness just as there is for depression (if, in fact, these are different states).

Loneliness is qualitatively different from depression in that it results primarily from a deficiency or perceived dissatisfaction in social relationships (Peplau and Perlman, 1982). It is the experience of hunger for human contact, and it is a pain felt so deeply that a person can quite literally die of love starvation.

Francine was mistakenly diagnosed by her psychiatrist as depressed. Indeed she appeared depressed—lethargic, mournful, despondent, unresponsive. Since she was married and holding down a decent job in a large office, there was no reason to assume that a longing for human contact was the source of her pain. In fact, the condition of loneliness is not part of the usual vernacular of the therapist; it is not even listed in the index of the *Comprehensive Textbook of Psychiatry* or in the *Dictionary of Pscyhology*.

Francine may have looked depressed, but inside she felt incredibly lonely. That her psychiatrist kept insisting she was really depressed (and gave her medication for that condition, which could be cured) only made her feel more alone and less understood. She had lost the feeling of being connected to others. She longed for greater closeness to those around her and craved being held and communicated with intimately.

For years she had tried to talk to her spouse, but received for her efforts only ridicule and rejection. Her husband claimed to love her, and probably did, but was utterly unable or unwilling to express the slightest affection. Twice per week they had sex in which she felt mounted, violated, and discarded like an animal. She tried to talk to friends about her feelings, but they were appalled by her disloyalty and impropriety in even discussing the matter.

Her friendships were dominated by ritual and routine, but with a distinct lack of real closeness. Within them, it was acceptable to discuss clothes, jobs, and family in a general way, but off-limits were "sticky subjects"—that is, intimate feelings, fears, doubts, and innermost thoughts. She thus felt estranged from all relationships and desperately wanted to be understood by someone.

Francine had the misfortune to select a therapist who believed in the value of objectivity and passivity to foster the transference relationship. To her, he simply appeared cold, aloof, bored, and uncaring. But since she was used to such treatment from her father and husband, it never occurred to her to complain. This, after all, must be her fate in life — to be condemned to superficial, unsatisfying, withholding relationships.

Twice per week she would see her therapist, pour her heart out, and cry continuously. The good doctor would watch from behind his large desk and write copious notes. In the several months she had been seeing him, he had not offered a single comment other than to tell her she should be patient and keep taking her antidepressant medication. When she would speak of her loneliness, he would occasionally ask a redirective question about her dreams or her family history. She felt so alone it was as if she were the only person in the world. Nobody seemed to care or understand her, even this doctor she was seeing for that very purpose.

So consumed with her loneliness and, yes, depressed that it would never end, Francine died of isolation. Of course, she did not actually fall dead off a chair one day; death by loneliness is more subtle. On a day not unlike many others, she awoke to the feel of dried semen on the bedsheets and a sense of hopelessness that anything in her life would ever change. She went into the bathroom where her husband was shaving and attempted to make contact with him: did he enjoy the lovemaking last night? What would he like for dinner? How were things going at work? To all her questions he responded gruffly and impatiently, telling her to leave him in peace. Defensively, he challenged her to tell that stuff to her shrink.

Francine left work at lunchtime for her scheduled therapy session. Throughout the interview she departed from her usual tearful monologue and attempted to engage the doctor in some sort of genuine dialogue, to get him somehow to look up from his notes and really see her as a person. She finally lost her patience and screamed at him that he was just like everybody else — that he didn't really care about her.

The doctor glanced up for a moment, actually looked as if he might say something, but then nodded slowly and asked her to continue. He wrote in his notes that the transference was proceeding quite satisfactorily. At the session's end he said, "I'll see you on Thursday, then." Francine didn't reply.

She walked out into the cold, cloudy, windy day with a tightness behind her eyes so intense she felt blinded by the meager light. Her breathing seemed labored, as if it were an effort just to stand there. She looked out at the busy street and saw hundreds of cars on their way to somewhere they had to be. She noticed a couple across the street, huddled from the cold in deep conversation. It was then that she realized there was nowhere she had to be. If she walked off the face of the earth she wondered how long it would take for somebody to notice. Although superficially connected to hundreds, perhaps thousands of people (and their faces momentarily came into view, especially the acquaintances who treated her kindly — the boy who does yard work, the woman who cuts her hair), she felt close to no one. There was nobody to love, and nobody who loved her.

For the first time in months, something made sense. Francine began to walk purposively across the boulevard headed apparently toward a row of stores. (Afterward, the police surmised that she must have been going to the drug store because in her pocket there was a prescription for antidepressant medication.) Suddenly, she stopped in the busy street and seemed to find something that caught her attention in the grey sky just as a

minivan caught her below the knees. It was then that her loneliness finally ended.

As tragic as these so-called "accidents" may be, a greater
sadness is found in realizing how many walking wounded there
are — those who are alive only in the token gestures they offer as
they drift through life in isolation. Loneliness is *the* most preva-
lent problem of mental health, even if it has not yet found its way
into textbooks.

Clients like Francine are among the most challenging to
treat. They do not respond to medication because, strictly
speaking, they are not depressed so much as they are stuck in a
passive, withdrawn mode of life. The client's sense of hopelessness often infects the mood of the therapist as well. Markowitz (1991, p. 26) describes the utter despair and sense of dread
lodged in the pit of the therapist's stomach when confronted by
a severely depressed and lonely client: "By definition, depression
attacks hopefulness, the very basis of a client's motivation to
work in therapy, and depressed clients are notorious for their
draining effect on the clinician's own sense of self-worth and
hopefulness."

I am aware when I am working with stubbornly lonely,
passive people — the ones who are not endogenously depressed,
but who have chosen their life style and are determined to hold
on to it no matter what I do — how relieved I am that I am I and
they are they. Their attitude of total surrender to their condition
is infuriating: How dare you give up when there is so much that
you could do!

As to what is most likely to be helpful to the passive, lonely
client, the literature suggests anything and everything! This
includes helping the client to appreciate better and make more
creative use of solitude (Hulme, 1977; Storr, 1988), increase her
desire to change by exaggerating isolation (Reynolds, 1976;
Suedfeld, 1980), become less dependent on a lover for hap-
piness (Russianoff, 1982), talk to herself differently about her
predicament (Young, 1982), use loneliness as an opportunity to
love (Moustakas, 1972), and take a more active role in life (Rosenbaum and Rosenbaum, 1973; Slater, 1976).

A number of other treatment strategies are also sometimes helpful with persistently lonely, passive clients (Kottler, 1990):

1. Facilitating greater risk taking in both reaching out to others and facing oneself without the need for distractions
2. Turning off radios, televisions, and other external entertainment/escapist media in order to deal more directly with what one is running away from
3. Understanding the significance of private time as a potentially endless source of creativity and self-expression
4. Reframing the perception of loneliness as a more active form of solitude
5. Using solitude to acknowledge more honestly one's cravings for intimacy

In summary, most therapeutic efforts are directed toward helping clients find greater meaning in their suffering, coupled with offering them support and encouragement to break out of their shells of isolation. The therapeutic relationship, of course, becomes the fulcrum by which this leverage is applied. What Francine longed for most from her therapist (and she confessed this to me the day before she died) was for him to look at her and respond to her as a person, not as a "patient," or "client," or "depressed woman," or subject to write notes about. She just wanted some compassion and understanding.

Clients Who Do Not Talk at All

Of Nordic stock, Phil embodies the essence of the word "stoic." He suffers, but oh so silently. He suffers like a man should. No tears. No feeling. No unseemly displays. Just a sad-eyed dog face and a low rumble of a voice that sounds like its battery needs replacing.

Phil is depressed and despondent because his wife left with their children. He does not much like the idea of therapy, but he thinks perhaps this gesture will convince his wife he is serious about changing. As to what it is he wants to change — that is a bit elusive. His wife, however, has stated in no uncertain terms that she can no longer live with someone who is so cold and unfeeling. Phil explains: "She says I'm empty inside. I have no feelings, or at least none that I'm aware of. Maybe she's right."

Although Phil really wants help, he does not know what to do, how to proceed, or where to go next. This uncertainty is not so unusual for a man cut off from his feelings. But Phil, not given much to introspection in any form, has no earthly idea about how to be a client in therapy. He is a man of few words and believes that talking in general is a waste of time. When queried about what is on his mind, he shrugs. When invited to bring up what is bothering him, he responds simply: "My wife left," and then looks at me expectantly as if I should go get her and bring her back.

"Your wife left you?"

"Ah, yuh."

"Can you tell me more about it?"

"Not much to tell. I came home from work last week and she was gone. So were the kids."

"Well, how do you feel about that?"

"She shouldn't have done that without at least telling me first."

"You sound pretty angry."

"Anger doesn't do a man much good. I just think that she should come home."

Working on a cognitive level, naturally, appeared more comfortable for him. And that is just where we stayed for awhile, each of our sessions seeming to last for hours of awkward silence: talking about the mechanics of living alone, what he should tell friends and family, ways he could fall asleep at night. He would begin each session with a single question and then fully expect me to talk the whole hour. Phil remained mute during our sessions; he claimed he had nothing to say.

"Fine," I said in relief, hoping to get rid of him. "Then I see no reason for us to reschedule."

But if Phil quit therapy he could lose the last chance he had to get his wife to come home, or so he believed. No, he was going to keep coming until his wife decided what she was going to do. But meantime, what were we to do with our time?

Each session was excruciating. Even if Phil wanted to talk, he did not know how. That left me with more than my share of the responsibility for what we did, unless I wanted to continue rambling, trying to fill up forty-five minutes with an answer to his initial question. I jabbered on, giving pep talks, trying to engage a flicker of interest in something. We tried fishing and hunting (subjects I know nothing about); sometimes we attempted to talk about what he feels or thinks inside (subjects he knew little about). Somehow we would get through the hour and then he would straighten his back as if preparing himself for the next dose of foul-tasting medicine and schedule another appointment.

I would like to think that Phil got something out of our time together, even if his wife never did return. After six months he did become a little less reticent. And I learned a lot about hunting and fishing. He eventually normalized his life once again, decided he would find another wife who could love him the way he was, or barring that, at least agree to live with him.

Phil was different from most clients who don't talk in therapy as he was not being the least resistant. He was trying to cooperate; he just did not know how. There are, of course, other clients we see who do not talk because they refuse to play by our rules.

Clients may remain silent for a number of reasons. Some resent intrusions into their privacy and the only way they can retain an illusion of autonomy is by controlling the flow of what comes out of them (verbally, anyway). Other clients appear quiet because they do not know what to say or what is expected of them; they wait until they can figure out how to provide what the therapist wants. Still others are expressing passive-aggression, withholding themselves in an effort to be punitive or controlling (Harris and Watkins, 1987).

Working with the Silent Client

Children and adolescents are among the most proficient at employing silence as a weapon in therapy. Marshall (1982) collaborated with one ten-year-old client who was especially skilled at avoiding any interaction whatsoever through a variety of means—detachment, indifference, disengagement from any-thing the therapist might try. Because this child was so brilliantly adept at ignoring questions, he was recruited to help write a list of what it takes to be the most difficult client possible. Marshall therefore suggested that if other children want to be like him and frustrate their therapists, they should say *only* the following in response to any question:

> "I don't know."
> "Sometimes."
> "It doesn't matter."
> "I guess so."
> "That's about it."
> "I don't care."
> "I forget."
> "Yes."
> "No."
> "Sort of."
> "I don't remember."
> "It doesn't make any difference."

Of course, once the therapist and client had made a game out of their rigid patterns of communication, making the rules explicit, they could laugh at themselves and thereby remove some of the barriers preventing them from exploring other areas.

Of all the responses we get from the silent client, "I don't know" may be the most difficult of all. Sack (1988) has cata-logued several of the most common ways a therapist might respond to a client who says "I don't know" to any query that is initiated. I have presented the therapeutic options in progres-sive order of how intrusive they might be. My assumption is that we try to do as little as possible to produce the greatest impact. Only when our most benign interventions fall on deaf ears should we resort to more potent strategies.

Therapist's Response Options to the Client Response of "I don't know."

1. *Silence.* Respond to silence with silence.
2. *Reflection of content.* "It is difficult for you to articulate what is going on for you."
3. *Reflection of feeling.* "You really feel resentful that you have to be here to answer these questions."
4. *Probe.* "What is it like for you not to know?"
5. *Labeling of behavior.* "I've noticed that you say 'I don't know' a lot."
6. *Invitation to pretend.* "Imagine that you did know. Take a wild guess as to what form it would take."
7. *Confrontation.* "I sense that you may know a whole lot more than you have decided to share with me right now."
8. *Self-disclosure.* "I'm having a hard time working with you when you answer 'I don't know' so often. It is as if you expect me to know what is going on inside you without your offering much help."

These are just some of the response options that are available to us when we are confronted with one common ploy passive resisters use to keep us at bay. On a larger scale, there are even more interventions that are sometimes effective in counteracting exaggerated silence or extreme passivity:

9. *Relabel the behavior.* "You seem to be quite good at staying within yourself. Most people can't stay quiet as long as you can.
10. *Schedule a silent session.* Continued silence now becomes a cooperative response.
11. *Prescribe the silence.* "I appreciate your keeping so quiet. That will make it so much easier when I discuss the problems with your parents. I'd like you to stay silent so I don't become confused by hearing your side of things."
12. *Provide structure.* "You don't seem to know what to do with our time together. I wonder if it would be easier for you if I asked you a series of questions?"

13.   *Provide freedom.* "I respect your desire not to talk right now. I am willing to wait as long as it takes for you to open up."
14.   *Create a game.* I'll ask you a series of questions in which you won't have to say a word. Just nod your head when I ask you a question or shrug if you don't know."
15.   *Use nonverbal sources.* "As it seems difficult for you to communicate verbally, maybe you could draw a picture describing how you feel." Other variations include bringing in photos, playing favorite music, playing a game, or going for a walk.

Doing More by Doing Less

I have read so many books and articles, attended so many workshops, consulted with so many colleagues about child and adolescent therapy that I can easily spout the party line. Provide a sanctuary of trust for the child. Communicate with the child on his or her own level. As play is the primary form of expression, do a lot of play therapy.

Well, even with all the training I have had and permission I have been given from supervisors I admire, I still feel the need to *do* something in my work. Cases in point: I am seeing three adolescents right now whom I would describe as difficult because they refuse to talk. Their parents insist they get help, feeling guilty about the monsters they believe they have created, so they drop them off at my office once a week for some brainwashing.

All three boys are defiant and surly. They have declared to me that they may have to come but they don't have to talk. "Fine," I tell them, "what, then, would you like to do with the time we have together?" I feel proud of myself. I am being supportive, concentrating on being with them on any level at which they can function. With one boy, we play cards—poker and gin rummy. He is not interested in learning any other games, and he will not respond to any question if it does not relate to the game. Another boy brings a ball and we play catch outside. He will not talk either, but I convince myself that on a metaphoric plane we are communicating on a deep level. The third boy walks with me to a drugstore where I buy him some chips and a Coke. He mumbles thank you and then promptly ignores me.

I have been seeing each of these boys for a period of months. I cannot see that their behavior when they are with me has changed at all. We have settled into a routine in which we know what is expected. The real surprise is that the parents of two of the boys claim there has been substantial improvement in their demeanor and school performance. Sometimes they are even nice to their sisters. The parents think I am some kind of magician and ask me what I've been doing. Trade secrets, I tell them. But I think to myself, *This is ridiculous. No fancy confrontations or brilliant interpretations. I just play cards and go for walks. I can't believe I get paid for this!*

So why are these kids possibly improving? It must be that they sense I really do care, that I *am* trying to help them. I try to be completely honest, and they know I will not tolerate any crap. I suppose they also realize that I am in a position to get them into even more trouble if they do not cooperate minimally. Maybe I will even be able to do them a favor someday.

The act of *not* doing psychotherapy is difficult for those of us who are so attracted to progress and change. Yet passively resistant clients do not respond too well to direct intervention. And sometimes with adolescents, the best therapy is to suspend any therapeutic activity temporarily so they do not feel so cornered (Anthony, 1976). I suppose it is awfully arrogant of us to believe that nothing much happens in therapy unless we make it happen; some of our best work comes from allowing resistant clients to move along at their own pace and speed without having to cater to our expectations.

PART FOUR

Managing Difficult Cases

CHAPTER FOURTEEN

Confronting
Unresolved Issues

Therapists are not only caring and giving; we are also *reciprocally* altruistic, that is, we expect some degree of appreciation and gratitude in return for our helping efforts. The trouble is that some clients are unable to acknowledge that they have been influenced or affected by us (or anyone), for to do so would be to dilute their own fragile power. On the other hand, if they can devise a way to make their therapist feel impotent and helpless, they raise their own sense of power.

Feeling helpless is inevitable for the therapist when working with difficult clients, as are accompanying feelings of anger, vulnerability, and sometimes even hatred. It is in exploring these countertransference feelings that we find the clues both to the most advantageous treatment plan for reaching the client and to the optimal course of growth in ourselves. Adler (1982) has suggested that many of our extreme negative feelings toward some clients has to do with our own fantasies about our omnipotence and ability to rescue. Our feelings are compounded by the regressive client's own projective fantasies in which the therapist is placed in the role of a perfect parent.

Saving the World, or Perhaps Ourselves

Possibly like many of you who gravitated to this field because of a drive to become more fully functioning as a person, I felt powerless and helpless throughout many of my early years. When I was about six I tied a cape (towel) over my shoulders and tried jumping off couches to fly like my superheroes Mighty Mouse and Superman. I believed the problem was that I was not trying hard enough. When I was eleven, my parents divorced because, I thought, I had failed to keep them together. My adolescence was marked by one failure after another—not being able to control my body, to date the girls I liked the best, to be part of the right group, to understand algebra or work a lathe in shop class, to win my parents' approval. Even in early adulthood, I felt out of control most of the time, unable to get what I wanted, or even to feel the way I wanted. Surely there had to be a better way.

When I first heard about the helping professions—that is, that you can get paid to show other people how to take charge of their lives—I thought to myself, "Finally, I will learn to fly!"

And I was not so far off the mark. Training to be a therapist plugged into my most grandiose fantasies of rescuing others, and myself in the process. Everyone knows that therapists can read minds, predict the future, and get people to do whatever they want. That seemed almost as interesting as x-ray vision.

So here I am, unabashedly admitting that I want to save the world, or as an alternative, at least everyone who asks for my assistance. Do I think this fantasy is a bit ridiculous if not downright psychotic? Certainly. Do I seem to be a little stuck in my egocentrism, inflating my sense of power? Assuredly so. But then, I do not tell many people about these delusions of grandeur. In fact, I hide these irrational beliefs so well that most of the time even I do not know I have not outgrown them. Time after time, I have my fantasies of omnipotence exorcised by supervision, but I never seem to get the roots out and they grow back—if not quite as lush, then more cleverly disguised. It takes a difficult client to find them again, even after months of repeating to myself and to others the mantras:

"There are limits to what I can do."

"It is up to the client to change."

"I can't help everyone all of the time."

The counterpart to these public prayers is the very private whisper that goes something like this:

"You don't believe that, do you? You *are* powerful. You have magic. You can talk to people; you can understand them. You have skills. You have books. You have diplomas. You can do *anything*."

I run for my cape. I tie it carefully around my neck. I climb on top of the couch. I try really, *really* hard to fly. Then I pick myself up off the floor.

Harnessing Countertransference Feelings

The reason we do this type of work is because we are both highly skilled and motivated to get through to people who have trouble communicating to others. Yes, they are boring or insensitive or hostile or manipulative: that is why they are in therapy to begin with. Either they or someone very close to them feels that they could use some help not to be so difficult.

In spite of our training and best intentions, we find ourselves stuck in a room with someone we do not like much. We have done our best to remain attentive, compassionate, and responsive, but we can feel ourselves drifting away, leaving the session whenever possible, taking fantasy trips inside our heads, anything to escape the ordeal of being with this client.

One of the most honest portrayals of this internal struggle that goes on inside a therapist's mind is described by Yalom (1980, p. 415), who offers this account of how he was able to regain contact with a difficult client:

> I listen to a woman patient. She rambles on and on. She seems unattractive in every sense of the word — physically, intellectually, emotionally. She is irritating. She has many off-putting gestures. She is not talking to me; she is talking in front of me. Yet how can she talk to me if I am not here? My thoughts wander. My head groans. What time is it? How much longer to go? I suddenly rebuke myself. I give my mind a shake. Whenever I think of how much time remains in the hour, I know I am failing my patient. I try then to touch her with my thoughts. I try to understand why I avoid her. What is her world

like at this moment? How is she experiencing the
hour? How is she experiencing me? I ask her these
very questions. I tell her that I have felt distant from
her for the last several minutes. Has she felt the
same way? We talk about that together and try to
figure out why we lost contact with one another.
Suddenly we are very close. She is no longer unat-
tractive. I have much compassion for her person,
for what she is, for what she might yet be. The clock
races; the hour ends too soon.

Freud ([1910] 1957) originally viewed all feelings that
therapists have toward their clients, both positive and negative,
as disruptive to the therapeutic process. Roth (1990) labeled this
form of countertransference *totalistic*, that is, it includes all the
thoughts, feelings, attitudes, and perceptions that the therapist
has toward the client. This countertransference is distinguished
from several other varieties, including *classical*, in which unconscious reactions develop in response to the client's transference,
and the most common type described by Yalom—*interactive*.
Both the therapist and client react to one another in profoundly
personal ways in response to what the other is doing as well as
what he or she is perceived to be doing.

As Freud originally conceived most countertransference
feelings, they were labeled as evidence of the clinician's own
unresolved issues, and once these were fully worked through in
supervision, the therapist could again regain a state of benevolent but neutral interest. Although Freud was unable to practice what he advocated for other professionals, having analyzed
many friends and even his own daughter, his cautionary advice
became a mandate for a generation of practitoners who strived
for this elusive objectivity and disengagement. The paradox
became this: how do I care about my clients without caring *for*
them?

Natterson (1991) confronts his owns subjective contribution to conflicts with his clients, a phenomenon he considers to
be much more than mere countertransference. In fact, he believes that clinicians' feelings toward their clients are the most

essential ingredients of treatment. He further asserts that nobody can be truly understood without the subjectivity that is an
implicit part of empathy. Even interpretations, the lifeblood of
the analyst, contain the seeds of the therapist's own unconscious
processes, just as they do the client's. It is senseless, therefore, to
argue that we can be connected with and to a client in therapy
without both of us being emotionally involved (Kottler, 1986).

Many other psychoanalysts now contend that it is not only
impossible to maintain strict neutrality and impassivity in the
therapeutic encounter but that it is also undesirable. Clinicians'
feelings toward their clients are now a legitimate tool of assessment, one that has become the essence of the analytic interaction (Giovacchini, 1989).

Many other therapists, such as McElroy and McElroy
(1991), believe that our countertransference feelings toward
difficult clients are the best clues available as to how to help
them. Once we become aware of what internal chords are being
strummed by our interactions with a particular client—whether
it is anger, frustration, anxiety, helplessness, defensiveness, revulsion, sexual attraction, or boredom—we are not only well on
our way to neutralizing their negative effects but also to formulating a more effective treatment plan.

Form a mental list of your current caseload. Better yet,
peruse your weekly calendar for the next several days. As you see
each person's name and conjure up an image of him or her
seated in your office, observe what internal reactions are going
on inside you. When I complete this exercise, not without a
certain amount of resistance, I feel relieved to note that I eagerly
anticipate seeing most of my clients. I wonder what they are
doing this moment. A smile comes to my face as I replay certain
interactions or recall some conversation that was especially
touching or funny or dramatic.

My breath catches, though, as a few other clients come to
mind. These are people whom I absolutely dread seeing. They
are demanding and obnoxious. Most of all, they don't appreciate
me very much. I can feel their disdain. Because they have not
improved much, I have repeatedly asked them why they keep
coming back to haunt me. Nowhere else to go, they might retort.

Manny is the most dreaded of all. I even fix myself an extra special lunch on those days I must see him. It takes me the rest of the afternoon to recover after he has come in, so I try not to schedule anyone else. Manny reminds me of fingernails scraped across the blackboard, of a mosquito bite I can't reach, of being trapped inside a room from which I can't escape.

It is no small consolation that Manny's referring physician warned me he was really ornery. That, in fact, was why he was sending him to me — because the good doctor was tired of dealing with him. There was nothing he could do to help him, medically anyway. He just needed someone to complain to.

Manny's idea of good therapy is for me to listen to him bitch about how unfair life is as he recounts all the injustices that have been heaped upon him. He has made it clear that he has no intention of changing anything about himself; it is the rest of the world that must accommodate to his needs. If I have anything that I absolutely feel I must say to him, I should be brief and not interrupt him; he will not listen, anyway.

Manny is perfectly content with the way things have been proceeding in our sessions together. He intends to keep coming forever, or until one of us dies or has a nervous breakdown. I think he will outlast me.

Now why, I ask myself, does Manny get to me so thoroughly? I can understand feeling mildly irritated and impatient; he is, after all, unwilling to play by the rules: he will not listen, respond, or change. But why do I dread his appointments with such intensity?

Manny, I come to realize, is my worst nightmare. It is not that he is so difficult to be with; in some ways he is quite interesting and entertaining. It is that he is the embodiment of everything I have learned to fear. He is so externally controlled, so unwilling to accept *any* responsibility for his life, that he is a professional victim. And if there is one thing I cannot stomach for even a few minutes, it is having someone else pulling the strings of my life. Flashback — to adolescence when my moods were completely under the spell of half a dozen girls I was in love with; to my mother, whose life was completely dictated by other people's whims; to my father, who left without asking my permission; to my first supervisor, who listened to my sessions through the wall and rapped hard whenever I said something she did not like.

Yes, Manny had become the monster I feared the most — the helpless, embittered victim. And on some level, I wondered if it might be contagious.

I found the clue to helping him in my irrational fears of becoming like him. I could not allow him to be the way he was; he had to change, to be more independent, more internally controlled and more compulsive. Just like me. Yet once I uncovered the principal source of my own discomfort, I realized that he could stay essentially the way he was and still get something out of therapy, even if it was just having a person who would listen to him without interrupting. Now this certainly was not the way I prefer to do therapy, but Manny is utterly convinced that he is getting his money's worth.

Incidentally, things did become more relaxed and fluid between us after I stopped trying to convince him to be different. And he actually started to change, a very little bit at a time. As for me, separating Manny's issues from my own is only the first step in working them through. In the rest of this chapter, we consider some of the other ways that therapists attempt to resolve countertransference issues and protect themselves from psychic damage in this line of work.

Not Taking It Personally

The single best way to protect oneself against the onslaught of difficult clients is to apply Freud's most basic dictum of professionalism: detachment. By maintaining appropriate distance from clients — close enough to be empathic, yet far enough away to avoid becoming overly emotionally involved — we are able to stay more objective, tough-minded, and clearly focused (Smith and Steindler, 1983). For example, in a study of burned-out mental health professionals, Pines and Maslach (1978) concluded that the most helpful strategy for preventing deterioration is adopting a stance of "detached concern" in which our feelings of compassion and caring are tempered with a degree of psychological withdrawal.

Basch (1982) has observed that while this detachment is easier said than done with obstructive clients, one of the most important things we can do is to remind ourselves that they are doing more to themselves than they are to us. "Resistance is a much more frustrating phenomenon if we believe on some level that the patient is willfully opposing us and could, if he were only a nicer person and less bent on making our life miserable, do something about it" (p. 4).

This belief, that clients are being difficult with us rather than with themselves, is easy to understand; it certainly seems as if they are out to get us. One of the prerequisites, however, to working through the resistance is to separate out our own unresolved issues. This is especially true with regard to wanting others to meet our expectations and imposing on our defensive clients the images of other people from our past who have given us a hard time.

Trying to Do Too Much

Strean (1985) catalogues the mistakes that therapists make while working with resistant clients, the most common of which he believes is trying too hard to resolve the presenting problems. When clinicians become overzealous, overactive, and overly committed to making things work single-handedly, clients who are already skittish may back off further. Although coming from a conventional psychoanalytic perspective that stresses detachment, Strean nevertheless reminds practitioners of all orientations to remember the limits of what can be done without the client's active participation.

Sometimes we have no choice but to accept the limits of what we can do for people who are determined to stay miserable. I recall how helpless I felt with my most difficult client— *anyone's* most difficult client—my own child. My son was suffering terribly after we relocated to a new state. He missed his friends. He felt lonely and lost. And worse, from his nine-year-old perspective, he could not imagine there would ever be a time when he would be happy again.

As I watched tears rolling down his cheeks and listened to him talk about how awful he felt, I mentally checked off the therapeutic options I might have chosen if he were my client. (What good is it to be a therapist, I reasoned, if I can't help my own son during his time of need?) I tried reflecting his feelings regarding his loneliness and pain, demonstrating that I understood what he was going through; he sobbed even more uncontrollably. Next, I tried self-disclosure: I told him about my own feelings of estrangement, how hard it was for me to make new friends, and that I, too, missed people we had left behind. "So what," he countered, "this was *your* decision to come here. Nobody gave me a choice." He had a point there. So much for his feeling we were in the same boat.

I tried reasoning with him next, helping him to recall that once before we had moved and he had had to make new friends. It had taken awhile, but eventually he was even better off than before. While this argument made perfect sense to me, he quickly dispensed with it by insisting that the circumstances of this situation were not the same.

"OK," I said, "then let's accept the fact that you are here, there is nothing you can do about that; but how are you going to make the most of a difficult situation?"

He had an answer for that one, too.

I tried reassurance, problem solving, and everything else I could think of until I finally admitted to him that no matter what I said or did he seemed determined to feel sorry for himself.

His lip quivered. He looked at me with accusing eyes. And then he burst into tears once again.

All I could do was hold him.

There are times when clients (or family members) are determined to keep their pain, no matter what we (or perhaps anyone else) might do or say. At least they are not operating on the same time schedule that we are. They seem difficult to us because they are not as ready as we are for them to change. It is during such times that all we can do is offer comfort, to sit patiently until they finally become sick of themselves the way they are. Certainly there are things we can do to accelerate this process, but only within certain parameters. The strongest anti- biotics or antidepressents still take a number of days to make a difference. Among the most challenging things that we are required to do is to wait and try not to do too much or take too much responsibility for the client's decisions. Sometimes, all we can do is to offer support.

Getting Support

Just as our most difficult clients need support, so do we. Those therapists who are least well equipped to withstand the pres- sures of difficult clients feel isolated and cut off from their peers. They have no support system for talking about their cases, their frustrations, and their problems. They are no longer certain about the meaning their work holds for them.

Other specialists who are in the same situation and expe- rience similar feelings of stress and impairment when subjected to difficult clientele include dentists, dermatologists, and oph- thalmologists (Smith and Steindler, 1983). Yet among all these professionals who work in an isolated environment, therapists are subjected to the most intense degree of interpersonal bom- bardment. This is why building a network of supportive and caring friends and colleagues is so crucial to working through the pressures that we experience.

Practitioners in private practice are the most notorious for neglecting their own needs for interpersonal nourishment. Most of their schedules are individually designed according to the major criteria of bunching clients together so as to maximize production per day. Because time to the private practitioner is measured in hourly rates, it is not unusual for the clinician to reason as follows:

"Well, I could meet some friends for a leisurely lunch. But can I really afford to give up two billable hours, plus the cost of a meal, just to sit around and swap a few stories? And if I do meet them and talk about one of my cases, all they will point out are things that I have already tried anyway."

Fiore (1988) believes the the greatest need of therapists

who are struggling with difficult clients is not further insulation or more treatment suggestions from colleagues. So often the response to supervision advice is "I already tried that" or "I have been doing that for awhile." No, what therapists need most is the opportunity to talk about their feelings, to feel validated and supported, to dissipate energy that builds up from stressful encounters. "One of the things that makes the difficult patient difficult is that he implictly and often consistently questions the meaning of life and the value of relatedness. Because of the patient's affective intensity, and therapist's empathic linkage, the therapist may lose sight of the fact that he is functioning at a different level. The patient's questioning and forlornness chal-lenge the therapist's beliefs about life generally and his capacity to care specifically" (Fiore, 1988, p. 96).

This is said so well! We do reach an altered state of con-sciousness or enter a different realm of awareness when we are engaged with a difficult client. We think about the person at odd moments. We feel powerless. The texture of our fantasies changes. We start questioning whether we want to continue doing this kind of work. The last thing in the world we need at that moment are more treatment options that we may have missed.

Our initial belief when we consult with peers is that they can see something that perhaps we have missed or know some-thing that we do not. And, of course, while this is usually true, it is mostly irrelevant. I have noticed that when I tell friends in the profession about a case I am struggling with, the first thing they do (which is also what I do whan I am called upon to respond) is to try to find the brilliant strategy that I have missed. Because I am smart enough to consult with colleagues who I believe are cleverer than I, I am rarely disappointed. I often get some wonderful ideas about how to proceed with the client that I never would have considered. I even write them down.

I rarely use the suggestion, however. By the time I get back into the session, somehow the idea does not fit quite so clearly as it did over lunch. What does linger is the renewed strength I feel from friends who have listened to me and supported me. I do not feel so alone. I feel I have been given permission not to know what to do; I've been told it is all right to struggle with a client. I am reminded that with sufficient patience and caring and clarity, I usually do help the client to get through the impasse. I also especially appreciate my colleagues' sympathy, their telling me that they also would feel frustrated, that anyone would. Yes, what helps most is hearing them say that I am not incompetent or stupid (as I sometimes tell myself) because I feel like I am completely blocked with a particular client. I need to let off steam, to be nurtured and taken care of for just a few minutes. And then I feel clear again, ready to resume the engagement, even eager to get back to the work at hand.

Remembering That Two Heads Are Better Than One

Sometimes support is not enough. Getting a hug from a loved one, a few encouraging words from a friend, a pat on the back from a colleague feels great, but many times it is not nearly enough. There are times when we do miss obvious or subtle clues, when we are doing things that are not working, but we cannot figure out why or think of anything else to do. It is during such times that consulting with a colleague or supervisor for input is crucial.

The days of the eccentric but brilliant genius, working in isolation, are over. Once the Edisons, Fords, Bells, Freuds, and Einsteins could labor in relative obscurity, creating revolutionary models of space, time, matter, or mind when left to their own devices. We have even come to associate innovation with the single-minded effort of a lone scientist or thinker.

In contrast, Diebold (1990) describes the development at Bell Laboratories of the transistor, an invention that has perhaps changed modern life more than any other, and observes that one-person accomplishment is now a rarity. Modern problems are so complex and multifaceted that they virtually demand collaborative efforts in order for researchers to unravel all their components and find an innovative solution. Three scientists were awarded the Nobel Prize for developing the transistor, but they were supported by dozens of physicists, chemists, engineers, metallurgists, and managers who pooled their expertise in solving technical problems.

The collaborative model has now become commonplace in several mental health training centers, especially those that specialize in family therapy. Recognizing the complexity of some families that manifest extreme interactive pathology and resistance, practitioners work as teams with some behind one-way mirrors monitoring carefully what goes on during sessions and offering input as needed. Although this arrangement is not practical for those who operate in solo practices or who do not have access to the resources available in these training centers, it does illustrate the value of collaboration when we are working with clients who are especially troublesome.

Above all, Saretsky (1981, p. 247) believes that getting good supervision and peer consultation is the key to resolving therapeutic impasses with difficult clients. He comments that in "narcissistically threatening predicaments" even the best clinicians "are temporarily deprived of their ordinary good sense and adaptive capacities." The regressive tendencies that manifest themselves in therapists during these times — extreme emotional reactions, feeling bored or restless, trying too hard to be liked, being abrupt, soliciting praise, ruminating about sessions — can all be worked through with the help of an able consultant. Process-oriented supervisory sessions as well as creative brainstorming often help us to regain our compassion and empathy while surrendering omnipotent authority roles.

Certainly seeking supervision when we feel stuck or when countertransference issues get the best of us is not a novel idea, but too often supervision is considered only for beginning practitioners who are still satisfying licensing requirements or for more experienced therapists who are meeting the standards for continuing education. It is too often thought of as something we have to participate in because it is mandated rather than as a process that we willingly undergo during times of need.

Stop Complaining

Much of the activity that takes place during supervision and peer consultations involves a litany of complaints about how awful some of our clients are to work with. During staff meetings, discussions can escalate to the point that people try to outdo one another with stories of who has the most difficult caseload or the nuttiest, most obstructive client. We hear ourselves and our colleagues say over and over that we can't believe the latest indignity heaped on us. Complaining about our difficult clients to a sympathetic audience does feel cathartic, but it also seems to legitimize that activity as appropriate. We must remember that complaining only begets further misery and gives us permission to continue feeling like victims.

When a therapist complains about a client's abrasiveness, Greenberg (1984) wonders what motives are operating. In his experience, labeling people as difficult is more a statement about the therapist than the client. "The longer I am in practice the more tolerant I find I have become of patients' communicative styles. I now no longer find a patient's communicative style irritating or offensive when I have the option to be curious or find it interesting instead" (p. 57).

Robbins, Beck, Mueller, and Mizener (1988) remind us that although we would much prefer to work with clients who are cooperative and appreciative, the mandate of our profession is to understand, accept, and manage those who are often bizarre, maladjusted, and obnoxious. In other words, it is senseless to complain about what we are being subjected to; such is the nature of this work. We would be better advised to look at our own unresolved countertransference issues, let go of excessive responsibility for therapy outcomes, and concentrate not on our frustrations but rather on what we can do within the circumstances.

CHAPTER FIFTEEN

Thinking Constructively, Feeling Compassionately

The way we think about our clients and their concerns dictates, to a great extent, how we feel about our work and what interventions we might choose to circumvent apparent resistance. These internal formulations about our cases arise, in part, from reactions to how clients present themselves, from our own personal issues, and as a contagious effect of how others influence us.

In their classic book on burnout, Pines and Maslach (1978) noted an inverse correlation between frequency of staff meetings and therapists' negative feelings toward clients. It seems that in most agencies and institutions, case conferences and meetings offer surprisingly little encouragement while fostering terribly counterproductive attitudes toward clients. When a difficult client is brought up for discussion, rather than helping the clinician look at personal blocks that may be getting in her way, her colleagues often direct their attention to how obnoxious the client is. Often it sounds as if the clients who so crave caring and empathy are discussed in terms we would usually reserve for an enemy. These meetings, therefore, can make things considerably worse for the practitioner who still naively wants to help the person whom others find so hard to be around.

Of Mockingbirds and Being Versatile

Versatility, flexibility, and pragmatism are the keys to working with difficult clients. And those who are most adept at working with these cases are clinicians who are able to draw on a vast reservoir of strategies and interventions, regardless of their conceptual frameworks or theoretical origins. These professionals, while they may be original and innovative in their methods, are also talented collectors and imitators of what other effective therapists can do. They are the mockingbirds of the profession in all the best sense of what it means to be a true artist.

> Mockingbirds are the true artists of the bird kingdom. Which is to say, although they are born with a song of their own, an innate riff that happens to be one of the most versatile of all ornithological expressions, mockingbirds aren't content to merely play the hand that is dealt them. Like all artists, they are out to *rearrange* reality. Innovative, willful, daring, not bound by the rules to which others may blindly adhere, the mockingbird collects snatches of birdsong from this tree and that field, appropriates them, places them in new and unexpected contexts, recreates the world from the world [Robbins, 1990, p. 6].

In these words novelist Tom Robbins describes in the mockingbird exactly what is necessary for the therapist to get through to difficult clients—the willingness and ability to do and be whatever it takes to get the job done. In a summary of all the research to date on therapy outcomes. Seligman (1990) heartily agrees that the hallmarks of clinician effectiveness are flexibility and adaptability. This means that the most successful practitioners are able to alter their levels of directiveness, treatment methods, and styles according to the client's presenting complaints, personality variables, and specific needs.

As an example, Seligman analyzes supportive versus probing forms of therapy to illustrate how both might be used by the same therapist with different kinds of difficult cases. The more confrontive, expressive methods would be recommended for those clients whose defenses will not permit nurturance as well as those who are highly motivated and psychologically minded. By contrast, supportive methods are more helpful with clients in crisis, those who are extremely vulnerable, or those who have limited goals (Wallerstein, 1986). Of course, there are also times when we may alternate between both treatment styles with the same client as therapy progresses.

A Pragmatic Approach

Our initial clinical judgments regarding client difficulty can often create problems if these diagnostic impressions remain rigid. In a study of therapists' initial assessment of client difficulty, Rosenbaum, Horowitz, and Wilner (1986) found consistent agreement among practitioners as to which cases would present the greatest challenge; however, these predictions often turned out to be inaccurate based on what actually transpired during treatment. So many of the difficulties we initially perceive — such as a client who does not seem to be very psychologically minded or sophosticated — eventually work themselves out through the educational process that is the essence of therapeutic change. The researchers concluded from their investigations that client difficulty should not be perceived as a static and stable condition impervious to change but rather as behavior that is a reflection of pain that will be surrendered when other alternatives are developed.

The strategies that work with difficult clients are essentially the same ones that are most helpful with clients who are maximally cooperative, but they need to be applied in greater quantity and intensity. The essential element is the therapist's adaptability to changing conditions and circumstances and his willingness to do whatever is called for in a given situation.

No longer can we afford the luxury of a parochial allegiance to a single therapeutic approach without considering the contributions from a number of competing schools of thought; there are just too many wonderful new contributions to the field from so many diverse sources to ignore what they have to offer.

Many authors such as Beutler (1983), Prochaska and DiClemente (1984), Lazarus (1986), Beitman, Goldfried, and Norcross (1989), and Mahrer (1989) have constructed integrative models of helping that combine the best features of most systems. These approaches may be likened to the effects of broad-spectrum antibiotics that are injected into the body to kill infection when we have no idea which culprit is causing the problem. If one weapon does not stop the problem, another one will. This conception is also helpful in the treatment of especially resilient client resistance. Rather than limiting the attack to a single strategy that may or may not prove effective, practitioners use a pragmatic model of functioning that allows them to draw on a variety of tools. These can target all three of the most prominent change agents: affective experiencing, cognitive mastery, and behavioral regulation (Karasu, 1986).

When clients are offered a number of conditions, interventions, and structures that seem to be universal among insight and action approaches, and cognitive and affective theories, they are more likely to find some therapeutic ingredient they can connect with. The following variables, described in a previous work (Kottler, 1991), have been found useful, regardless of a therapist's theoretical base:

Altered States of Consciousness

Improving the client's receptivity to influence through the use of rituals designed to maintain interest and attention.

"When I turn my back and face you again you will notice a profound change in the way I appear and how you feel about me—even if that change is simply an awareness of how difficult it is for you to tell me what you see."

Placebo Effects

Communicating our confidence and expectation that the client will eventually improve after a few setbacks.

"I'm not all that surprised that this would be rocky for you. In fact, these difficult times are a sign that you are getting even closer to your ultimate goals."

Therapeutic Relationship

Capitalizing on the difficult client's craving for intimacy and trust to override apprehensions and reluctance.

"I want so much to get close to you and I sense that you want to trust me as well."

Cathartic Processes

Facilitating the free expression of anger and frustration in more healthy and direct ways.

"Instead of mumbling under your breath and sneering, I wonder if you might tell me to my face what you are thinking and feeling right now."

Consciousness Raising

Increasing the client's awareness of patterns of resistance and the meaning this behavior has.

"So why do you think that every time you care for someone you find a way to destroy that love?"

Reinforcement

Applying basic learning principles to extinguish inappropriate behavior and reward efforts to be cooperative.

"I am amazed that you just made it through a whole sentence without saying a single negative thing."

Rehearsal

Helping the client to practice new ways of thinking, acting, and feeling.

"Just now you attempted to tell me to back off, but you did so in a way that could be interpreted as rude and insensitive. I would like to see you try it again, but this time try to be a bit more gentle and diplomatic."

Task Facilitation

Constructing a series of therapeutic activities that counteract destructive tendencies.

"You say that you are tired of being dependent on others, including me, for approval and validation. Let's talk about a few ways that you could deliberately do some things that YOU want to do that others would not necessarily like."

Major Demolition

Shaking up the client's view of himself or herself and the world in an effort to recreate a different, healthier reality.

"I don't think I can help you, or that anyone else can, either. I see no way out for you other than to lose everything you have. After you have lost your job, your family, and all your resources to your drug addition, THEN come back and we will talk."

Modeling Effects

Using the force of our personalities to provide a healthy model for the client to emulate.

"Notice that I am not pleased with the way things are going, either. But rather than pouting, blaming myself or you, I would rather spend my time carefully analyzing what is going on and what it means. I am talking to you about how I feel rather than keeping everything inside. Rather than feeling helpless or immobilized or frustrated, I concentrate instead on how challenged I am to get to the bottom of this."

Patience

Respecting the client's own pace in progressing at a level that is most comfortable.

"I hear what you are saying—that you can't stand it any longer. But apparently you CAN stand it a little longer or you would let go of what is holding you back. I can wait for you as long as it takes."

When we review these variables, which operate as part of most effective therapies, it isn't necessary for us to choose which ones to use and which to ignore. They can all be valuable on some level. In fact, when working with clients who do not respond to our preferred method of operation, we must be even more pragmatic than usual. The only way we can ever hope to get through is by capitalizing on as many of these factors as possible to increase the pressure on the client to stop being so difficult with himself or herself and with others.

The Dangers of Rigidity

A major source of resistance in therapy that stems directly from the clinician is a posture of certainty whereby the therapist communicates absolute parameters of right and wrong, good and bad, to the client (Bauer and Mills, 1989). These rigid beliefs regarding what constitutes reality or what clients *really* mean when they act in certain ways are bound to stir up rebelliousness in many otherwise cooperative clients. Not only does such an attitude communicate disrespect for the client's capacity to determine for herself what is best, but it also implies that there is a single reality to which everyone must swear allegiance.

Confronted by a client who suddenly becomes stubborn, it is often helpful to ask ourselves in what ways we are being overly rigid. As a beginner in this field, I looked with awe on those supervisors and mentors who always seemed to know the right thing to say or do, no matter what circumstances arose in a session. During an encounter with one supervisor, he informed me that while he might *appear* to know what he was doing most of the time, often he felt confused and uncertain. Furthermore, he claimed, he was very suspicious of any therapist who *did* claim to know what was happening in any moment. "Worry not when you don't know what to do with a client," he cautioned, "but when you think you do."

I have always taken this advice to heart, and I have found that of the dangerous traits with which a therapist can hurt people, rigidity can be the most lethal. I have learned to be suspicious of therapists who believe they have found truth, not only for themselves but also for the rest of the world. Further, I have discovered that when I face a client who seems to be digging in for a fight, I look first to myself to see what trenches I have dug for myself. Quite often, I find that I have been spouting some variation of "I know-what-is-best-for-you-damn-it! Just-do-what-I-say!"

A Mental Checklist

A comprehensive and accurate assessment of client and therapist contributions to therapeutic impasses is crucial to formulating successful treatment strategies. These contributions would also include, of course, interactional effects as well as external influences that often sabotage progress—meddling family members, impoverished environments, and the like.

When clients are resistant, it is important to examine carefully the positive adaptive functions of their symptoms. Because causality is so hard to ascertain—that is, who is creating the problems by doing what—the remedy is to examine all four possible factors that could be contributing influences: *interpersonal issues*, which help to show how the resistant behavior aids in maintaining the client's stability; *individual issues*, which provide clues to the intrapsychic and psychodynamic values of the symptoms; *family history data*, which can reveal cultural and ethnic factors and codependency issues; and *external factors*, which are operant reinforcers in the client's environment that discourage change.

A more specific approach to assessment is offered by Dyer and Vriend (1973), who tackle the problem of reluctant clients by running through a mental checklist much the way a pilot does before beginning any takeoff. They recommend that when therapists feel stuck, they ask themselves a series of questions such as the following:

Who is the *real* client who needs help?
Which negative attitudes and self-defeating beliefs does the client subscribe to that are interfering with his or her ability to change?
What payoffs is the client enjoying as a result of his or her behavior?

What meaning does the resistance have for the client?
What expectations do I have that the client is unwilling or
  unable to meet?
How is my own impatience becoming an obstacle?
How am I personalizing the difficulties in such a way that I
  feel like a target?

Focusing this assessment process to even greater specificity, it is desirable to follow a similar pattern every time we
encounter trouble. For example, one of the most common ways
that clients become uncooperative is to fail to complete homework assignments — either those prescribed by their therapist or
those tasks that they initiate on their own. A therapist's mental
checklist might then proceed as follows: were the instructions
clear? Was the task beyond the client's capabilities at this time?
Was the assignment irrelevant to the client's needs? What is the
client communicating by his or her noncompliance? Who is
working behind the scenes to sabotage progress? What appears
to be most threatening to the client if he or she completed the
task? "By exploring the possibilities raised by each of these
alternatives," Lazarus and Fay (1982, p. 119) explain, "it is often
possible to reframe the assignments, reeducate the patient, and,
if necessary, reexamine the therapeutic relationship and re-
evaluate the patient's family system or social network."

One other assessment procedure a therapist can use when
encountering resistance is the differentiation between normal
versus characterologically reluctant clients. Dowd and Seibel
(1990) make the following distinctions between the two:

Normally Resistant	*Characterologically Reactant*
Situationally ignited behaviors	Chronic interpersonal style
Overt oppositional behaviors	Subtle manipulative ploys
Adaptive functions	Maladaptive functions
Healthy expression of autonomy	Destructive expression of need for control

Protection against rapid changes	Protection against *any* changes
Reponsiveness to direct intervention	Responsiveness to indirect intervention
Desire for a resolution of conflict	Preference for oppositional position

Dowd and Siebel (1990) find it extremely valuable when interpreting the behavior of difficult clients to determine whether the interactive problem is unique to the therapeutic encounter, or whether these clients find themselves constantly in conflict with others. One person may experience trouble in virtually all his relationships, in which he is seen as inflexible, controlling, and caustic. Another person may generally get along with most of his peers but seem to have consistent trouble only with those in positions of power. Still another possibility is the client who has difficulty only in therapy because of unique factors inherent in that encounter. It is important to determine which of these situations we are dealing with before we construct an appropriate response.

The client who is difficult with the therapist but no one else will profit from an intensive examination of transference-countertransference dynamics as well as the personal meaning this encounter has for her. As I have mentioned before, it would also be helpful for the therapist in this circumstance to consider her own contributions to the problem because of the unique interactive effect.

The client who is generally oppositional to authority figures will find it quite helpful to reach an accommodation with the therapist as a representative authority figure who can be trusted. The client thus learns to create a new conceptual schema for power figures: those who are exploitive versus those who are benevolent. This is an intermediary step before such clients learn eventually to empower themselves.

The client who is difficult with almost everyone requires quite a different strategy, one that seeks a major reorganization of the client's perceptual and interactive systems. With this person we tend to work more cautiously and in smaller increments.

Although we may exhibit greater patience for the progress of the characterologically reactant clients than we would for those who are situationally resistant, we will tolerate a lot less acting out from the former and feel the need to establish firmer boundaries with them.

A Behavioral Profile

One way the therapist's assessment process is applied to these temperamentally difficult clients is through attention to those specific behaviors that are most obstructive. In their book on chronically difficult children, Turecki and Tonner (1985) offer advice to parents that is equally appropriate for therapists who are struggling with clients who are uncooperative. They recommend constructing a profile of exactly those types of behavior that are viewed as disruptive or counterproductive, including specific examples, the situations in which they occur, and what usually results from these actions. They feel that we must have a thorough understanding of exactly what it is about a difficult client that we find troublesome before we can ever hope to break the destructive cycle.

　　One of the hardest things for therapists to do is to resist simplifying complex clients into simple diagnostic categories; this simplification is often more important for our own need for structure than it is for treatment planning. Emily, for example, has been a continual challenge for me over a period of many years. She has so many problems, that may or may not be psychosomatic in origin, that I never really have had a handle on what I am helping her with. She was originally referred by her physician because of suspected self-mutilation of her vagina. While she vehemently denied touching herself in any way, she offered no other explanation for the vaginal bleeding that never seemed to diminish. When one time she was caught by a nurse trying to raise the thermometer temperature artificially with a match, I decided to do away with a "borderline" diagnosis. She seemed to be exhibiting a rare Munchausen syndrome in which she continuously found ways to seek medical attention for ap-

parently fake maladies. But her situation was a lot more complicated than that.

Emily was also very depressed, sometimes suicidal. She
had a number of learning disabilities, and although she refused
to talk much during sessions, I strongly suspected there had
been some severe sexual abuse in her family. Only after several
years of therapy did she finally confess that her older brother
had been coming into her room at night since she was five years
old (she refused to elaborate). Contributing to her problems, she
was going nowhere vocationally and she was socially isolated;
she had never dated a boy during the twenty-five years of her life.
But regardless of the diagnosis I could select—borderline, hysterical, Munchausen syndrome—Emily was a chore to be with.
She could be alternately withdrawn, petulant, or entertaining,
depending on her mood and perhaps how far she believed she
could push me on any given day.

And yes, I *was* taking this case very personally; I felt as if
she were playing with me. I tried many different strategies
during our tenure together. On occasion I would try waiting out
her silences; once we managed a whole session in which neither
one of us said a single word for forty-five minutes until I broke
the spell by asking her if she wanted to reschedule. Of course she
said yes. At times I confronted her, interpreted her behavior,
shared my frustrations, provoked her, supported her, mimicked
her. All these worked. And at times, nothing did. Yet whatever I
did with Emily, however much *I* was frustrated, there was no
doubt she was improving consistently. I was completely at a loss
to explain how and why.

I knew that behavioral profiles can sometimes be helpful
in planning treatment. We use them to target interventions that
are likely to be more successful than what we are already doing.
So I tried constructing a behavioral profile describing the aspects of her that I found most difficult (see Table 15.1).

From this exercise I learned that there was a pattern
operating (a brilliant conclusion), but I could not see what it
was. I studied all the evidence for a while and finally, the answer
hit me: the pattern was that there was *no* pattern! Emily was an
expert at change, a virtual chameleon who could change her

Table 15.1. Profile of a Difficult Client.

Type of Behavior	Behavioral Example	Situation	Consequences
Defiant	I mention that now she has enough money to move out of her parents' house, so she quits her job.	When her life is changing too quickly	Lets me know I must respect her
Withdrawn	She sits down and does not say a word; answers questions with monosyllables.	When she has me on a variable interval schedule	Frustrates the heck out of me
Obstructive	She cancels an appointment at the last minute.	Usually after an intense session the week before	Thinks she is punishing me for getting too close
Manipulative	She tells me she might not see me next week because she may decide to kill herself.	After I have been aloof from her games	Hooks me into threatening hospitalization
Complaining	She whines and complains that nothing will ever change.	After she has made some dramatic change	Denies responsibility for progress
Stubborn	She refuses to see a doctor for a chronic health problem.	After I contact her doctors	Establishes limits regarding what she considers safe to discuss
Helpless	She expresses her hopelessness that she could ever be different.	In reaction to any therapeutic task that requires effort	Avoids taking risks or increasing her vulnerability

Source: Adapted from Turecki and Tonner, 1985.

colors of camouflage as the situation required. She may have been learning disabled in math or reading, but she was one awfully smart lady. I told her so. I even showed her my chart (I was so proud of it I *had* to show it to someone).

Emily smiled enigmatically, but furiously denied that my theory had any merit. If nothing else, she seemed appreciative that I had devoted so much time to thinking about her. And I noticed, immediately, that she became more cooperative in the sessions that followed. Oh, she still kept me on my toes with new twists, but I could tell her heart was not in it. Even if doing this behavioral profile did not help her, it definitely helped me get a handle on the chaos I was trying to organize without resorting to writing her off as "another crazy borderline." Sometimes it is better if I just let go of that need for order I find so important. Once I realize I am in the vortex of a cyclone and I cannot do much about it, I might as well enjoy the ride. And while I can truthfully say that I never enjoyed much of our time together, I believe Emily improved most significantly once I was able to appease my own anxiety about the case by attempting to create some semblance of structure.

Reframing Resistance

One of the most helpful ways to circumvent impasses with difficult clients is to change the way we think about them, to alter our diagnoses to those that may be more useful. A useful diagnosis, according to Weltner (1988), is one that suggests a treatment plan that is easy, efficient, and effective. Such a diagnosis of the problem would meet the following criteria:

1. It is acceptable to the client and everyone else involved in the treatment.
2. It identifies something the client truly wishes to change, something she has demonstrated *behaviorally* that she has the power and willingness to change.
3. It involves a problem that is generally resolvable within the time parameters and resources that are available.

I know of no metaphor more applicable than *reframing* to describe how therapists reconceptualize client problems in order to deal with them more easily. Originally coined by Watzlawick, Weakland, and Fisch (1974) in their work on formulating client issues, the term *reframing* is discussed in different forms by a number of writers including Haley (1967), Palazzoli, Selvini, Cecchin, and Prata (1978), Madanes (1981), and Bergman (1985).

In this internal strategy we seek to take the work of art that the client creates and presents to us, retain its essence, and change its form to something the client will still recognize as his but which we can feel more comfortable dealing with. When reframing works well, the client's perceptions of his problems are forever altered in a way that feels more hopeful.

By illustration, the behavior of an angry adolescent can be recast as a "helpful" way to get attention for a problem that has been ignored. Then, the whole concept of "resistance" can be looked at in a different light.

Some clinicians believe there is no such thing as resistance, that the client is simply educating the therapist through a unique form of cooperation. Reframed in this way, the difficult client's behavior dictates the most appropriate way to respond. O'Hanlon and Weiner-Davis (1989) describe, for example, the four possible ways a client could respond to a homework assignment and offer appropriate therapist actions:

> If the client completes the task, give another one.
> If the client modifies the task, offer easily changeable assignments that are ambiguous.
> If the client does not do the homework at all, do not give any more.
> If the client does the opposite of what is suggested, give a paradoxical directive.

From this perspective, clients are never resistant, oppositional, or difficult; we have just been unable to decode the ways they are trying to cooperate. In advising therapists who work with difficult clients, Erickson (1980, p. 213) reminds us that behavior we might find obstructive or unreasonable is "part of the problem that brought [the client] into the office; it constitutes the personal environment within which the therapy must take effect; it may constitute the dominant force in the total patient-doctor relationship."

One of the major contributions of Ericksonian therapy is the novel and indulgent view that client behavior, no matter how bizarre, is a legitimate form of communication. This perspective requires the clinician to show a high degree of acceptance and flexibility in order to treat resistant behavior, paradoxically, as a valuable resource (Dolan, 1985).

Changing Our Expectations

The principal assumption that gets in the way of therapists as they work with difficult clients is the notion that resistance is an inevitable part of treatment and that people do not want to change (O'Hanlon and Weiner-Davis, 1989). Our expectations of what we will find most definitely influence what we actually observe; that is why we go to such lengths in conducting research to minimize "subjective pollutants." If we expect a client to be difficult or anticipate that we will encounter resistance, we are most likely to find what we are looking for—trouble.

An extreme position regarding this subject is advocated by de Shazer (1984), who has declared resistance to be a figment of the imagination. He further insists that when clients do not cooperate with their therapists, it is not at all because they are resisting; rather, they are teaching their therapists how to be most helpful, and also showing them the behavior they do not especially appreciate. If a client does not comply with a task, complete an assignment, or cooperate the way the therapist thinks she should, the problem is not with the client but with the therapist.

I get a kick out of this unusual perspective, as I do with any creative innovation; however, I do believe that resistance exists. I also find it helpful, in some circumstances, to expect a hard time; then I am able to be more understanding and patient, and I am willing not to take the reluctance personally. I also see the value of monitoring carefully what I am thinking, feeling, observing, and anticipating as I begin working with a new client. Whenever my gut-level internal voice is saying something like, *"Oh no, not another one of these!"* or *"What am I ever going to do with this one?"* I know it is time to stop, take a deep breath, clear my head of these negative thoughts, and start over again. De Shazer is indeed right on one score: every client has a unique way of communicating and cooperating in therapy; it is our job to discover what that way is and to make the best use of it.

CHAPTER SIXTEEN

Solidifying
Therapeutic Alliances

There are as many different ways to treat difficult clients as there are approaches to any other aspect of therapy. Each strategy appears to be enticing. "I must learn to do that," I say to myself, only to find another, sometimes conflicting, strategy that also has tremendous appeal.

I have been ruminating about a case I cannot make much headway with. I have tried everything I can think of—both with the client and with myself—so I don't become even more frustrated. Nothing yet seems to be getting through to her. I feel more than ready to get out of my comfort zone and try something new.

I reacquaint myself with paradoxical interventions suggested by Madanes (1990a) in which I can prescribe resistance, because that is what the client is determined to do anyway. I am both intrigued with and amused by a case Madanes describes in which a series of four different directives are offered to an anorectic girl and her alcoholic father. Their symptoms are linked by a contract in which each becomes responsible for the other's life: if the father stops drinking, the daughter must start eating. And vice versa.

Brilliant, I think, and start searching for a way I can apply a strategic approach to my own case. I am convinced now that this is the key. While Madanes and her colleagues can explain only superficially why such a strategy works—disrupting patterns and such—they claim that it doesn't really matter. What counts is fixing the problem. Makes sense, I reason; after all, it is

184

the client who wants satisfaction, not me. If I must live with the uncertainty of not knowing how I was helpful or understanding the exact mechanisms by which change took place, so be it.

Before I ever had the opportunity to put this approach into practice, I came across another conception of working with difficult clients that seemed diametrically opposed to what I was about to try. In a case with a young man who had been unable to engage with any of several reputable therapists over a problem related to a writing block, Basch (1982, p. 15) described what to him made the biggest difference: "A turning point in the therapy came when I found myself unable to follow the patient in something he was saying about his work in one particular session. He casually mentioned a book that gave a nontechnical overview for the interested layman of the particular subject we were discussing. Some weeks later when the topic came up again I was able to understand what he was saying, which surprised him. When I said that I had read the book he recommended and had enjoyed it, he burst out sobbing: 'You really do care,' he said."

How compelling that anecdote sounded! But should I concentrate on the conflicts in our relationship, or forget that stuff and go after the presenting problem? This very dilemma is what makes our work so deliciously complex. There is an infinite number of ways to facilitate change, depending on the situation or even our mood at the time. The important point in this instance is that I have options, lots of options, too many options. I can pick one of these strategies, or a dozen others, and will never feel stuck as long as I remember that all clients are difficult, life is difficult, and the reason I chose this line of work is because it is challenging.

Therapeutic Alliances

One interpretation of the behavior of clients who are being difficult is that they have been unable to bond with the therapist in a constructive alliance. Rogers (1980), in looking over his life's work, found that again and again he made the greatest impact on people and circumvented their reluctance to change through the authenticity of his personal encounters. Bugental (1990) also believes that clients *become* difficult when we are unable to reach them.

According to the bulk of empirical research, there is greater likelihood that a therapeutic effort will be successful when a relationship has been established that is mutually interactive, includes collaboratively structured roles, and is characterized by openness, acceptance, and empathy on the part of the clinician (Sexton and Whiston, 1990). More specific to severely disturbed clients, Campbell (1982) examined the texture and structure of the therapeutic relationship. After reviewing the positions of the major theorists who focus on treating borderline personality disorders, including the work of Kernberg (1975), Blanck and Blanck (1974), Masterson (1976), and Giovacchini (1982), she identified a consensus regarding the optimal therapeutic alliance.

The majority of writers agree that borderline disorders are characterized by both developmental arrest and inadequate separation/individuation issues. Thus it is crucial to construct a vehicle that permits further growth in these areas to occur. This plan would involve a long-term commitment to a relationship that permits the client to work through primitive dependency and aggressive needs without pushing the therapist to relinquish a position of technical neutrality. Campbell (1982) further emphasizes the inevitability that countertransference issues will arise and notes the importance of using these feelings to promote greater developmental maturity in the client.

A warning to therapists about disclosing their feelings to the client is certainly in order. Tansey and Burke (1989) caution practitioners to be careful when sharing their feelings to clients, especially when these reactions may be the result of countertransference processes.

Validation of the disclosure is the most important problem. If the therapist is feeling bored or frustrated, this condition is not necessarily because of what the client is doing. Second, even if the therpist's perceptions are accurate, sharing them with the client can do as much harm as good, especially considering the power that some clients attribute to therapists, seeing them as omniscient authorities.

The authors also note that how the disclosure is presented is just as important as what is said. Consider the difference between these two efforts:

1. (Said with an irritated, impatient, and sarcastic tone of voice): "Do you realize how long you have been talking about this? Sometimes I find it very hard to listen to you."
2. (Said softly and tentatively): "I notice you feel the need to spend a lot of time on this subject. My attention is moving on to other things you mentioned earlier, which could mean that you have exhausted this topic. Then again, perhaps we could look at it from a different angle. How do you react to what I just said?"

The first disclosure sounds punishing whereas the second is offered with caring and sensitivity. We can make certain the first situation is avoided if we ask ourselves (a) what am I trying to accomplish? (b) What is the evidence that my perceptions are accurate? (c) How can I say this in a way that it will be well received?

The essence of therapy with difficult clients—or any clients for that matter—is the quality of the therapeutic relationship. Once the clinician allows this alliance to become polluted by the client's manipulation or hostile traits, disengagement often follows. Every client wants to feel valued and understood by us; it is when we trade our compassion for cynicism that we loose the opportunity to be helpful.

Feeling Understood

In a qualitative research study on the experience of feeling understood, Dickson (1991) interviewed a number of people to get at the essence of significant personal transformation. Several of the people he interviewed described their experiences as similar to the following:

> The instant after you conveyed your understanding, I experienced a full pause. The frame froze. My

> feeling of urgency dissipated. For that moment, I
> had nothing to do and nowhere to go. What I had
> been struggling with seemed settled and resolved. I
> felt no urge to try to convince anyone of anything. I
> did not want to fight or bang pots. I felt like a
> person who found water after nearly dying of thirst
> in the desert. It was enough. Nothing else mattered.
> The craving had been fulfilled and the next con-
> cern was still down the road. When the time would
> come, I would be able to leave that moment and
> engage fully in the next. The issue felt complete
> [p. 86].

I think all people, whether perceived as difficult or not, respond more cooperatively to someone if they believe that person understands them. A client who has previously felt raw or vulnerable will sometimes let go of defenses designed to keep others away once he or she feels understood: "I have experi- enced a soothing quality to it, like warm oil. The oil is also protective. It adds freshness, healing in a sense. One is not so harshly exposed to the cruel elements. There is a renewal. It is really nurturing" (Dickson, 1991, p. 123).

Understanding someone, especially a person who is throwing up obstacles, smoke screens, and diversions, and who is changing forms so as to remain disguised, is an awesome, even an overwhelming task. Yet as Bugental (1990, p. 321) discloses, "The gift above all else that my clients have given me is the conviction that there is always more; that courage, persistence, and determination can always open possibilities where none has seemed to exist.

"We cannot do everything, but we can do so much more than we usually do. It is tragic how little we recognize this. It is breathtaking to recognize how much more is possible."

Empathy and compassion are the keys to helping clients feel understood and nurtured. These elements are crucial to any therapeutic relationship because they allow us to access the client's inner world and remind us we are dealing with real, live human beings—not just objects to be treated. Perhaps most important, empathy and compassion reduce our tendencies to view difficult clients as bad and evil (Book, 1991).

Family Relationships

Sometimes clients become difficult in therapy, not because it is their choice but because someone else is actively sabotaging treatment. A young wife, for example, starts out highly motivated to work on several issues... until her husband begins ridiculing her as weak and spineless because she is always running to her shrink for support. An adolescent would very much like to open up and deal with some things that are bothering him, but he is teased mercilessly by his brothers for attending sessions. A middle-aged man has been quite cooperative in the first session, but then things turn ugly thereafter; you learn that his mother is working behind the scenes to undermine his resolve because of her own fears that certain family secrets will come out into the open. In each of these cases, the client initially wants to be as cooperative as possible—that is, until an influential relative or friend seeks to destroy the therapeutic connection.

Once the source of the resistance is identified, recruiting that person into the treatment is often helpful. The husband is asked to come in to help the therapist understand the situation better. The siblings of the adolescent are invited in so that now the whole family is the "client" rather than the one child stigmatized as the problem. And in the last example, the mother can be called to let her know how important she is and how valuable her help could be.

A therapist obviously must use a great degree of tact and skill to involve the disruptive person in the treatment without aggravating the situation even more. Nevertheless, when there are systemic dysfunctions in a client's family, especially the kind that are working actively to resist change, the whole family must be involved in the treatment. In these cases, the difficult client is simply acting out the ambivalence toward change manifested in the system or in coalitions of the family structure.

Stanton and Todd (1981), specialists in the treatment of

difficult clients, believe that attempting to treat these clients without including their families is foolish. The authors find this especially true with drug addicts; not only are they the scapegoats of their families, delegated to act out on behalf of others, but they are sabotaged unconsciously if not overtly by those they love most.

In researching the techniques with greatest promise for engaging the most difficult of client populations — resistant heroin addicts and their families — Stanton and Todd found that the absolutely essential step is to identify the family members most capable of sabotaging or encouraging progress and to insist that they attend sessions, even if they or the client seems reticent about their involvement.

In other research on treating resistant families, Anderson and Stewart (1983a) suggest a number of guidelines that should be followed:

> *Create an alliance.* Join the family as a supportive and compassionate member.
>
> *Realize all families resist therapy.* Any system works actively to maintain its constancy and resist change of any kind.
>
> *Establish an alliance with the person who holds the power.* Without the support of the family power hierarchy, any change is doomed.
>
> *Accept the family's view of the problem.* Initially, it is best not to challenge the family member's perception of their problem. Slowly, it can be reframed.
>
> *Start where the family is.* Do not ask them to do anything they are not ready for.
>
> *Take the road of least resistance.* Avoid power struggles and concentrate on the areas that are initally most responsive.
>
> *Relabel resistance as helpful.* Rather than seeing uncooperative behavior as oppositional, view it instead as feedback.
>
> *Establish contracts.* Help members set goals that are realistic and complete tasks that are within their grasp.

All this advice has one central theme: stay loose and flexible. Put your own agenda aside. Rather than searching for something that is not there, or demanding something that the client(s) are not ready for, go with what they are giving you. Of utmost importance, concentrate your efforts on establishing the most constructive alliances possible with those in positions of influence.

Group Relationships

Most group therapy practitioners screen out difficult clients because of their disruptive influence on others and their potential to destroy the cohesive elements in a group. Leszcz (1989), however, believes that groups are ideal settings to help such people alter their maladaptive styles. When groups are structured to include not more than one or two character-disordered clients, these individuals are provided the opportunity to experience stable, affirming relationships under the tutelage of an empathic leader. This therapeutic experience can be invaluable for the difficult client who so needs opportunities for healthy interaction; it can also allow more normal-functioning clients to work on issues related to confrontation and conflict management.

I applaud the effort of any therapist who takes on the challenge of including difficult clients in group settings. My own experiences have been somewhat less than successful in this arena because of my inability to neutralize the negative effects of the difficult one on other group members. I am convinced, however, that this treatment modality is the ideal setting to alter dysfunctional interaction styles, *if it can be done without diminishing the therapeutic experience of other group members.* That is a tall order, indeed!

Assessment, naturally, is the key. In deciding whether a difficult client (expecially one manifesting classical symptoms of borderline or narcissistic disturbance) is appropriate for group treatment, Powles (1990) recommends that the therapist make a series of clinical decisions, based on these questions:

How severe is the psychopathology?

Is the client amenable to treatment at all?

What is the best indicated treatment modality? Intensive versus supportive versus behavioral? Individual therapy? Family therapy? Group therapy?

If so indicated, what kind of group therapy is likely to be most beneficial? Group guidance versus group counseling versus group therapy? Heterogeneous versus homogeneous group composition? Insight versus action-oriented approaches? Group-centered versus leader-centered formats?

Some difficult clients are accepted much more easily than others into group environments. They are potentially more responsive to confrontation and better able to adapt to group norms. Sam, the "boring client" of Chapter Twelve, was able to respond no better in a group than in individual sessions, but another client with similar problems did marvelously well in group therapy. Every time he began to ramble, to drone on about meaningless details, he was vigorously but lovingly confronted by others. He felt accepted by the group, so he did not pout too much when others told him to shut up. And when he would withdraw and feel rejected, the other members would draw him out and encourage him to share his deeper-level feelings.

Gradually, this client did learn to alter his communication style. But just as important, for the first time in his isolated life he had access to the personal world of others (something that had been available to him previously only through television). He was fascinated and greatly entertained by the more dynamic members of the group. Even though some of their behaviors were self-defeating, he began to model himself after their more engaging styles of expression. For the first time, he felt part of a group who cared for him.

Promoting Insight Within Therapeutic Relationships

Assuming that the source of greatest impediment to progress in therapy lies in the client's behavior rather than our own, Golden

(1983) recommends a problem-solving approach to identify contributing factors and to neutralize them. Often the most advantageous place to start this analysis is with a thorough exploration of those secondary gains or payoffs the client is receiving as a result of engaging in difficult behavior.

Applying a model suggested by Dyer and Vriend (1973), the therapist examines all behavior in terms of its helpfulness, even the most self-defeating acts imaginable. He also examines the payoffs that accrue to the hostile client. Anger is seen as a way of dominating and controlling others, instilling fear, keeping people on the defensive. This style of interaction holds people at a distance and protects the client against vulnerability and rejection. It gives her license to be abusive to others, and then to have a ready excuse: "I'm sorry about my outburst earlier, but you know I have a bad temper." It also allows the person to act out freely any residual anger and frustration that she has accumulated throughout her life.

Once we, and later the client, understand what she gets out of the difficult behavior, it is harder for her to continue it. I have seen this technique work quite effectively in a number of different settings, including a therapy group.

Patrick was Irish and damn proud of it. His flaming red hair and lilt were dead giveaways of his ethnic origin. Patrick announced to the group during this first introduction that he had been pressured into getting help for his bad temper, but he saw it as a hopeless cause: he had Irish genes that predisposed him to lose control sometimes. Everyone laughed nervously.

Soon Patrick showed us what he meant. His temper could be ignited without warning. His face would turn the color of his hair, his eyes would smolder, and he would virtually explode with anger over some imagined injustice — usually a feeling that he was slighted or ignored. Needless to say, Patrick demanded and got a *lot* of attention.

Eventually, one courageous group member decided to broach the subject during one of Patrick's calmer moments when he had announced that he was in a good mood. She very softly yet directly told him she did not feel safe with him in the group. She was tired of his ranting and raving and insisted that it would have to stop or she would leave the group. She had already endured enough from an abusive husband similar to Patrick and she did not intend ever again to subject herself to that sort of psychological torture. The group broke out into spontaneous applause.

Much to everyone's surprise, tears started to run down Patrick's face. He said that he wanted to change so badly but that he just could not, no matter what he tried. It was just part of his blood.

He was then challenged to consider whether that assumption was indeed true and what satisfaction he got from believing it. Patrick could think of absolutely nothing. "I *hate* being like this. It is awful being so out of control."

The leader asked him and other group members to consider that everyone gets *something* out of a particular behavior; if they did not the behavior would stop. Patrick agreed with that assumption, but could still not think of any payoffs to being so belligerent and hostile. "After all, I just end up alienating everyone."

"And what is the benefit of that?" one group member asked, picking up the cue.

The next half-hour was spent helping Patrick list all the "wonderful" things he got out of being the way he was—the attention he received, the power he wielded, the barriers he erected to protect himself. If ever insight can be an impetus to lasting change, it is in understanding the hidden secondary gains from self-defeating behaviors. No longer can you pretend you do not know what you are doing and why. Henceforth, every time Patrick began to erupt, before anyone else would say a word, a small smile would cross his face. He would shake his head, once, twice, take a deep breath and continue. Sometimes he would even giggle when he caught himself engaging in previous maladaptive patterns.

This model for looking at difficult client behavior in terms of the helpful functions it serves accomplishes a number of therapeutic tasks: (1) it focuses on the existence of values in even self-destructive acts, (2) it unveils the hidden motives behind behavior, (3) it makes clients assume responsibility for even their unconscious behavior, (4) it teaches clients a way to think about and to make sense of what they are doing, (5) it labels in concrete ways the meaning and purpose of even the most destructive acts, (6) it gives the therapist the leverage to confront the difficult client by labeling what he or she is doing and why, and (7) it takes destructive behavior out of the realm of the pathological and explains it as a legitimate coping mechanism that just has unfortunate side effects.

Models for facilitating insight are only as effective as the quality of the therapeutic relationship that has been established. Whether we are working in the context of individual, group, or family sessions, any interventions we try have a greater likelihood of success once the difficult client feels secure enough to risk experimenting with new ways of interacting with others.

CHAPTER SEVENTEEN

Practical Strategies
for Resolving Impasses

Helping difficult clients involves much more than adopting a particular set of attitudes or establishing an effective alliance; it requires intervening, sometimes quite forcefully, to stop a client's self-defeating patterns and to help channel energies in more constructive directions. The particular nature of these action strategies, whether variations of providing structure, using cognitive interventions, setting limits, or employing paradoxical techniques, is probably less important than the practitioner's willingness to equip himself with a variety of therapeutic options he can draw on as the situation requires.

This chapter is not meant to be a comprehensive compilation of all the action-oriented interventions that are at the therapist's disposal as much as a sampling of the most common possibilities. So often with difficult clients we are unable to apply "standard" strategies that have proved effective before; we are usually required to modify and adapt interventions to the unique requirements of a case.

Cognitive Interventions

At the heart of most forms of resistance is some underlying thought disorder in which the client distorts reality and applies erroneous, illogical, irrational, or self-contradictory reasoning processes (Ellis, 1962; Mahoney, 1974; Beck, 1976; Meichenbaum, 1977; Burns, 1980; Lazarus and Fay, 1982; Golden, 1983). This conception of client difficulty falls within the province of cognitive therapists but most practitioners also find it helpful to home in on what clients are thinking and processing that leads them to interpret and respond to the world the way they do.

Once clients, even very difficult clients, are helped to realize that their absolutist thinking is a gross distortion of reality, that the "shoulds," "musts," and other dogmatic demands that are part of their vocabulary are actually setting them up for failure, the stage is set for considering alternative ways to look at their situation.

Although greater patience and repetition is needed to reach clients with severe disturbances and thought disorders, they can often be led to understand that the following statements apply to them:

- You are the one creating the obstacles to getting what you want; it is not being done to you by others.
- Just because you are not progressing as fast as you would like does not mean you will not eventually reach your goals.
- Pain and discomfort accompany any growth; there is no sense in complaining about it because that will not make it go away.
- Setbacks are an inevitable part of life and simply signal that you need time to gather your momentum.
- Just because you are struggling in these few areas of your life does not make you a complete loser and failure.
- You have the capacity to stop making things difficult for yourself and others when you decide to think differently about your situation and your life.

In spite of claims by Ellis and others who argue that cognitive methods are successful in countering the resistant behavior of borderline personalities and even psychotic individuals, I would suggest that these methods are probably even more helpful when we use them with ourselves. One of the hallmarks of the cognitive therapist is supposed to be that he practices what he preaches. As almost any therapeutic impasse involves some contribution by the clinician, it is often necessary for us to challenge our own belief system to understand what is occurring. There are thus parallel processes operating simultaneously: on the one hand we are identifying those counterproductive beliefs that the client is using to sabotage progress; on the other we are confronting ourselves to let go our own irrational demands. These usually take the form of unrealistic expectations we hold for our own behavior or for that of the client, standards of perfection that can never be met.

Providing Structure

Some writers propose that the best way to face reluctant clients is to reduce the ambiguity of the therapeutic encounter by providing more structure (Manthei and Matthews, 1982; Day and Sparacio, 1980; Ritchie, 1986). People become most difficult when they are faced with situations they find threatening. And there are few encounters in life that feel more frightening than sitting across the room from someone you believe is studying you silently like a specimen, forming judgments that are probably not very flattering.

Client apprehensions can be reduced, anxieties soothed, and cooperation solicited if we accommodate clients who need more structure in order to feel safe. The most effective therapists of any theoretical persuasion tend to be those who are most flexible and pragmatic, who treat each client as an individual, and who design each treatment plan for the unique requirements of a given individual, set of symptoms, and therapeutic situation.

So many ex-clients who dropped out of therapy prematurely or who hold some special animosity for members of our profession complain about how distant and withholding their helper was: "He just sat there staring at me. Every time I asked a question or requested some help, he just looked at me with his smug smile and crossed his arms. Sometimes he would say: 'What do *you* think?' but more often he would just wait. I wanted to strangle him. And no, he didn't remind me of my father!"

There are indeed some clients in whom we bring out the worst when we insist that they conform to our rules regarding conduct during sessions. These rules include demanding that clients trust us before they know us, spill their innermost secrets, and be very patient with us until we can get a handle on what is happening.

These rules seem perfectly reasonable to you and me; they are, in fact, crucial to getting much work done. But I can also appreciate how some people might have a little trouble with them, especially left-brained folks who live in a concrete world where everything has its place. Some people can indeed become quite difficult to deal with when we place them in an unfamiliar environment where everything they do best does not count and where we expect them to violate many of their basic values. Consider, for example, the prototype of the macho man. He has been taught his whole life that (1) if you show your feelings you are weak, (2) if you admit you cannot handle your own problems you are a failure, (3) reflection and introspection are evidence of laziness and avoidance of real work, (4) being sensitive and communicative is for women and sissies, (5) you keep your innermost thoughts and feelings (if you have any) to yourself, and (6) you do not trust shrinks. Now we are asking this guy, whose marriage is probably ending because his wife has had enough of his macho crap, to abandon his basic values. Even more incredible, we are asking him to do the opposite of everything he ever learned: be open, trusting, sensitive, vulnerable, reflective, and flexible.

It is amazing how often clients such as the man described above do change considerably in therapy, but that can happen only if we offer enough structure in the beginning to allow him to feel at least a little familiarity with the environment. I remember one insurance adjuster I saw who absolutely insisted that he have some specific goal he could work on between sessions. When I was seeing him, I had just sworn off behavioral interventions in lieu of a more insight-oriented approach, so I gave him a hard time about his need for concrete results: "I guess this is exactly what your wife means when she says that you are so rigid." Understandably, he became quite ornery with me until I realized there could not be any harm in humoring him for awhile until he felt more comfortable with this ambiguous enterprise we call psychotherapy. He did eventually stop doing con-crete homework assignments every week (although that did seem to be helpful to him) as he experimented with a less structured way of working on himself.

Resistance can often be managed by providing more structure until the client feels less threatened. Sometimes this requires you to explain more than you usually do about what you are doing and why, where things are headed, and what you expect from the client in order to be helpful to him or her: "You seem confused by my request that you report on what happened during the week. I am trying to get a handle on what you thought about and how you felt after our last session. I wonder what ideas, if any, you found useful. And I am interested in what changes you may have noticed that have taken place inside you. This information will allow us both to decide what has been helpful to you and in which direction we should head next."

There are instances, of course, when we provide structure in sessions more to appease our own anxieties than to aid the client. There are times when it is best to allow the client to flounder a bit and find his or her own way out of the maze of uncertainty. But it is also important to assess the reasons a particular client may be uncooperative. If, as an experiment, we reduce the ambiguity of the therapeutic encounter and provide more direction and then notice that the client becomes more responsive, we have some idea that instituting more structure may be just what the client needs in order to function more effectively.

Accentuating the Positive

Any discussion of difficult cases seems to focus on problems, negative factors, failure, and what has gone awry. This focus is easy to understand: resistant clients are themselves obsessed with disaster. They revel in their role as tragic heroes—misun-derstood, hopeless, doomed to spend their lives as failures. In therapy they talk about what is not working, what is going bad in their lives, and how useless it feels to try anything different.

Often, we inadvertently reinforce their tragic roles by

allowing them to complain on and on about their troubles. We even ask them how things are going, knowing what to expect. We are, after all, trained to examine the pathological and ask people about their troubles. Some clients who have more than their fair share of problems can easily spend hundreds of hours listing everything that is annoying, disappointing, and frustrating for them.

It is quite a departure from our normal mode of operation to follow a path suggested by O'Hanlon and Weiner-Davis (1989) and to concentrate almost exclusively on what is going right and what is working well. Granted, for some difficult clients, we must dig quite deeply and probe very patiently to get them to admit that *anything* is going well. But unless we can move away from a focus on the negative aspects of a case, and get the client to do the same, we will go around in endless circles listening to others complain, and then complain ourselves about their complaints.

Some of the more solution-oriented brief therapists advocate spending most of the time exploring what is already working for the client instead of what is not working. This technique allows us to find exceptions to the presenting problem as well as a hint about the directions we might move toward. "It is as if there is a television screen that gets filled with whatever is in front of the camera of therapeutic conversation. If the camera is focused mainly on problems and pathology, both therapists and clients perceive problems and pathology. In a similar manner, if clients can be brought to either perceive or act upon strengths and solutions outside of the session, that perception or experience will fill the screen of their lives outside of therapy as well" (O'Hanlon and Weiner-Davis, 1989, pp. 39-40).

When I read the preceding quotation for the first time I happened to be stumped with a case that was proving to be beyond my resources. I definitely thought we were spending altogether too much time on the client's various complaints— that her health was failing, that her husband was neglecting her, that her children were a burden, that her mother was a nag, that her colleagues were insensitive, and, yes, that I was not being much help. In fact, we both seemed to have defined the structure

of therapy as an opportunity for her to dump everything that
was bothering her.

One day, I decided to try a novel approach suggested by
the quote above. As soon as the client sat down, but before she
had a chance to open her mouth, I held up my hand for silence. I
told her to indulge me, that I wanted to try an experiment. I
wondered if she would depart from our usual plan and talk
about something a little different. She seemed somewhat hurt
but eventually agreed (but not before extracting a promise that
we could stop whenever she wanted to). I simply asked her to tell
me only about what was going well in her life, only the things she
felt good about, only the areas that were smooth.

"Well, I suppose relatively speaking, my stomach problems have gotten a little better. I only had to go to the bathroom
four times this morning, and, I have got to tell you, I'm getting
sick of this. These doctors. . ."

"Wait. Wait. Wait. Hold on. Remember our experiment?
We are only going to talk about the positive."

"I would like to talk about the good things, but frankly,
there aren't any that I can think of."

"I like the way you put that (*I was trying to be positive*). At the
end of your statement, you said 'any that you can think of.'
Whether you realize it or not, you implied that there may be
positive things going on in your life, but they just don't immediately come to mind."

We went on like this for awhile. It was not easy by any
stretch of the imagination. I almost longed for the usual litany of
complaints; then, at least, I could daydream. But this was like
pulling teeth—just to get her to admit that there were a few nice
things that were happening. With perseverance and determination I continued pushing, drawing her out, but stopping her
whenever she would lapse into complaining. Fortunately, she
forgot she had the power to stop our little game whenever it grew
tiresome. Or maybe she sensed unconsciously that however
difficult it was for her to change her focus, such a task was
necessary if she was ever to improve.

Although I would not have counted the experiment an
unqualified success, it did break the monotony of our routine.

Actually, I was fully prepared to return to our usual pattern in the very next session. But when she came in, I noticed that there was a perceptible change in her behavior: she spent five whole minutes in the beginning of the session telling me about a good thing that happened to her during the week! Then she returned to her monologue.

Over time, the distribution of our energy eventually reached a fifty-fifty split with a significant part of our time together spent focusing on what was going well in her life in addition to the ugly stuff. I thought this shift was truly remarkable. I realized that in my training, in my discussions with colleagues, even in the internal conversations I have with myself about cases, I focus mostly on psychopathology, symptomology, problem areas, impasses, and mostly difficult cases in which I do not understand what is going on. I also noticed a pattern in which those clients I like the least are those who complain the most. It occurred to me that maybe that is what they think I want to hear, that the appropriate role for a client in therapy is to come in and bitch. Further, it seemed quite possible to reduce all this attention on what is wrong and to spend at least some part of every session devoted to the positive dimensions of a client's life.

Clients improve more quickly when we balance the difficult aspects of life with those that are relatively stable. In addition, they learn to pay attention to what is working for them and to do those things more often. Such a conceptual switch makes the sessions *feel* more productive for the therapist as well. When our morale improves, the client's positive attitude quickly follows.

Managing the Therapeutic Environment

Difficult clients have little respect for external boundaries established by others. They often feel entitled to operate under their own rules of convenience. If they want extra time after a session has ended, they take it. If they feel like letting loose a barrage of abuse, what is a therapist for if not to be a receptacle for garbage? If they wish to call us late at night for a consultation,

instant gratification is just a phone call away. If there is something about the fee structure, time schedule, office arrangement,
or therapy style that they don't like, it is a simple matter to insist
that we do whatever needs to be done to change it.

It is Sklar's contention (1988) that while working through
the difficult client's intrapsychic conflicts is certainly important,
the greatest priority should be placed on managing the therapeutic environment with its accompanying boundaries. The
disturbed client's rage, fear, anxiety, resistance, and need to
control are most often expressed in her efforts to circumvent
whatever rules have been established. This often includes coming late to or breaking appointments, creating crises, and challenging clinicians to alter the customary practice of their
profession.

These terrorist tactics can begin in several seemingly
innocent ways. An example is a sweet, little old lady who requested a session on the first floor because she didn't like
climbing the stairs, and then escalated her demands to include
appointments at odd hours. Another client expressed a preference to sit somewhere other than in the waiting room before the
session began. Still another client asked for a glass of water as
each session began, knowing that the therapist would have to
walk to the other end of the building for it. When the therapist
refused, she began a series of coughing fits that lasted until she
got what she wanted.

Once we understand the meaning and function that
ground rules have for difficult clients, we can establish and
maintain a therapeutic environment that is secure, stable, and
predictable (Langs, 1976). This is, of course, standard operating
procedure for many psychoanalysts and also those practitioners
who spend much time treating borderline disorders. The point
is that *any* client who is being difficult is probably playing with
boundaries and testing limits. Many outcome failures occur not
only because therapists intervene at inappropriate times but
also because they do not do enough to set limits on provocative
and obnoxious behavior (Fiore, 1988). It is our job to institute
whatever limit setting is necessary to keep the client within
acceptable bounds.

The most challenging part of this task is to establish and enforce limits in a firm manner while still retaining our tact and compassion (Groves, 1978). Along these lines, Hamilton, Decker, and Rumbaut (1986) distinguish between "punitive limit setting" and "therapeutic limit setting." Imagine, for example, a borderline client who has repeatedly threatened suicide, but as yet, has not followed through on any gesture. The most natural inclination is to inform him that such behavior will no longer be tolerated and that if he will not cease this manipulative behavior, you will no longer work with him. Although on the surface this appears to be the most clinically appropriate response, the therapist is actually feeling abused and angry. The ultimatum is delivered coldly, conveying a message the client has probably heard many times before from his parents: "Unless you follow my plan I won't love you any more and I will leave you."

Therapeutic limit setting, on the other hand, delivers the needed firm message that certain behaviors can no longer be tolerated, but it does so with caring: "This is the fourth time you have threatened to kill yourself. That is four times I have been seriously concerned about you. If you do decide to kill yourself, I will feel sad, but there is not much I can do to stop you. If you and I are going to continue working together, you have to develop some other ways to cope. The next time you tell me that you intend to kill yourself, I will interpret that to mean that you are out of control and you are asking me please to put you in the hospital. I will do that because I care for you and realize that you would be asking for my help."

The difference between these two styles of limit setting is not so much what you do, or even precisely how the message is delivered, as much as how you feel inside as you work with clients. When we are clearheaded and do not take the clients' actions personally, we are able to establish limits without striking back or punishing them to meet our own needs for retribution.

The same is true for the use of confrontation when we are working with difficult clients. Confrontation, like limit setting, comes in two major forms: the kind that originates from the therapist's indignation and the kind that stems from a deep caring. In the first variety, we feel angry and frustrated. We lash back under the guise of being helpful. The "confrontation" in this situation is actually a punishment designed to put the client back in her place. This behavior is contrasted with confrontation that is truly intended to help the difficult person to accept responsibility for behaviors that are hurtful, both to her and to others.

Warner (1984) describes himself as having been traumatized by a controlling client who did everything possible to defeat both him and the therapy. Such clients feel powerful when they are able to find ways to obstruct progress. They delight in getting under other people's skin and enjoy irritating powerful figures like therapists most of all.

For this reason, Warner (1984) reminds us that working with abrasive people is qualitatively different from working with other kinds of clients. You must do something; you cannot ignore their obstructiveness; it will not go away by itself. "They find far more reassurance in your confronting them with what they are doing that is really *un*acceptable" (p. 34).

Even psychoanalytic practitioners such as Kernberg (1984), who advocates technical neutrality as the ideal therapist posture, will, when faced by a difficult client, adopt a more aggressive and confrontive stance: "My point is that it is better for the therapist to risk becoming a 'bull in a china shop' than to remain paralyzed, lulled into passive collusion with the patient's destruction of time. At the very least, an active approach reconfirms for the patient the therapist's concern, his determined intolerance of impossible situations, and his confidence in the possibility of change" (Kernberg, 1984, pp. 245–246). Most practitioners of varying theoretical approaches would therefore stress the importance of being more confrontive and more conscious of setting limits with those clients who are interpersonally difficult.

Paradoxical Interventions

The physicist Niels Bors invented the complementarity principle to describe the paradoxical nature of light that exists as a particle of solid matter and yet behaves as an oscillating wave. Until Bors's time, every aspect of the physical world was classified as having either-or properties. He pointed out that almost everything about Nature is paradoxical and therefore expressed as polarities of good and evil, yin and yang, useful and useless (Goldberg, 1990).

What we often call difficult behavior in clients may alternatively be viewed as their attempts to exercise freedom in spite of the efforts of a therapist who is diligently trying to eliminate choices (even if they were self-destructive) that previously were avialable to them. An example of this reactance theory, originally conceived by Brehm (1966), is described by Tennen, Rohrbaugh, Press, and White (1981, p. 15): "Thus if a therapist implicitly or explicitly tells the client what to do, the client could restore freedom *directly* by disobeying or doing other than what the therapist requests. Or s/he could do it more *indirectly*, by implication—for example, by complying now but disobeying the therapist's next request." The authors then suggest that the best way for the therapist to avoid eliciting reactance in the client is to employ strategies that are designed to arouse defiance instead. This, of course, is exactly the rationale for paradoxical techniques.

It would be nice to have another name for these techniques that can be so manipulative. "Nondirective" interventions is much less obtrusive sounding, implying that the therapist does something by not doing something. And certainly there are few alternatives more attractive to us than those strategies that do not involve butting heads with clients who are obstinate. There is something brilliantly simple and elegant about refusing to acknowledge the existence of a boundary that the client has just dared us to cross.

Some clients are difficult not only because of attempts to defend their turf or because of characterological defects but also because of specific patterns of communication that take place between therapist and client (Watzlawick, Weakland, and Fisch, 1974). Erickson (1964) pioneered a series of techniques with which to manage resistance that stems from interactive effects, the most famous of which involve paradoxical methods of encouraging the difficult behavior. He discovered something that every parent knows: if you want a child to stop doing something, tell her to keep doing it. The theory behind this method is that people cannot oppose us if we are ordering them to be oppositional; resistance is transposed into cooperation once we join the difficult client in his efforts to resist change (Otani, 1989b).

At about the same time that Erickson was experimenting with indirect directives in the United States, Frankl (1960) created paradoxical intention in his efforts to apply logotherapy to resistant clients. It seems supremely ironic that two such different practitioners might approach several clients in quite similar ways. An insomniac might be ordered to deliberately stay awake. A stutterer would be directed to stutter more often and for longer periods of time.

Predicting a Relapse

One of the infuriations about working with difficult clients is the persistence and rigidity with which they maintain dysfunctional behavior. The self-defeating patterns seem impervious to all but the most dramatic interventions. About the only weapon that seems available to the therapist is the ability to anticipate these behavioral configurations. Shay (1990) suggests that we capitalize on our ability to predict what will happen next as a way to disrupt the sequence before it fully unfolds. For example, a client goes on a spree of overeating whenever she faces a Saturday night without a date; a child gets kicked out of school every time his parents have a major fight. The therapist jumps in at the opportune moment: "So, Jacob, I suppose since your parents had a real knock-down skirmish this weekend, we can expect you will find a way to leave school."

It is fairly important that these predictions be accurate or one loses a lot of credibility as an expert—unless, of course, the prediction was designed to be wrong. The simple elegance of this technique is illustrated in Haley's (1973) description of "predicting a relapse." A client becomes easily discouraged. She has just made some minor advance in her efforts to expand her social world, but you can feel her trepidations that her progress is short-lived. Surely something disappointing will happen. Again. And you utter your worst fears aloud: "I want to warn you that this probably won't work out the way you expect it to. At least half the plans you made will fall through."

If this prediction turns out to be true, then the client has been adequately prepared to hold off a disastrous relapse; she can take the disappointment in stride. And if the prediction turns out to have been unduly pessimistic, then the client feels even better about her ability to prove the therapist wrong.

With those cases who are even more stubborn, Haley (1973, p. 31) describes a method by which you not only predict a relapse, but *encourage* one. "I want you to go back and feel as badly as you did when you first came in with the problem because I want you to see if there is anything from that time that you wish to recover and salvage."

Doing the Opposite

The essence of creative problem solving, according to Rothenberg (1990) in his study of Nobel Laureates, is the resolution of polarities or the blending of opposites. So often, he observes, new discoveries in science, art, or philosophy are the opposite of previously held ideas. "Even more surprising is this: not only is the opposite true, but both the opposite and the previously held idea are operative and true" (p. 25).

Nowhere is this more evident than in our own field where we have learned that the following opposite polarities can coexist:

1. Nurturing clients facilitates change, but so does confronting them; blending the two techniques is even better.
2. Dealing with unexpressed feelings promotes insight, as does exploring underlying thought processes; combining the two strategies is ideal.
3. Seeing clients in individual sessions is quite effective, as is working with them in groups or families; sometimes a combination approach is even more powerful.

4. Dealing with the past promotes changes in the present; looking at present behavior helps explain the past; both approaches combined make for a more productive future.

Some practitioners employ insight as their principal tool; others prefer to ignore self-understanding altogether and concentrate on action strategies. Some clinicians stay objective and detached in the therapeutic relationship; others present themselves as authentic and genuine. It is apparent, therefore, that our whole profession is grounded in polarities that contradict one another and that reconciling opposites is a requirement of the practitioner.

Creative professionals tend to think in the language of opposites. When administered a free association test, Nobel prize winners are more likely to respond to a stimulus word by supplying its opposite. Rothenberg (1990) cites several examples of how this Janusian Process (from Janus, the Roman god of beginnings who faces in opposite directions at the same time) operates in problem solving. Albert Einstein had been greatly perplexed as to how he could develop an all-encompassing general theory of relativity similar to his special theory of relativity applied to light. He was convinced that there was some underlying order to the physical world, that "God does not play dice with the universe." The idea came to him that if a man was falling from a building he would be in motion and yet at rest relative to an object falling from his pocket. The reconciliation of this paradox led to Einstein's most famous theory.

I believe this same process underlies our most creative work in therapy. When we are stymied with a difficult case, it is usually because we are trying the same things over and over again. Therefore, the simplest prescription for practitioners who feel stuck is to apply the strategic dictum of doing the opposite of what has already been tried. This could involve several strategies mentioned by Dolan (1985):

1. If talking doesn't work, become silent; if silence doesn't work, try talking.

2. If you feel stuck while sitting, start moving; if you feel stuck while moving, try sitting immobile.
3. If the mood is impersonal, soften it; if the situation is emotional, shift to a more objective tone.
4. If you feel anxious, take a few deep breaths to relax; if you feel bored, do something to heighten the intensity.

The formula for becoming unstuck in any situation is to identify your pattern of ineffective responses and then to alter something in a systematic way—whether it is the style, the content, the context, the direction, the pace, the intensity, the frequency, the force of impact, the speed of action, the amount of pressure, or the degree of investment in the outcome. Tinkering with individual variables might be plotted something like this: the therapist asks the client pointed questions about her history and background, after which she becomes evasive. The therapist then tries using more open-ended inquiries, but the client begins to ramble and drift off track. Finally, the therapist stops asking questions altogether and tries the opposite—sitting quietly. This time the client volunteers useful information.

Fabian Tactics: Doing the Unexpected

The strategy of confusing an opponent in an adversarial position by adopting an unexpected series of moves is described by Goldberg (1990) as Fabian Tactics. Named for the Roman general Quintus Fabius Maximus, who was able to out-maneuver Hannibal during the Punic Wars, this approach seeks to avoid direct confrontation in those situations where one is clearly overmatched. Throughout history, other military leaders have defeated vastly superior forces by using tactics designed to delay, harass, and confuse. Thomas J. (Stonewall) Jackson during the Civil War, Francis Marion (the Swamp Fox) during the Revolutionary War, and Erwin Rommel (the Desert Fox) during the North African campaign of World War II were able to throw opponents off balance with completely unpredictable and incongruous behaviors.

The strategy of General Fabius against Hannibal was not

simply to evade battle or stall for time; it was designed to destroy the enemy's will to fight, to so thoroughly demoralize and frustrate him that he would give up and go home. This was also the strategy of the Viet Cong that proved so effective during the Vietnam War.

Difficult clients are hardly "enemies" or "opponents," even if they sometimes see us in that role. Yet the principle of avoiding direct confrontation and employing indirect interventions with an entrenched and resistant client was a particular favorite of Milton Erickson. Many of his hypnotic induction procedures that proved potent, even with those most determined to resist, were based on Fabian Tactics of doing the unexpected.

When Marshall enters the office and demands that I accommodate every one of his detailed requests before he will agree to work with me, he is expecting me to turn him down so he has an excuse to fire me. He tells me that in order for us to proceed further (Marshall is an attorney), I will have to agree to the following:

1. Schedule appointments on a week-by-week basis with his secretary.
2. Bill his office once a month and wait for payment until he has received insurance reimbursement.
3. Agree not to schedule anyone else immediately before or after him so he will not be seen entering or leaving my office.
4. Allow him to bring his portable telephone into the session in case anything from the office needs his immediate attention.
5. Permit him to sit in *my* chair because it has maximum support for his back problem.
6. Stick to *his* agenda of matters he would like to address. If he does not wish to talk about something, I will agree not to push him.
7. Keep on hand for his exclusive use his brand of herbal tea, which he will supply.

I was so stunned by the sheer audacity (not to mention volume) of his demands that at first, I did nothing except stare at him openmouthed. While Marshall adjusted his posture in *my* chair (that had been his first request to which I had innocently acquiesced), I considered my options. If I told him what I really thought—that I would not stand for his manipulative, controlling behavior, nor would I tolerate his games to undermine my position—then it seemed clear that therapy with Marshall was over. I must say that idea appealed to me tremendously. Next, I considered what would happen if I tried to negotiate with him. I mean, this man was a professional litigator. He chews people up and spits them out for a living. He even carries a telephone with him so he can intimidate someone whenever the mood strikes him! And I think I am going to go up against this guy and get him to back down? I felt like General Fabius facing Hannibal's hordes astride their elephants.

I therefore considered my third option: give in to his demands, but with a few conditions of my own. This I reasoned, might disarm him completely and we could stop with the jousting.

"Sure," I said. "What you are asking sounds perfectly reasonable to me. I have no objection to anything you ask. In fact, I like a person who states what he needs. That is why I will accept your conditions if you will accept mine."

Wary now, Marshall's initial signs of triumph evaporated. "What do you have in mind?" he asked in his silkiest, lawyer-like voice.

"Nothing much. Just a few modifications of your requests. First, if you are going to sit in my chair, I ask you not to lean back, as sometimes it tips over. Second, you are more than welcome to keep your tea here—I think that's a great idea—but you will also need to bring your own cups, sugar, spoons. Oh yes, and a teapot. I think it would be best if you made your tea with your own things.

"As for your portable phone, that's fine. But if you are going to take calls during the session, I would like to do the same thing. And the scheduling arrangement, I would be happy to arrange things with your secretary—that is, if you will remind me the day before I am supposed to call her . . ."

I continued no further as his laugh interrupted my "negotiations." (I was just warming up, too!) He moved out of my chair with the exasperated remark that he did not know shrinks were so temperamental about where they sat. But now we had an understanding, even an alliance of sorts.

I am not saying this guy did not continue to be a challenge to deal with, but I found that whenever he did resort to similar controlling tactics, I could best neutralize them through indirect, unexpected means.

The Use of Adjuncts

Audio and video recorders are excellent devices by which to help difficult clients hear and observe themselves in action. To a large extent, they get away with their games because they do not have to admit that they are acting inappropriately. Consequently, hard, documented evidence is an invaluable tool for helping them to face themselves. Often, the therapist does not even have to point out what is occurring, thus avoiding the danger that the client will lose face or feel humiliated. Some clients are quite able to find the patterns themselves once they have the opportunity to monitor their behavior in a less threatening situation.

During a therapy group one young woman persisted in denying she had any bone to pick with the leader. She maintained this position even though every time he spoke to her, no matter how gentle his approach or how inane his comment, she would flinch as if she had been struck and then retaliate with sarcasm and hostility.

Several times the group leader pointed out the pattern in a number of different ways, including a very direct approach:

Group leader: I notice every time I open my mouth you seem to become enraged. I wonder how you feel about me?

Hostile client: I don't feel anything one way or the other. Why do you always pick *me* out to ask these stupid questions?

Group leader: See, even now, you are doing what you say you don't do. It's almost as if I remind you . . ."

Hostile client: Never mind. Since I can't seem to say anything right, to say it the way *you* think I should, I'll just keep my mouth shut. Somebody else talk. You won't hear another word from me.

Group leader: Backing away isn't going to change the pattern that keeps recurring here. Has anyone else noticed the dynamics of what occurs between us? Maybe someone else could describe this in a way that you can understand.

Hostile client: I just told you: *I DON'T WANT TO TALK ABOUT THIS. ARE YOU DEAF?*

The therapist had a policy of recording each session and giving the tape to the client who had received the most time during the group session. This practice allowed the client to review what had transpired but to do so at a time and in a place less emotionally charged. The client would then bring the tape back the following week to protect confidentiality of members and then report on issues he or she had heard that were missed during the actual group session.

This structure provided a major breakthrough for the young woman. She was absolutely stunned to hear how she sounded on tape—so angry, so cantankerous, and so unwilling to hear what others had been saying to her. She was now painfully aware of what she had been doing and was prepared to explore its meaning. She could ward off confrontation, tune out what she did not want to hear, and attack rather than be defensive. What she could not do, however, was ignore what she sounded like to herself on the tape recorder.

Developing a Multidimensional Plan

We can be virtually certain that none of the strategies mentioned in this chapter, or throughout the book, are likely to be successful with the truly difficult client unless they are integrated into an overall treatment plan. Sex offenders, for example, are among the most challenging populations to work with because of the complexity of their disorder and everything that maintains it—high intensity arousal, compulsive drives, low motivation to change, and low probability of being caught. The *only* thing that works is a multidimensional attack combining no less than five different treatment efforts offered simultaneously: social skills training, victim empathy, hormone suppression medication, sex education, and direct attacks on deviant arousal (LoPiccolo, 1985).

This same multipronged approach is necessary in our work with most difficult clients. We simply cannot afford to stay with a narrowly focused treatment strategy that neglects some crucial element that helps to maintain the dysfunctional patterns. Other "rules of engagement" follow in the next chapter.

CHAPTER EIGHTEEN

Rules
of Engagement

The wealthy neighborhoods of Lima, Peru, hold stunning mansions behind their high walls. Each sprawling estate houses, in addition to the family in residence, the obligatory gardener, chauffeur, bodyguards, maids, and a nanny for each child. While the rest of the city languishes in the squalor of abject poverty, these pristine residential areas gleam with affluence. They would indeed be a sight to behold if not for one irritating problem: any time, day or night, you will find wandering around the city's streets, sleeping in the shrubs, howling at the moon, lost hordes of psychotic people.

The hospitals and mental insititutions of Peru have long been filled to capacity. With inflation running over 1,000 percent, an economy on the verge of bankruptcy, and terrorists seeking to overthrow the government, the bureaucrats have more on their minds than what to do about the mentally ill, who have no money, no friends in high places, and no power. With no hospital beds available and no doctors who can treat these patients, they are left to wander the streets.

For reasons that should be obvious, these homeless individuals gravitate toward the nicer neighborhoods where there is less competition for garbage to eat and where they can hallucinate in peace. They occupy these immaculate residential areas as if they were discarded, portable litter.

For years the landowners have struggled with the problem. "What can we do with these people? Clearly we can't allow them to live among us, to pester us and create such disturbances.

Why doesn't the government do something?" But alas, even if the city should decide to clean up this mess, there are no funds available to pay for such a project. For this reason the home-owners decided to take matters into their own hands.

One neighborhood ingeniously hired a van to patrol the area and round up the vagrants, just as a dogcatcher retrieves stray animals. That was the easy part. Unfortunately, with no place available to store these people—it was highly impractical to drive them around continuously—the vans would relocate their cargo to another place, open the doors, and herd them out where they would now be someone else's problem. Eventually, *every* neighborhood caught on to this idea and hired its own van.

Picture this situation now. Every night, vans patrol the neighborhoods picking up the homeless and transporting them to other neighborhoods to be released—where they are rounded up once again by *that* neighborhood guard and perhaps even driven back to the place they started! These people, who have no place to go, spend their lives in transit.

I think of Lima when I refer a difficult client to a friend for better treatment. I have probably reached the end of my pa-tience, or the client and I are tired of one another, or in certain cases, something just did not click between us. If I have learned anything from experience in this profession, it is how to identify a potentially difficult client from the first telephone encounter.

"What? I am the fifth therapist you have called this year? Let me give you the number of someone who specializes in your problem."

"Oh, I see. You can only make time for me every other Wednesday and that is when you are in town. I'm so sorry. I have no Wednesday appointments available."

"You say it was your astrologer who referred you to me? You want to know when my birthday is before you will set up an appointment? I know a great Sagittarian colleague who would be perfect for you."

However ridiculous this sounds, we all have exquisitely sensitive antennae for screening out those people we don't believe are right for our style of practice. And this is as it should be, for nobody, no matter how skilled, no matter how flexible or pragmatic, can work with every person. Perhaps the best predictor of successful treatment is a good match between what the client needs and what the therapist can offer. And it is for this very reason that we occasionally refer to a colleague those clients who are beyond what we can (or want to) handle.

This is, of course, the easiest way to deal with difficult clients: refuse to see them at all and limit your practice only to those who are the most motivated and least disturbed; refer the rest to a member of your organization who is lower in the pecking order. (If *you* are the lowest in the pecking order, make the case seem interesting enough that a more senior staff member will be intrigued by the challenge.) Humor aside, the idea of referring clients you feel uncomfortable with is a strategy advocated by some short-term analysts who use screening techniques to eliminate prospective clients who may prove to be resistant (Mann, 1973; Sifneos, 1973b).

On a more subtle level, most practitioners do get rid of those clients they believe will be troublesome or who are not likely to profit from the kind of treatment they offer:

"Let me refer you to a colleague who works on a sliding scale." READ: *You can't pay me enough for the aggravation you will dish out.*

"The only time I have available next week is Thursday at 2:00. Would you like the names of a few therapists who have a more flexible schedule?" READ: *I know some people so hard up for new referrals, they will see* anyone.

"I would like to work with you, but. . ." READ: *I don't want to work with you.*

"What you seem to be saying is that you have your doubts as to whether this is the right place for you." READ: *That is what I am saying.*

"You seem to be disappointed in the way I am handling things." READ: *My feelings are hurt. Go find someone else to pester.*

"I don't do that sort of work." READ: *With you.*

"Maybe you would like to take some time to think about it before we reschedule another appointment." READ: *Don't call me; I'll call you.*

If we are true professionals, we decide to refer a client solely on the basis of helping someone to find a better match in terms of expertise, specialty areas, or interactive compatibility; we definitely do *not* refer based on the ability to pay; on ethnic, religious, or racial dissimilarity to us; or because a client, at first glance, seems difficult. How can we ever grow as therapists if we do not tackle new challenges and move beyond our comfort zones? How can we truly make a difference in the world if we refuse to assist people who need our service the most?

There is, of course, tremendous strength in knowing our limitations, in knowing what we cannot do well, in being able to sense when it would be in the client's best interest to see someone else. These could be legitimate reasons that we might routinely refer substance abuse cases, victims of sexual abuse, or bulemics. We might truly want to be able to treat every case that walks in the door, but we cannot be everything to everyone.

I am fascinated by how the Lima Phenomenon operates in our profession: there are difficult clients who are being passed from one therapist to another because they are so resistant. Almost a decade ago I worked with a young woman I tried to help for a few weeks. I quickly realized that we were not on the same wavelength, so I gave her the name of a friend as an alternative to dropping out of therapy altogether. A dozen therapists later, she recently called me. She had been referred to me again! This time we tried to work things out, and whether it is a function of the progress she made with her other therapists or the development of my own maturity, we got along famously — at least until she abruptly stopped coming, never to be heard from again (at least by me).

Maybe the best arrangement of all is the one we set up naturally: a network of colleagues we can trust to handle certain kinds of cases. I have one friend who loves working with young children, but refuses to see adolescents (she has three teenagers at home). I, in turn, especially enjoy kids who are high school age, but I avoid treating younger children. I play enough games at home with my own son.

With certain exceptions, difficult clients are in the eye of the beholder. Some therapists thrive on working with people whom other clinicians would pay to get rid of. That is why it is so interesting to hear about alternative perspectives:

"I like working in substance abuse because I get to treat myself over and over. As a recovering addict, I need the constant reminders that my own demise is just a single impulse away. These people who are my clients are street people, just like me. I know their games and their lies. I get such a kick out of seeing myself in them."

"I get a lot of referrals from other therapists in the area. Send me your borderlines, I tell them. Some colleagues have said to me cynically that I have a guaranteed annuity from some of these patients who will need to be in therapy for most of their lives. But the truth is that I really enjoy long-term relationships. Some of these people can be a gigantic pain in the ass, but once I have my limits in place, I can deal with the acting out. I am just very patient and I don't mind waiting a long time to see results."

"Among my favorite clients are those others discard. If anything, I have developed a reputation for dealing with hopeless cases. I feel much more freedom to be creative and experimental when I know that other therapists, some quite accomplished in their own right, have already tried and failed with traditional methods. There is no sense in my doing what has already been done, so I have the opportunity to invent something quite original as a result of interacting with this supposedly 'resistant' client."

"I am known in my agency as 'The Terminator.' I close cases where others fear to tread. I like this a lot. I don't know, maybe I overidentify with these people because I was such trouble when I was younger. In one sense, I know this is true.

Nobody wanted to have anything to do with me because I would get in his face and make him deal with me on equal terms. When I was younger it seemed like everybody wanted to control me and tell me what to do. So now I have this opportunity to work with people who are kind of the way I was. To tell you the truth, I don't understand how people in my field can call themselves therapists when they are only willing to work with the people who don't really need their help in the first place.

"I like it when some of my colleagues give up on some cases and send them over to me. I can't lose. Nobody really expects very much, so if I help the person at all, I'm a miracle worker. It doesn't even seem all that hard to get through to them. They seem to recognize me as one of their tribe."

"To me, each person holds his or her own mysteries, and when I think about cases in terms of adventures, I don't feel frustrated when I encounter obstacles. Rather, I am a tinkerer. I study things a bit. Apply a little oil here and there. Maybe tighten a loose screw. If I have to, I will turn the thing upside down to see how it looks from another angle. But if the client will stay long enough and be patient with me, then I am certainly willing to put up with whatever he or she wants to dish out along the way. Hey, what fun would an adventure be without a few obstacles along the way?"

A Summary of Rules of Engagement

Fun indeed! If we might distill the essence of what experts have been saying about the most important operating principles when working with difficult clients, most of them would have to do with fun. This is the first of several rules of engagement.

Keep Your Sense of Humor

It *is* funny, as well as tragic — the extent to which some people will go to get attention. What makes clients difficult is how inventive and creative they are in their attempts to control relationships. They live by another set of rules. It sometimes helps us to keep things in perspective when we realize the absurdity of what we are witnessing—a client who is trying to bait us by testing what she can get away with, another who saves the best stuff for the last five minutes of every session, or still another who weeps uncontrollably every time we get close to something important.

In a survey of how therapists cope with stress induced by working with difficult clients, one of the most adaptive strategies relied on was optimistic perservance tempered by an appreciation for humor (Medeiros and Prochaska, 1988). Siegel (1982) tells the story of an obnoxious patient who was giving her doctor a particularly hard time over the cost of every procedure he suggested. When he recommended a cortisone injection in her knee to relieve arthritic pain, she asked how much *that* would cost. As a courtesy, he replied that he would charge her half his usual fee—$10—to which she became outraged that he would charge so much for less than a minute's work. The doctor then countered that if it would make her feel any better, he would leave the needle in longer.

Do Not Retaliate

Therapy is lost once we have been sucked so far into the trap that we begin entertaining fantasies of how to get even with the client. It is the difficult client's job to try to upset our equilibrium. It is only business, nothing personal.

It is our job to find a way to absorb or rebuff direct attacks in such a way that we don't suffer emotional injury and the client learns that such conduct is unacceptable, and ultimately self-destructive.

When the situation calls for firmness, it is important that we enforce necessary limits without losing our compassion and without becoming punitive. Favored ways that we are prone to retaliate when we feel hurt or angry include withdrawal, "emotional spankings" inflicted under the guise of confrontation, ridicule masked as dry wit, or more direct forms of aggression—calling the client names or even "firing" him in anger.

Define Rules and Roles

Clearly spell out what you are willing to do and not willing to
do. Explain the consequences of going outside the boundaries. Enforce the rules calmly and consistently. Do not make
exceptions.

Stay Flexible

Although the external boundaries of therapy are fairly sturdy, it
is important internally to remain loose. Difficult clients are
unpredictable. They come at us from directions that we do not
expect. As long as we remind ourselves anything can happen at
any time, we are prepared to go with the flow, to counter with a
response in an ever-changing situation.

Be Pragmatic

We get into trouble with *any* client when we persist in continuing
with a treatment strategy that is not working. The more difficult
the client, the more quickly things will deteriorate if we do not
adapt our methods to fit the unique requirements of a given
situation.

    Take inventory of everything that has already been tried
with the client and has not worked: Do not do any of those things
any more. Do something else. Again. And again. Until you find
the right combination of factors that make a difference.

    Sometimes the therapeutic alliance itself will provide
sufficient leverage to keep the client in line. Other times you will
need to keep matters more behaviorally focused or more cog-
nitively centered or more affectively oriented. Eventually, with
sufficient time and patience, we usually find the key to eliciting
greater cooperation.

Use Self-Disclosure Effectively

One of the most useful tools at our disposal is our own reactions
to a client's behavior. This is especially true with those who have

trouble trusting people to begin with; the last thing in the world they need is a shell of a person hiding behind a professional role (Miller and Wells, 1990). The therapist's genuine reactions, when conveyed sensitively and compassionately, can often be turning points for the alliance.

Confront, Confront, Confront

Certain people have discovered the secret for how to irritate the hell out of others and get away with it. They can be obnoxious or insensitive or manipulative or controlling without disastrous consequences to themselves. They know that other people may not like them very much, but the successfully obnoxious client has learned to stop just short of sparking violent retribution.

Our job, then, is to be one of the few people in the client's world from whom she will tolerate honest confrontation without running away. If we are to be helpful at all, we must have license to tell clients they are out of line without fear that they will flee. This practice works only when clients are sure that we are confronting them with love and concern rather than anger and hostility. The ones who *do* leave are not good candidates for change to begin with; if they stick around, they are saying by their behavior, "I don't like what you are doing, but I realize I need it."

Be Patient

Seligman (1990) reminds us that the most essential rule for treating difficult clients is to remember that therapy can sometimes take a long time. Trust is built only gradually. Because difficult clients struggle with trust issues more than most people, we must often exercise extreme patience until a therapeutic alliance is firmly established.

Decode the Meaning of the Resistance

All forms of resistance are communicating some message to us — "I hurt," "I'm scared," or perhaps "I enjoy the power I feel in controlling others." Once we have figured out the meaning underlying a client's behavior, we can then find a way to deal with it. Ideally, helping clients to understand what they are doing and why helps them to change their self-defeating behavior.

Be Compassionate

Keep in mind that all the preparation and training in the world will not equip us with every tool we need to handle problematic people. "With difficult patients, more often than not, we have to rely on intuition, on belief, and on professional dedication" (Lowenthal, 1985, p. 153).

It is interesting that the quote above is not from a therapist but from a dentist who is describing what is necessary to handle unpleasant patients. Yet, in whatever setting a helper practices, he will encounter rude and demanding consumers who require even more than the usual dose of kindness, compassion, and understanding in order to feel cared for.

When All Else Fails

"I am a pretty good therapist and I have been doing this for a number of years. I have done everything I can think of. I am flat out of ideas. You are probably going to be like this for the rest of your life unless you can come up with something that you think would be helpful" (LoPiccolo, 1991).

After this startling speech, LoPiccolo then demonstrates what he believes is a crucial skill for clinicians: to let go when there is nothing else that can be done. There comes a time, after we have tried everything we can think of and consulted every resource that is available, that we have no choice (other than to drive ourselves crazy with feelings of inadequacy) but to put the ball back in the client's court: "OK, you win. Collect your prize. You get to stay the way you are. So now what do you want to do next?"

Framo (1990) notes that when he was young and idealistic he zealously took on the challenge of any case who walked in the door; he reluctantly admits now that there are some clients, and some families, who are so difficult to work with that they defy treatment by almost any expert on earth. Their feelings of entitlement can drive even the most experienced and patient practitioner to lash out in frustration.

Framo's best advice when encountering such cases is to give up the fantasy of omnipotence, the belief that you can reach anyone all the time. There are some people whom no therapist alive can help. And there are some who are simply beyond what you can do.

I find this to be wonderful advice indeed! The only problem is that I have an awful time following it. My fear is that if I regularly accept my limitations and give up my sense of omnipotence, I also sacrifice a potent weapon that has, on occasion, served my work well. My stubborn reluctance to give up, to let go of seemingly hopeless cases, has on (admittedly) rare occasions produced miraculous results. Granted, the success rate is probably one in a hundred, and that means ninety-nine times I feel thwarted and frustrated. Yet, I think it is a price worth paying to help that one client who seemed so hopeless.

Is this a neurotic flaw in me? Most definitely. Would I enjoy my work more and stretch out my career if I eased up a bit? I am working on it. But in the meantime, until I can let go of hopeless cases, I am stretching myself in ways I never could imagine, challenging myself to discover new ways to work with difficult clients.

References

Adler, G. "Helplessness in the Helper." In P. C. Giovacchini and L. B. Boyer (eds.), *Technical Factors in the Treatment of the Severely Disturbed Patient.* Northvale, N.J.: Jason Aronson, 1982.

Allgood, S. M., and Crane, D. R. "Predicting Marital Therapy Dropouts." *Journal of Marital and Family Therapy*, 1991, *17*, 73–79.

Altshul, J. A. "The So-Called Boring Patient." *American Journal of Psychotherapy*, 1977, *31*, 533–545.

American Psychiatric Association. *Diagnostic and Statistical Manual of Mental Disorders.* (3rd ed., revised) Washington, D.C.: American Psychiatric Association, 1987.

Anderson, C. M. and Stewart, S. *Mastering Resistance: A Practical Guide to Family Therapy.* New York: Guilford Press, 1983a.

Anderson, C. M., and Stewart, S. "Meeting Resistance in Ongoing Treatment." *Family Therapy Networker*, Jan./Feb. 1983b, pp. 32–39.

Anthony, E. J. "Between Yes and No: The Potentially Neutral Area Where the Adolescent and His Therapist Can Meet." *Adolescent Psychiatry*, 1976, *4*, 323–344.

Basch, M. F. "Dynamic Psychotherapy and Its Frustrations." In P. L. Wachtel (ed.), *Resistance: Psychodynamic and Behavioral Approaches.* New York: Plenum, 1982.

Bauer, G. P., and Mills, J. A. "Use of Transference in the Here and Now: Patient and Therapist Resistance." *Psychotherapy*, 1989, *26*(1), 112–119.

Beck, A. T. *Cognitive Therapy and the Emotional Disorders.* New York: International Universities Press, 1976.

Beitman, B. D., Goldfried, M. R., and Norcross, J. C. "The Movement Toward Integrating the Psychotherapies: An Overview." *American Journal of Psychiatry,* 1989, *146*(2), 138–147.

Bellak, L., and Faithorn, P. *Crises and Special Problems in Psychoanalysis and Psychotherapy.* New York: Brunner/Mazel, 1981.

Bergman, J. S. *Fishing for Barracuda.* New York: W.W. Norton, 1985.

Beutler, L. E. *Eclectic Psychotherapy: A Systematic Approach.* Elmsford, N.Y.: Pergamon Press, 1983.

Bion, W. R. *Seven Servants: Four Works by Wilfred R. Bion.* New York: Jason Aronson, 1977.

Blanck, G., and Blanck, R. *Ego Psychology: Theory and Practice.* New York: Columbia University Press, 1974.

Book, H. E. "Is Empathy Cost Efficient?" *American Journal of Psychotherapy;* 1991, *45*, 21–30.

Boulanger, G. "Working with the Entitled Patient." *Journal of Contemporary Psychotherapy,* 1988, *18*(2), 124–144.

Bowlby, J. *Attachment and Loss.* New York: Basic Books, 1973.

Boy, A. V. "Psychodiagnosis: A Person-Centered Perspective." *Person Centered Review,* 1989, *4*(2), 132–151.

Brehm, J. W. *A Theory of Psychological Reactance.* New York: Academic Press, 1966.

Brehm, S. S., and Brehm, J. W. *Psychological Reactance: A Theory of Freedom and Control.* Orlando, Fl.: Academic Press, 1981.

Brenner, A. "From Acting Out to Verbalization." *Journal of Contemporary Psychotherapy,* 1988, *18*(2), 179–192.

Breuer, J., and Freud, S. "Studies on Hysteria." In J. Strachey (ed.), *Standard Edition of the Complete Psychological Works of Sigmund Freud.* London: Hogarth Press, 1893.

Brothers, B. J. "Rocks and Glaciers (and Psychosis): A Weaning Away, as of Rocks by Glaciers. . ." In E. M. Stern (ed.), *Psychotherapy and the Abusive Patient.* New York: Haworth Press, 1984.

Bugental, J.F.T. *Intimate Journeys: Stories from Life-Changing Therapy.* San Francisco: Jossey-Bass, 1990.

Burns, D. *Feeling Good.* New York: Morrow, 1980.

Cahill, A. J. "Aggression Revisited: The Value of Anger in Therapy and Other Close Relationships." In S. C. Feinstein and J. G. Looney (eds.), *Adolescent Psychiatry: Developmental and Clinical Studies.* Chicago: University of Chicago Press, 1981.

Campbell, K. "The Psychotherapy Relationship with Borderline Personality Disorders." *Psychotherapy,* 1982, *19*(2), 166–193.

Colson, D. B., and others. "An Anatomy of Countertransference: Staff Reactions to Difficult Psychiatric Hospital Patients." *Hospital and Community Psychiatry,* 1986, *37*(9), 923–928.

Cormier, W. H., and Cormier, L. S. *Interviewing Strategies for Helpers.* (3rd ed.) Pacific Grove, Calif.: Brooks/Cole, 1991.

Csikszentmihalyi, M. *Flow: The Psychology of Optimal Experience.* New York: Harper & Row, 1990.

Davis, H. "Impossible Clients." *Journal of Social Work Practice,* May 1984, pp. 28–48.

Day, R. W., and Sparacio, R. T. "Structuring the Counseling Process." *Personnel and Guidance Journal,* 1980, *59,* 246–249.

DeChenne, T. K. "Boredom as a Clinical Issue." *Psychotherapy,* 1988, *25*(1), 71–81.

de Shazer, S. "The Death of Resistance." *Family Process,* 1984, *23*(1), 11–17.

Dickson, M. "On the Experience of Feeling Understood." Unpublished doctoral dissertation, Union Graduate School, Cincinnati, 1991.

Diebold, J. *The Innovators.* New York: Dutton, 1990.

Dixon, D. N. "Client Resistance and Social Influence." In F. J. Dorn (ed.), *The Social Influence Process in Counseling and Psychotherapy.* Springfield, Ill.: Thomas, 1981.

Dolan, Y. M. *A Path with a Heart: Ericksonian Utilization with Resistant and Chronic Clients.* New York: Brunner/Mazel, 1985.

Dowd, E. T., Milne, C. R., and Wise, S. L. "The Therapeutic Reactance Scale: A Measure of Psychological Reactance." *Journal of Counseling and Development,* 1991, *69,* 541–545.

Dowd, E. T., and Seibel, C. A. "A Cognitive Theory of Resistance and Reactance: Implications for Treatment." *Journal of Mental Health Counseling,* 1990, *12*(4), 458–469.

Dyer, W. W. *Your Erroneous Zones.* Ramsey, N. J.: Funk & Wagnalls, 1976.

Dyer, W. W., and Vriend, J. "Counseling the Reluctant Client." *Journal of Counseling Psychology,* 1973, *20*(2), 240–246.

Dyer, W. W., and Vriend, J. *Group Counseling for Personal Mastery.* New York: Sovereign, 1980.

Ellis, A. *Reason and Emotion in Psychotherapy.* Secaucus, N.J.: Citadel, 1962.

Ellis, A. *Overcoming Resistance.* New York: Springer, 1985.

Epstein, L. "The Therapeutic Function of Hate in the Countertransference." In L. Epstein and A. H. Feiner (eds.), *Countertransference.* Northvale, N.J.: Jason Aronson, 1979.

Erickson, M. H. "A Hypnotic Technique for Resistant Patients." *American Journal of Clinical Hypnosis,* 1964, *7*, 8–32.

Erickson, M. H. "The Use of Symptoms as an Integral Part of Therapy." In E. L. Rossi (ed.), *The Collected Papers of Milton H. Erickson.* New York: Irvington, 1980.

Esman, A. H. "Some Reflections on Boredom." *Journal of the American Psychoanalytic Association,* 1979, *27*, 423–439.

Feiner, A. H. "Comments on the Difficult Patient." *Contemporary Psychoanalysis,* 1982, *18*(3), 397–411.

Fiore, R. J. "Toward Engaging the Difficult Patient." *Journal of Contemporary Psychotherapy,* 1988, *18*(2), 87–106.

Ford, C. V. *The Somatizing Disorders.* New York: Elsevier Biomedical, 1981.

Framo, J. L. "An Intergenerational Approach." *Family Therapy Network,* Sept./Oct. 1990, pp. 83–85.

Frankl, V. "Paradoxical Intention: A Logotherapeutic Technique." *American Journal of Psychotherapy,* 1960, *14*, 520–535.

Franz, C. *The People's Guide to Mexico.* Santa Fe, N.M.: John Muir Publications, 1990.

Fremont, S. K., and Anderson, W. "What Client Behaviors Make Counselors Angry? An Exploratory Study." *Journal of Counseling and Development,* 1986, *65*(2), 67–70.

Fremont, S. K., and Anderson, W. "Investigation of Factors Involved in Therapists' Annoyance with Clients." *Professional Psychology,* 1988, *19*(3), 330–335.

Freud, S. "The Future Prospects of Psychoanalytic Therapy." In

J. Strachey (ed.), *The Standard Edition of the Complete Psychological Works of Sigmund Freud.* Vol. 11. London: Hogarth Press, 1957. (Originally published 1910.)

Freud, S. "On the History of the Psychodynamic Movement." In J. Strachey (ed.), *The Standard Edition of the Complete Psychological Works of Sigmund Freud.* Vol. 14. London: Hogarth Press, 1957. (Originally published 1914.)

Freud, S. "Observations on Transference-Love." In J. Strachey (ed.), *The Standard Edition of the Complete Psychological Works of Sigmund Freud.* Vol. 12. London: Hogarth Press, 1957. (Originally published 1915.)

Freud, S. "Analysis: Terminable and Interminable." In *Freud: Therapy and Technique.* New York: Collier Books, 1963.

Gelman, D. "A Much Riskier Passage." *Newsweek,* Summer/Fall 1990, pp. 10–17.

Giovacchini, P. L. "Structural Progression and Vicissitudes in the Treatment of Severely Disturbed Patients." In P. L. Giovacchini and L. B. Boyer (eds.), *Technical Factors in the Treatment of the Severely Disturbed Patient.* Northvale, N.J.: Jason Aronson, 1982.

Giovacchini, P. L. *Countertransference Triumphs and Catastrophes.* Northvale, N.J.: Jason Aronson, 1989.

Giovacchini, P. L., and Boyer, L. B. (eds.). *Technical Factors in the Treatment of the Severely Disturbed Patient.* Northvale, N.J.: Jason Aronson, 1982.

Goldberg, P. *The Babinski Reflex.* Los Angeles: Jeremy P. Tarcher, 1990.

Golden, W. L. "Resistance in Cognitive-Behavior Therapy." *British Journal of Cognitive Psychotherapy,* 1983, *1*(2), 33–42.

Goldstein, A. *Structured Learning Therapy: Towards Psychotherapy of the Poor.* San Diego, Calif.: Academic Press, 1973.

Greenberg, G. "Reflections on Being Abrasive: Two Unusual Cases." *The Psychotherapy Patient,* 1984, *1*(1), 55–60.

Greenberg, L. S., and Johnson, S. M. *Emotionally Focused Therapy for Couples.* New York: Guilford Press, 1988.

Greenson, R. *The Technique and Practice of Psychoanalysis.* New York: International Universities Press, 1967.

Groves, J. E. "Taking Care of the Hateful Patient." *New England Journal of Medicine,* 1978, *298*(16), 883–887.

Haley, J. (ed.) *Advanced Techniques of Hypnosis and Therapy: Selected Papers of Milton H. Erickson.* Philadelphia: Grune & Stratton, 1967.

Haley, J. *Uncommon Therapy.* New York: Norton, 1973.

Haley, J. *The First Therapy Session.* San Francisco: Jossey-Bass, 1989. Audiotape.

Hamilton, J. D., Decker, N., and Rumbaut, R. D. "The Manipulative Patient." *American Journal of Psychotherapy*, 1986, *60*(2), 189–200.

Harris, G. A., and Watkins, D. *Counseling the Involuntary and Resistant Client.* College Park, Md.: American Correctional Association, 1987.

Hartman, C., and Reynolds, D. "Resistant Clients: Confrontation, Interpretation, and Alliance." *Social Casework*, April 1987, pp. 205–213.

Hulme, W. E. *Creative Loneliness.* Minneapolis: Angsburg, 1977.

Issacharoff, A. "Barriers to Knowing." In L. Epstein and A. H. Feiner (eds.), *Countertransference.* Northvale, N.J.: Jason Aronson, 1979.

Jahn, D. L., and Lichstein, K. L. "The Resistive Client: A Neglected Phenomenon in Behavior Therapy." *Behavior Modification*, 1980, *30*, 303–320.

Jones, E. E. "Psychotherapists' Impressions of Treatment Outcome as a Function of Race." *Journal of Clinical Psychology*, 1982, *38*, 722–732.

Jones, E. E., and Zoppel, C. L. "Impact of Client and Therapist Gender on Psychotherapy Process and Outcome." *Journal of Consulting and Clinical Psychology*, 1982, *50*, 259–272.

Jurich, A. P. "The Jujitsu Approach: Confronting the Belligerent Adolescent." *Family Therapy Networker*, July/Aug. 1990, 43–49.

Karasu, T. B. "The Specificity Versus Nonspecificity Dilemma: Toward Identifying Therapeutic Change Agents." *American Journal of Psychiatry*, 1986, *143*, 687–695.

Kernberg, O. F. *Borderline Conditions and Pathological Narcissism.* Northvale, N.J.: Jason Aronson, 1975.

Kernberg, O. F. *Internal World and External Reality.* Northvale, N.J.: Jason Aronson, 1980.

Kernberg, O. F. *Severe Personality Disorders.* New Haven, Conn.: Yale University Press, 1984.

Kitzler, R., and Lay, J. "Bread From Stones." In E. M. Stern (ed.), *Psychotherapy and the Abusive Patient*, New York: Haworth Press, 1984.

Kottler, J. A. *Pragmatic Group Leadership.* Pacific Grove, Calif.: Brooks/Cole, 1983.

Kottler, J. A. *On Being a Therapist.* San Francisco: Jossey-Bass, 1986.

Kottler, J. A. *Private Moments, Secret Selves: Enriching Our Time Alone.* Los Angeles: Jeremy Tarcher, 1990.

Kottler, J. A. *The Compleat Therapist.* San Francisco: Jossey-Bass, 1991.

Kottler, J. A., and Blau, D. S. *The Imperfect Therapist: Learning from Failure in Therapeutic Practice.* San Francisco: Jossey-Bass, 1989.

Kottler, J. A., and Brown, R. W. *Introduction to Therapeutic Counseling.* (2nd ed.) Pacific Grove, Calif.: Brooks/Cole, 1992.

Kroll, J. *The Challenge of the Borderline Patient.* New York: Norton, 1988.

Krystal, H. "Alexithymia and Psychotherapy." *American Journal of Psychotherapy*, 1979, *33*, 17–31.

Krystal, H. "Alexithymia and the Effectiveness of Psychoanalytic Treatment." *International Journal of Psychoanalytic Psychotherapy*, 1982, *9*, 353–378.

Kushner, M. G., and Sher, K. J. "The Relation of Treatment Fearfulness and Psychological Service Utilization: An Overview." *Professional Psychology*, 1991, *22*, 196–203.

L'Abate, L. "Pathogenic Role Rigidity in Fathers: Some Observations." *Journal of Marriage and Family Counseling*, 1975, *1*, 69–79.

Langs, R. *The Therapeutic Interaction.* Northvale, N.J.: Jason Aronson, 1976.

Langs, R. "Some Communicative Properties of the Bipersonal Field." *International Journal of Psychoanalytic Psychotherapy*, 1978, *7*, 87–135.

Langs, R. *Interactions.* Northvale, N.J.: Jason Aronson, 1989.

Larke, J. "Compulsory Treatment: Some Practical Methods of Treating the Mandated Client." *Psychotherapy*, 1985, *22*(2), 262–268.

Lasky, R. "Primitive Object-Relations and Impaired Structuralization in the Abrasive Patient." In E. M. Stern (ed.), *Psychotherapy and the Abrasive Patient.* New York: Haworth Press, 1984.

Lazarus, A. A. "The Need for Technical Eclecticism." In J. K. Zeig (ed.), *The Evolution of Psychotherapy.* New York: Brunner/Mazel, 1986.

Lazarus, A. A., and Fay, A. "Resistance or Rationalization? A Cognitive-Behavioral Perspective." In P. L. Wachtel (ed.), *Resistance: Psychodynamic and Behavioral Approaches.* New York: Plenum, 1982.

Leiderman, D. B., and Grisso, J. A. "The Gomer Phenomenon." *Journal of Health and Social Behavior*, 1985, *26*(3), 222–232.

Leszcz, M. "Group Psychotherapy of the Characterologically Difficult Client." *International Journal of Group Psychotherapy*, 1989, *39*(3), 311–334.

Liebenberg, B. "The Unwanted and Unwanting Patient: Problems in Group Psychotherapy of the Narcissistic Patient." In B.E. Roth, W. N. Stone, and H. D. Kibel (eds.), *The Difficult Patient in Group.* Madison, Conn.: International Universities Press, 1990.

Lipsitt, D. R. "Medical and Psychological Characteristics of 'Crocks.'" *International Journal of Psychiatry*, 1970, *1*, 15–25.

LoPiccolo, J. Workshop on Sex Therapy, Charleston, S.C., 1991.

LoPiccolo, J., and Friedman, J. "Sex Therapy: An Integrative Model." In S. Lynn and J. Gurske (eds.), *Contemporary Psychotherapies: Models and Methods.* New York: C. E. Merrill, 1985.

Lowenthal, V. "A Dentist's Approach to Difficult Patients." *Journal of Oral Medicine*, 1985, *40*(3), 151–153.

Luborsky, L., Crits-Christoph, P., Mintz, J., and Auerbach, A., *Who Will Benefit from Psychotherapy? Predictions and Therapeutic Outcomes.* New York: Basic Books, 1988.

Luther, G., and Loev, I. "Resistance in Marital Therapy." *Journal of Marital and Family Therapy*, Oct. 1981, pp. 475–480.

McElroy, L. P., and McElroy, R. A. "Countertransference Issues in the Treatment of Incest Families." *Psychotherapy*, 1991, *28*, 48–54.

McGuire, W. (ed.), *The Freud/Jung Letters.* Princeton, N.J.: Princeton University Press, 1974.

McHolland, J. D. "Strategies for Dealing with Resistant Adolescents." *Adolescence,* 1985, *20,* 349–368.

Madanes, C. *Strategic Family Therapy.* San Francisco: Jossey-Bass, 1981.

Madanes, C. *Metaphors and Paradoxes.* San Francisco: Jossey-Bass, 1990a. (Tape series)

Madanes, C. Workshop on Strategic Family Therapy. Lansing, Mich., 1990b.

Madden, D. J. "Voluntary and Involuntary Treatment of Aggressive Patients." *American Journal of Psychiatry,* 1977, *134*(5), 553–555.

Mahoney, M. J. *Cognition and Behavior Modification.* New York: Ballinger, 1974.

Mahrer, A. R. "The Care and Feeding of Abrasiveness." In E. M. Stern (ed.), *Psychotherapy and the Abusive Patient.* New York: Haworth Press, 1984.

Mahrer, A. R. *The Integration of Psychotherapies.* New York: Human Sciences Press, 1989.

Mann, J. *Time Limited Psychotherapy.* Cambridge, Mass.: Harvard University Press, 1973.

Manthei, R. J., and Matthews, D. A. "Helping the Reluctant Client to Engage in Counselling." *British Journal of Guidance and Counselling,* 1982, *10,* 44–50.

Markowitz, L. M. "Better Therapy Through Chemistry?" *Family Therapy Networker,* May/June 1991, pp. 23–31.

Marshall, R. J. *Resistant Interaction.* New York: Human Sciences Press, 1982.

Martin, J. *The Resistant Patient.* Kensington, Australia: New South Wales University Press, 1979.

Martin, P. "The Obnoxious Patient." In P. L. Giovacchini (ed.), *Tactics and Techniques in Psychoanalytic Therapy,* New York: Jason Aronson, 1975.

Masterson, J. F. *Psychotherapy of the Borderline Adult.* New York: Brunner/Mazel, 1976.

Medeiros, M. E., and Prochaska, J. O. "Coping Strategies that

Psychotherapists Use in Working with Stressful Clients." *Professional Psychology*, 1988, *19*(1), 112–114.

Meichenbaum, D. *Cognitive Behavior Modification*. New York: Plenum, 1977.

Mens-Verhulst, J. van, "Perspectives of Power in Therapeutic Relationships." *American Journal of Psychotherapy*, 1991, *45*(2), 198–210.

Merbaum, M., and Butcher, J. N. "Therapists Liking of Their Psychotherapy Patients: Some Issues Related to Severity of Disorder and Treatability." *Psychotherapy*, 1982, *19*(1), 69–76.

Miller, L. "Man Without Passion." *Psychology Today*, 1989, pp. 20–22.

Miller, M. J. "The Invisible Client." *Personal and Guidance Journal*, 1983, *62*(1), 30–33.

Miller, M. J., and Wells, D. "On Being 'Attractive' with Resistant Clients." *Journal of Humanistic Education and Development*, 1990, *29*, 86–92.

Milman, D. S., and Goldman, G. D. "Introduction to Resistance." In D. S. Milman and G. D. Goldman (eds.), *Techniques of Working with Resistance*. Northvale, N.J.: Jason Aronson, 1987.

Morrant, J. C. A. "Boredom in Psychiatric Practice." *Canadian Journal of Psychiatry*, 1984, 29, 431–434.

Moustakas, C. *Loneliness and Love*. Englewood Cliffs, N.J.: Prentice-Hall, 1972.

Munjack, D. J., and Oziel, L. J. "Resistance in the Behavioral Treatment of Sexual Dysfunction." *Journal of Sex and Marital Therapy*, 1978, *4*(2), 122–138.

Murphy, G. E., and Guze, S. B. "Setting Limits: The Management of the Manipulative Patient." *American Journal of Psychotherapy*, 1960, *14*, 30–47.

Natterson, J. *Beyond Countertransference*. Northvale, N.J.: Jason Aronson, 1991.

Nelson, G. *The One-Minute Scolding*. Boulder, Colo.: Shambala Press, 1984.

Nichols, W. C. "Polarized Couples: Behind the Facade." In J. F. Crosby (ed.), *When One Wants Out and the Other Doesn't*. New York: Brunner/Mazel, 1989.

O'Connor, J. J., and Hoorwitz, A. N. "The Bogeyman Cometh: A

Strategic Approach for Difficult Adolescents." *Family Process*, 1984, *23*, 234–249.

O'Hanlon, W. H. "Establishing the Agenda: A Solution-Oriented Approach." *Family Therapy Networker*, Nov./Dec. 1990, pp. 69–70.

O'Hanlon, W. H., and Weiner-Davis, M. *In Search of Solutions: A New Dimension in Psychotherapy.* New York: W.W. Norton, 1989.

Otani, A. "Client Resistance in Counseling: Its Theoretical Rationale and Taxonomic Classification." *Journal of Counseling and Development*, 1989a, *67*, 458–461.

Otani, A. "Resistance Management Techniques of Milton H. Erickson." *Journal of Mental Health Counseling*, 1989b, 11 (4), 325–334.

Palazzoli, M., Selvini, B. L. Cecchin, G., and Prata, G. *Paradox and Counterparadox.* New York: Jason Aronson, 1978.

Patterson, C. P. *Theories of Counseling and Psychotherapy.* (3rd ed.) New York: Harper & Row, 1980.

Peplau, L. A., and Perlman, D. (eds.). *Loneliness: A Sourcebook of Current Theory, Research, and Therapy.* New York: Wiley, 1982.

Pines, A., and Maslach, C. "Characteristics of Staff Burnout in Mental Health Settings." *Hospital Community Psychiatry*, 1978, *29*(4), 233–237.

Pope, K. S., and Garcia-Peltoniemi, R. E. "Responding to Victims of Torture: Clinical Issues, Professional Responsibilities, and Useful Resources." *Professional Psychology*, 1991, *22*, 269–276.

Pope, K. S., Keith-Speigel, P., and Tabachnick, B. C. "Sexual Attraction to Clients." *American Psychologist*, 1986, *41*(2), 147–158.

Powles, W. E. "Problems in Diagnosis and Group Treatment Design of Borderline Personalities." In B. E. Roth, W. N. Stone, and H. D. Kibel (eds.), *The Difficult Patient in Group.* Madison, Conn.: International Universities Press, 1990.

Prochaska, J. O., and DiClemente, C. C. *The Transtheoretical Approach: Crossing the Traditional Boundaries of Therapy.* Homewood, Ill.: Dow Jones-Irwin, 1984.

Puntil, C. "Integrating Three Approaches to Counter Resistance in a Noncompliant Elderly Client." *Journal of Psychological Nursing*, 1991, *29*, 26–30.

Purcell, P., and Wechsler, S. "Stalking the Wild Cricket." *Family Therapy Networker.* Jan./Feb. 1991, pp. 62–65.

Redl, F. *When We Deal with Children.* New York: Free Press, 1966

Reynolds, D. K. *Morita Psychotherapy.* Berkeley: University of California Press, 1976.

Ritchie, M. H. "Counseling the Involuntary Client." *Journal of Counseling and Development,* 1986, *64,* 516–518.

Robbins, J. M., Beck, P. R., Mueller, D. P., and Mizener, D. A. "Therapists' Perceptions of Difficult Psychiatric Patients." *Journal of Nervous and Mental Diseases,* 1988, *176*(8), 490–496.

Robbins, T. *Skinny Legs and All.* New York: Bantam, 1990.

Roberts, R. "Treating Conduct-Disordered Adolescents and Young Adults by Working with the Parents." *Journal of Marital and Family Therapy,* Jan. 1982, pp. 15–28.

Rogers, C. "A Process Conception of Psychotherapy." *American Psychologist,* 1958, *13,* 142–149.

Rogers, C. *A Way of Being.* Boston: Houghton Mifflin, 1980.

Rosenbaum, J., and Rosenbaum, V. *Conquering Loneliness.* New York: Hawthorne Books, 1973.

Rosenbaum, R. L., Horowitz, M. J., and Wilner, N. "Clinician Assessments of Patient Difficulty." *Psychotherapy,* 1986, *23*(3), 417–425.

Roth, B. E. "Countertransference and the Group Therapist's State of Mind." In B. E. Roth, W. N. Stone, and H. D. Kibel (eds.), *The Difficult Patient in Group.* Madison, Conn.: International Universities Press, 1990.

Roth, B. E., Stone, W. N., and Kibel, H. D. (eds.). *The Difficult Patient in Group.* Madison, Conn.: International Universities Press, 1990.

Rothenberg, A. *Creativity and Madness.* Baltimore, Md.: Johns Hopkins University Press, 1990.

Russianoff, P. *Why Do I Think I Am Nothing Without a Man?* New York: Bantam, 1982.

Sack, R. T. "Counseling Responses When Clients Say 'I Don't Know.'" *Journal of Mental Health Counseling,* 1988, *10*(3), 179–187.

Saretsky, T. *Resolving Treatment Impasses.* New York: Human Sciences Press, 1981.

Schlesinger, H. J. "Resistance as Process." In P. L Wachtel (ed.), *Resistance: Psychodynamic and Behavioral Approaches.* New York: Plenum, 1982.

Schofield, W. *Psychotherapy: The Purchase of Friendship.* Englewood Cliffs, N.J.: Prentice-Hall, 1964.

Seligman, L. *Selecting Effective Treatments.* San Francisco: Jossey-Bass, 1990.

Sexton, T. L., and Whiston, S. C. "A Review of the Empirical Basis for Counseling: Implications for Practice and Training." *Counselor Education and Supervision,* 1990, *30,* 330–334.

Shay, J. J. "The Wish to Do Psychotherapy with Borderline Adolescents—And Other Common Errors." *Psychotherapy,* 1987, *24*(2), 712–719.

Shay, J. J. "Rules of Thumb for the All-Thumbs Therapist: Weathering the Marital Storm." *Journal of Integrative and Eclectic Psychotherapy,* 1990, *9*(1), 21–34.

Shelton, J. L., and Levy, R. L. *Behavioral Assignments and Treatment Compliance.* Champaign, Ill.: Research Press, 1981.

Shochet, B. R., Levin, L., Lowen, M., and Lisansky, E. T. "Dealing with the Seductive Patient." *Medical Aspects of Sexuality,* 1976, *10*(2), 90–104.

Siegel, I. M. "Time and a Half." *Journal of the American Medical Association,* 1982, *247*(7), 972.

Sifneos, P. E. "The Prevalance of 'Alexithymic' Characteristics in Psychosomatic Patients." *Psychosomatics,* 1973a, *22,* 255–262.

Sifneos, P. E. *Short Term Psychotherapy and Emotional Crisis.* Cambridge, Mass.: Harvard University Press, 1973b.

Singer, J. "Transference and the Human Condition: A Cognitive-Affective Perspective." *Psychoanalytic Psychology,* 1985, *2*(3), 189–219.

Sklar, H. "The Impact of the Therapeutic Environment." *Journal of Contemporary Psychotherapy,* 1988, *18*(2), 107–123.

Slakter, E. (ed.). *Countertransference.* Northvale, N.J.: Jason Aronson, 1987.

Slater, P. *The Pursuit of Loneliness.* Boston: Beacon Press, 1976.

Smith, R. J., and Steindler, E. M. "The Impact of Difficult Patients upon Treaters." *Bulletin of the Menninger Clinic,* 1983, *47*(2), 107–116.

Stanton, M. D., and Todd, T. C. "Engaging Resistant Families in Treatment." *Family Process*, 1981, *20*(3), 261–293.

Steiger, W. A. "Managing Difficult Patients." *Psychosomatics*, 1967, *8*(6), 305–308.

Stern, E. M. (ed.) *The Psychotherapy Patient*, 1984, *1*(1)

Stiles, W. B., Shapiro, D. A., and Elliot, P. "Are All Psychotherapies Equivalent?" *American Psychologist*, 1986, *41*(2), 165–180.

Storr, A. *Solitude: A Return to the Self.* New York: Free Press, 1988.

Stuart, R. B. *Helping Couples Change.* New York: Guilford Press, 1980.

Strean, H. S. *Resolving Resistances in Psychotherapy.* New York: Wiley, 1985.

Strong, S. R., and Matross, R. P. "Change Processes in Counseling and Psychotherapy." *Journal of Counseling Psychology*, 1973, *20*, 25–37.

Strupp, H. S. "Invited Address: A Little Bit of Bad Process Can Go a Long Way in Psychotherapy." New Orleans: American Psychological Association Convention, 1989.

Suedfeld, P. *Restricted Environmental Stimulation.* New York: Wiley, 1980.

Taffel, R. "The Politics of Mood." Family Therapy Networker, Sept./Oct. 1990, 49–53.

Talmon, M. *Single-Session Therapy.* San Francisco: Jossey-Bass, 1990.

Tansey, M. J., and Burke, W. F. *Understanding Countertransference.* Hillsdale, N.J.: Analytic Press, 1989.

Taylor, G. J. "Psychotherapy with the Boring Patient." *Canadian Journal of Psychiatry*, 1984, *29*, 217–222.

Tennen, H., Rohrbaugh, M., Press, S., and White, L. "Reactance Theory and Therapeutic Paradox: A Compliance-Defiance Model." *Psychotherapy*, 1981, *8*(1), 14–22.

Thomas, L. *The Lives of a Cell.* New York: Viking, 1974.

Turecki, S., and Tonner, L. *The Difficult Child.* New York: Bantam, 1985.

Vandecreek, L., Knapp, S., Herzog, C. "Malpractice Risks in the Treatment of Dangerous Patients." *Psychotherapy*, 1987, *24*(2), 145–153.

Wallerstein, R. S. *Forty-Two Lives in Treatment.* New York: Guilford Press, 1986.

Walters, M. "The Codependent Cinderella Who Loves Too Much. . . Fights Back." *Family Therapy Networker,* July/Aug. 1990, pp. 53–57.

Warner, S. J. "The Defeating Patient and Reciprocal Abrasion." In E. M. Stern (ed.), *Psychotherapy and the Abusive Patient.* New York: Haworth Press, 1984.

Waters, J. "Bring Back the Juvenile Delinquent." *Newsweek,* Summer/Fall Special Edition, 1989.

Watzlawick, P., Weakland, J., and Fisch, R. *Change: Principles of Problem Formation and Problem Resolution.* New York: W.W. Norton, 1974.

Welpton, D. F. "Confrontation in the Therapeutic Process." In G. Adler and P. G. Meyerson (eds.), *Confrontation in Psychotherapy.* New York: Science House, 1973.

Welt, S. R., and Herron, W. G. *Narcissism and the Psychotherapist.* New York: Guilford Press, 1990.

Weltner, J. "Different Strokes: A Pragmatist's Guide to Intervention." *Family Therapy Networker,* May/June 1988, pp. 53–57.

West, M. "Building a Relationship with the Unmotivated Client." *Psychotherapy,* 1975, *12*(1), 48–51.

Winnecott, D. W. "Hate in the Countertransference." *International Journal of Psycho-Analysis,* 1949, *30*, 69–74.

Winnecott, D. W. *The Maturational Processes and the Facilitating Environment.* New York: International Universities Press, 1960.

Wise, T. N., and Berlin, R. M. "Burnout: Stresses in Consultation-Liaison Psychiatry." *Psychosomatics,* 1981, *22*(9), 744–751.

Wolstein, B. (ed.) *Essential Papers on Countertransference.* New York: New York University Press, 1988.

Wong, N. "Perspectives of the Difficult Patient." *Bulletin of the Menninger Clinic,* 1983, *47*(2), 99–106.

Yalom, I. *Existential Psychotherapy.* New York: Basic Books, 1980.

Yalom, I. *Love's Executioner.* New York: Basic Books, 1989.

Young, J. "Loneliness, Depression, and Cognitive Therapy." In L. Peplau and D. Perlman (eds.), *Loneliness: A Sourcebook of Current Theory, Research, and Therapy.* New York: Wiley, 1982.

Youngren, V. R. "Opportunity's Hard Knocks: Clinical Training in Adolescent Milieu Therapy." *Psychotherapy*, 1991, 28, 298–303.

Zukav, G. *The Dancing Wu Li Masters.* New York: Bantam Books, 1979.

Index

factors, 5; control needs, 29; and countertransference, 24–25; dangerous, 37–39; defensiveness, 29; demanding behavior, 28–29; diagnostic descriptors, 33; and difficult therapists, 15, 20–21; empty, 27; engendering, 52–54; externalization, 29; fear/anxiety, 40–41, 64–65; and gomerism, 16; in group therapy, 191–192; hidden agendas, 22; homeostasis model, 12–14; hopeless, 27; impatient, 25; impulse control, 28–29; inarticulate, 26; insight, 192–195; interactive style, 17; intimacy fears, 23–24; literal (concrete), 26–27; measures of difficulty, 37–38; medically, 65–66; negative attitudes, 200–201; physiological disorders, 21–22; positive behavior functions approach, 193–195; preference for, 17–18; prescreening, 5, 218–219; referring out, 219–220; refusal of responsibility, 22–23; resistant families, 189–191; rules of engagement, 222–227; self-unawareness, 14; similarities to therapist, 65–66; survival tactics, 14; and therapeutic environment, 203–206; therapeutic models, 5–6; and therapist expectations, 42–43, 81–82, 182–183; and therapist frustration tolerance, 46; and therapist mismatch, 24; and therapist perceptions, 51–52; and therapist self-blame, 4–5; and therapist self-dissatisfaction (example), 61–63; and therapist self-examination, 66–68; therapists as, 49–50, 56; as threatening, 54–56; treatment risks, 86–87; treatment strategies, 169–173. *See also* Adolescent clients; Borderline clients; Boring clients; Clients; Combative couples; Controlling clients; Hostile clients; Lonely clients; Passive resistant clients; Silent clients

Dolan, Y. M., 182, 210
Dowd, E. T., 7, 17, 29, 90, 175, 176
Dyer, W. W., 10, 33, 174, 193

E

Elliot, P., 31
Ellis, A., 56, 196
Epstein, L, 45
Erickson, M. H., 6, 181, 207
Esman, A. H., 133

F

Fabian Tactics, 211–213
Fay, A., 21, 138, 175, 196
Feiner, A. H., 35, 51, 127
Fiore, R. J., 34, 42, 90, 91, 162, 163, 204
Fisch, R., 6, 121, 138, 181, 207
Ford, C. V., 10, 65
Framo, J. L., 226
Frankl, V., 208
Franz, C., 43
Fremont, S. K., 42, 112, 113
Freud, S., 6, 38, 43, 60, 156

G

Game playing. *See* Clients: game playing; Therapeutic game playing
Garcia-Peltoniemi, R. E., 16
Gelman, D., 111
Giovacchini, P. L., 3, 101, 157, 186
Goldberg, P., 207, 211
Golden, W. L., 21, 192, 196
Goldfried, M. R., 169
Goldman, G. D., 38
Gomerism, 16
Greenberg, G., 33, 94, 166
Greenberg, L. S., 120
Grisso, J. A., 16
Group therapy: audio/videotaping, 215–216; and difficult clients, 191–192. *See also* Interventions; Psychotherapy